DEATH OF A WORLD

by DR. MICHAEL ESSES

THE PROPHECIES OF THE BOOKS OF DANIEL
AND THE REVELATION,
REGARDING THE END TIMES WE LIVE IN;
AND THE SECOND COMING OF CHRIST.
A COMMENTARY, A STUDY, AN EXPOSITION
by DR. MICHAEL ESSES

ESSES PUBLISHING COMPANY
PEORIA, ARIZONA

DEATH OF A WORLD

Peoria, Arizona

ISBN Number 0-945730-00-4

Library of Congress Catalog Card Number: 88-91036
ESSES PUBLISHING COMPANY

International Standard Book Number 0-945730-00-4

DEDICATED
To
MY FATHER IN-LAW
WALTER C. DAVIS SENIOR
Who Has Shown Me The Love And Devotion
Of A Real Father

To Billie Jean Esses, My Lovely Wife

**MY EZER KA-NEGDI; MY HELPMEET; WHO HAS
MET ME AT EVERY POINT OF MY NEED, AS GOD
HAD INTENDED FROM THE FOUNDATIONS OF THE
WORLD, AND WITHOUT WHOM THIS BOOK WOULD
NOT AND COULD HAVE NOT BEEN WRITTEN**

TO
HAROLD AND JO ANN KENT
WHO'S WALK MATCHES THEIR
TALK IN CHRIST TO PRODUCE
CHOICE FRUIT FOR THE KINGDOM OF GOD!

CONTENTS

Part II The Revelation According to St. John

PREFACE

It is indeed a privilege for me, a man born of The Hebrew Faith, who has found his Messiah, to write this book on THE DEATH OF A WORLD; in regards to the times we are living in and the Second Coming of Jesus Christ. Jesus said, in The Gospel According to John 6:44 "no one can come to me unless The Father who sent Me draws him, and I will raise him up at the last day." I thank God that in the fortieth year of my life, My Father in Heaven revealed to me that Jesus is My Lord and Savior. I am now 65 years old and I really don't know what I would have done with out Jesus these last 25 years. My afflictions, trials and tribulations have been many; but I praise God for His Word and His many promises for He Has Delivered me out of them all! His Word in Psalm 34:19 states; "many are the afflictions of the righteous: but the Lord delivereth him out of them all." Thrill with me in God's Word of yesteryear in these Books of Daniel, and The Revelation which have been given to us for today, as we see God's Timeclock winding down to the end of the age; to our soon coming King, Jesus Christ. Be ready with me for The Rapture if it happens to be pre-trib, or mid-trib, or post-trib; the main thing being to be ready for That Glorious Event when it does occur; to be watching and waiting knowing that Our Redemption Draweth Nigh Unto Us! Be ready with me to go to The Wedding Feast of The Marriage Supper of The Lamb! Jesus said, "Blessed are they who share in The First Resurrection." Be ready with me to come back with The Next Visitor to Planet Earth; Jesus, and fight in The Battle of The Armageddon as His Saints, for we have read the end of The Book, and We Win! We Win! We Win! Now let us spend 1,000 years together in The Time of The Millennium, in perfect peace, in perfect love, in the blessedness of Jesus Our Leader, Who still continues to bless us in every area of our lives; **Spiritually, Physically, Emotionally, Financially!**

Because Jesus is My Lord, Your Humble Servant, Michael Esses

ACKNOWLEDGMENTS

Scripture quotations herein are from The Holy Bible, New International Version copyright © 1978 by New York International Bible Society. Published by The Zondervan Corporation, Grand Rapids, Michigan 49506. Used by permission, The Holy Bible, New International Version © 1978 by New York International Bible Society.

THE FALL OF MAN

GEN 3:1 Now the serpent was more crafty than any of the wild animals the Lord God had made. He said to the woman, "Did God really say, 'You must not eat from any tree in the garden'?" The woman said to the serpent, "We may eat fruit from the trees in the garden, but God did say, 'You must not eat fruit from the tree that is in the middle of the garden, and you must not touch it, or you will die.' " "You will not surely die," the serpent said to the woman. "For God knows that when you eat of it your eyes will be opened, and you will be like God, knowing good and evil." When the woman saw that the fruit of the tree was good for food and pleasing to the eye, and also desirable for gaining wisdom, she took some and ate it. She also gave some to her husband, who was with her, and he ate it. Then the eyes of both of them were opened, and they realized they were naked; so they sewed fig leaves together and made coverings for themselves. Then the man and his wife heard the sound of the Lord God as he was walking in the garden in the cool of the day, and they hid from the Lord God among the trees of the garden. But the Lord God called to the man, "Where are you?" He answered, "I heard you in the garden, and I was afraid because I was naked; so I hid." And he said, "Who told you that you were naked? Have you eaten from the tree that I commanded you not to eat from?" The man said, "The woman you put here with me—she gave me some fruit from the tree, and I ate it." Then the Lord God said to the woman, "What is this you have done?" The woman said, "The serpent deceived me, and I ate." So the Lord God said to the serpent, "Because you have done this, "Cursed are you above all the livestock and all the wild animals! You will crawl on your belly and you will eat dust all the days of your life." When God questioned The Women she freely confessed her sin to God, and God instantly forgave her. When God questioned the Man he blamed GOD and his WIFE; and he has been doing the same ever since!

ALL *BIBLICAL* PROPHECY MUST BE SEEN THROUGH WHAT GOD HAD STATED IN GENESIS 3:15 AS HE CURSED SATAN

GEN 3:15 And I will put ENMITY between you and the WOMAN, and between your SEED and her SEED ; HE will Crush your head, and you will strike his heel."

The word for Satan's seed in The Hebrew is PLURAL, whereas the word in The Hebrew for The Woman's Seed is SINGULAR. For in the distant future a WOMAN by the name of MARY who would be A VIRGIN, would carry a SEED OF HER OWN, and NOT THE SEED OF A MAN who would impregnate HER. She would be IMPREGNATED BY THE HOLY SPIRIT; and conception would take place by The HOLY SPIRIT!

This SINGULAR SEED, who is JESUS THE CHRIST, will CRUSH Satan's HEAD and all of his many PLURAL SEED with him on the CROSS OF CALVARY. Every sin of man from The Garden of Eden and onward; past, present, and future would be taken by JESUS to the CROSS. The only power and authority that Satan has ever had is as God has said: YOU, SATAN, WILL BE ABLE TO STRIKE AT THE HEELS OF JESUS' FOLLOWERS AND NO FURTHER. FOR MY SON, JESUS, HAS GIVEN MY POWER AND AUTHORITY TO ALL OF HIS FOLLOWERS TO BIND YOU, AND REBUKE YOU, SATAN, IN HIS NAME. For at The Name of Jesus, every knee must bow and every tongue

CONFESS THAT HE JESUS CHRIST IS LORD!

GEN 3:17 To Adam he said, "Because you listened to your wife and ate from the tree about which I commanded you, 'You must not eat of it,' "CURSED is the ground because of you; through painful toil you will eat of it all the days of your life. It will produce thorns and thistles for you, and you will eat the plants of the field. By the sweat of your brow you will eat your food until you return to the ground, since from it you were taken; for dust you are and to dust you will return." The Lord God made garments of skin for Adam and his wife and clothed them." A temporary covering; until Jesus came into our world and COVERED all of mankind with HIS SPOTLESS BLOOD.

Chapter 1

The Life Of Daniel

The available data in our Jewish History indicates that Daniel was a boy of about fourteen years of age when he was driven,together with his three companions, Hananiah, Mishael, Azariah, into captivity into Babylon. He and his three companions were of royal descent of the house of David. In Babylon, under Nebuchadnezzar, he received, together with other chosen lads of his rank and ability, an education in the arts and sciences of the time.He gave early signs of brilliance and character. The entire time he staunchly maintained the strict letter of the Mosaic Law, refusing to defile himself with forbidden food. His opportunity came when the king had a dream which he forgot; ordering his astrologers to divine and interpret the dream on pain of death. Daniel received from God the revelation both of the dream and its interpretation, which he declared to the king. In gratitude and admiration Nebuchadnezzar promoted him to high rank and honor. The wisdom God gave him brought him fame and responsibility. The Talmud asserted of Daniel that if he were placed in one scale of the balance and all the wisest heathens in the other he would have outweighed them all. When great king Nebuchadnezzar erected an image and ordered all of his subjects to worship it, Daniel escaped the ordeal of the fiery furnace experienced by his three companions, since the king sent him on a mission outside Babylon, knowing that if he stayed behind he would have incurred the same penalty as his friends. God gave Daniel wisdom and skill to minister not only in the court of Nebuchadnezzar, but also in the reigns of Belshazzar, Darius the Mede and Cyrus. He lived to an advanced old age and witnessed the return of the Jews to the Holy Land. He delegated his high office and many honors to Prince Zerubbabel and retired with the royal blessing of the many Kings he served to Shushan, where he spent the rest of his life in great piety.

The Book of Daniel was written in Hebrew and the vernacular Aramaic: From chapters 2:4 through 7:28 were written in Aramaic, the rest of the book was written in Hebrew. Upon the return from the captivity in Babylon, the Men of the Great Synagogue rewrote the entire book of Daniel in Hebrew. The Great Assembly or as known in Hebrew, as Keneset Ha-Gedolah was composed of Haggai, Zechariah, Malachi, Nehemiah, Mordecai, Bilshan, Jeshua, and Prince Zerubbabel and was under the leadership of Ezra. Daniel whose Hebrew name means, "God Is My Judge," was given the Aramaic name, as his three companions were, the name of Belteshazzar which when pronounced in the Aramaic is BALATSU-USUR which means O'Bel protect his life. Hananiah whose Hebrew name means, "He Who Depends Upon The Grace Of God," was given the Aramaic name of Shadrach; which is SHUDUR-AKU which means, he waits upon the command of Aku the moon-god. Mishael whose Hebrew name means, "Who Is Like Unto Thee O Lord," was given the Aramaic name of Meshach, which means he will be a servant of Chemosh the fire god. Azariah whose Hebrew name means, "My Help Cometh From The Lord," was given the Aramaic name of Abed-Nego; which is ABED-NEBO which means he will be a servant of Nebo the god Anubis who is in charge of the souls in hell for Satan. Daniel was carried into captivity, in the third year of Jehoiakim, in 605 B.C. This date marks the beginning of the times of the Gentiles, the prophetic period when all of Jerusalem is under Gentile control, and will remain so until the second coming of Christ. Daniel continued a most active and prominent and remarkable career of about 70 years from 605–535 B.C. When taken into the captivity; Nebuchadnezzar, King of Babylon was informed by his magicians, that from the line of David, King of Israel, would descend a King who would live forever and a Kingdom that would last for all of eternity. He was told that he held captive four of the Princes' of the tribe of Judah of the royal House of David. His magicians who served Satan, failed to realize, and understand; that as God placed blinders on their eyes, that they were holding five Princes. Daniel age 14, Hananiah age 13, Mishael age 12, Azariah age 11, and little Prince Zerubbabel age 6. And so when Nebuchadnezzar had all four Princes castrated; to prevent a King and a Kingdom which would live and last for all eternity from coming into the world; he missed The Little Prince Zerubbabel who was hidden in God's Hiding Place. And so let us pick up The Genealogy of Jesus as found in The Gospel According to Matthew 1:12–17.

"After the exile to Babylon: Jeconiah was the father of Shealtiel, Shealtiel the father of Zerubbabel, Zerubbabel the father of Abiud, Abiud the father of Eliakim, Eliakim the father of Azor, Azor the father of Zadok, Zadok the father of Akim, Akim the father of Eliud, Eliud the father of Eleazar, Eleazar the father of Matthan, Matthan the father of Jacob, and Jacob the father of Joseph, the husband of Mary, of whom was born Jesus, who is called Christ. Thus there were fourteen generations in all from Abraham to David, and fourteen from David to the exile to The Christ."

Praise God For His Never Failing Word! Jesus The King Who Lives Forever! Daniel's tomb in accordance with oral and written Babylonian Tradition; and Hebrew Tradition is shown in two places:

(1) In the royal vault in Babylon, a little west of the Acropolis.
(2) In one of the Synagogues of the Capital city of Susa.

Shushan or Susa was the winter capital of the kings of Babylon, and later on of the kings of Persia, or as is known today as Iran. Ecbatana was the summer residence of the kings of Babylon.

As we begin our study of The Book of Daniel, the first thing I want to call to your attention is this. Jesus referred to the book of Daniel more than any other book of the bible. We see in Matthew 24:15 that Daniel is called a prophet by Jesus. Jesus confirmed and vouched for the entire Old Testament. I do not have to apologize for God's word; God's word, who is Jesus, apologizes for me; as He still says" Father Forgive Them For They Know Not What They Do." We have people with us today like my so called friends, like one yo yo who

3

teaches apologetics. Here is how Websters Dictionary defines "apologetics." I quote, "That branch of theology by which Christians are enabled *scientifically* to justify and defend the precepts of their faith, and to answer its opponents." I do not have to justify and defend my faith in Jesus Christ. He justifies and defends me. Praise God! I believe The Bible to be The Word of God, Infallible and Without Error. When we say "Amen" to God's Word, we are saying three Hebrew letters; Aleph, Mem, Nun, which means, "God Our King Is Trustworthy." My God and My King is Jesus of Nazareth, King Of Kings and Lord Of Lords; and when He says something, I believe It and that settles it!

The Message Of The Book Of Daniel

This book is the key to all biblical prophecy. Setting aside the great endtime disclosures of this book, the entire prophetic portions of the book of Daniel must remain sealed until a later time. The great discourse Jesus gave The Disciples on The Mount of Olives; as shown to us in Matthew 24:–25; Mark 13; Luke 21; as well as 2nd.Thessalonians 2; and the entire book of The Revelation, can only be unlocked through the understanding of the prophecies of Daniel. The great themes of New Testament Prophecy, the revealing of the Antichrist the man of sin, The Great Tribulation, the second coming of The Messiah, the Times of The Gentiles, and The Resurrections and Judgments are all treated in this Book of Daniel.

DANIEL PRINCE OF THE TRIBE OF JUDAH; THE MAN OF CHARACTER

DAN 1:1 In the third year of the reign of Jehoiakim king of Judah, Nebuchadnezzar king of Babylon came to Jerusalem and besieged it. And the Lord delivered Jehoiakim king of Judah into his hand, along with some of the articles from the temple of God. These he carried off to the temple of his god in Babylonia and put in the treasure house of his god. Then the king ordered Ashpenaz, chief of his court officials, to bring in some of the Israelites from the royal family and the nobility—young men without any physical defect, handsome, showing aptitude for every kind of learning, well informed, quick to understand, and qualified to serve in the king's palace. He was to teach them the language and literature of the Babylonians.

The king assigned them a daily amount of food and wine from the king's table. They were to be trained for three years, and after that they were to enter the king's service. Among these were some from Judah: Daniel, Hananiah, Mishael and Azariah. The chief official gave them new names: to Daniel, the name Belteshazzar; to Hananiah, Shadrach; to Mishael, Meshach; and to Azariah, Abednego. But Daniel resolved not to defile himself with the royal food and wine, and he asked the chief official for permission not to defile himself this way. Now God had caused the official to show favor and sympathy to Daniel, but the official told Daniel, "I am afraid of my lord the king, who has assigned your food and drink. Why should he see you looking worse than the other young men your age? The king would then have my head because of you." Daniel then said to the guard whom the chief official had appointed over Daniel, Hananiah, Mishael and Azariah, "Please test your servants for ten days: Give us nothing but vegetables to eat and water to drink. Then compare our appearance with that of the young men who eat the royal food, and treat your servants in accordance with what you see." So he agreed to this and tested them for ten days. At the end of the ten days they looked healthier and better nourished than any of the young men who ate the royal food. So the guard took away their choice food and the wine they were to drink and gave them vegetables instead. To these four young men God gave knowledge and understanding of all kinds of literature and learning. And Daniel could understand visions and dreams of all kinds. At the end of the time set by the king to bring them in, the chief official presented them to Nebuchadnezzar. The king talked with them, and he found none equal to Daniel, Hananiah, Mishael and Azariah; so they entered the king's service. In every matter of wisdom and understanding about which the king questioned them, he found them ten times better than all the magicians and enchanters in his whole kingdom. And Daniel remained there until the first year of King Cyrus."

The third year of Jehoiakim's reign was the year 605 b.c., which marks the beginning of the "Times of the Gentiles," the prophetic period when Jerusalem is under Gentile control. It is evident from the scripture in 2nd. Kings 24:1–4 that the Kingdom of Judah would be under Gentile control from this time on.

2nd.Kings 24:1–4 "During Jehoiakim's reign, Nebuchadnezzar king of Babylon invaded the land, and Jehoiakim became his vassal for three years. But then he changed his mind and rebelled against Nebuchadnezzar. The Lord sent Babylonian, Aramean, Moabite and Ammonite raiders against him. He sent them to destroy Judah, in accordance with the word of The Lord proclaimed by His servants the Prophets. Surely these things happened to Judah according to The Lord's command, in order to remove them from His presence because of the sins of Manasseh and all he had done, including the shedding of innocent blood. For he had filled Jerusalem with innocent blood, and The Lord was not willing to forgive."

Our Jewish history reveals that King Manasseh of Judah, did not like the message The Prophet Isaiah; who was his cousin brought him by The Word of The Lord; so he had him sawn in half, and so he filled Jerusalem with innocent blood, that The Lord was not willing to forgive. The people of Israel knew what was happening, they stood by and said nothing, and did nothing; and so they became accessories during and after the fact. It was the same way in Germany during the time of The Holocaust, the German people said nothing and did nothing. In this first deportation Nebuchadnezzar took only the noble and most promising of the kingdom of Judah. Daniel was of royal birth, of The House of David, and was gifted by God and showed great promise. His moral faith and spiritual courage were proven in his godly separation from the defilement of Babylon. Babylon, the scene of Daniel's ministry, was a city of wonder in the ancient world. It was situated in the region which was near to The Garden of Eden. The City of Babylon was the favorite residence of of The Babylonian, Assyrian, and Persian Kings and also of Alexander The Great. Babylon was brought to the height of its power by Nebuchadnezzar, who was Daniel's friend and who, during his reign of 45 years never stopped building and beautifying its palaces and its temples. The great temple of Bel, adjoined The Tower of Babel, which was the most famous sanctuary in the entire Euphrates valley. It housed a golden image of Bel and a golden table which weighed 50,000 pounds. At the top were golden images of Bel and Ishtar, 2 golden lions, a golden table 40 feet long and 15 feet wide, and a human figure of solid gold 18 feet high. The Hanging Gardens of Babylon were one of the Seven Wonders of the ancient world; which were built by Nebuchadnezzar for his Median Queen, the beautiful daughter of Cyaxeres who had helped his father conquer Nineveh. Daniel's life in Babylon, extended from the first year of Nebuchadnezzar, through the succeeding reigns of 5 kings, past the fall of Babylon, into The Persian Empire, through the reign of Darius The Mede, and well into the third year of the reign of Cyrus The Persian. He was there from the 1st.year of The Jews captivity, till 2 years after the return of The Jews from the captivity. **GOD'S WITNESS IN THE PALACE OF THE EMPIRE THAT RULED THE WORLD.**

Chapter 2

Nebuchadnezzar's Dream

DAN 2:1 In the second year of his reign, Nebuchadnezzar had dreams; his mind was troubled and he could not sleep. So the king summoned the magicians, enchanters, sorcerers and astrologers to tell him what he had dreamed. When they came in and stood before the king, he said to them, "I have had a dream that troubles me and I want to know what it means." Then the astrologers answered the king in Aramaic, "O king, live forever! Tell your servants the dream, and we will interpret it." The king replied to the astrologers, "This is what I have firmly decided: If you do not tell me what my dream was and interpret it, I will have you cut into pieces and your houses turned into piles of rubble. But if you tell me the dream and explain it, you will receive from me gifts and rewards and great honor. So tell me the dream and interpret it for me." Once more they replied, "Let the king tell his servants the dream, and we will interpret it." Then the king answered, "I am certain that you are trying to gain time, because you realize that this is what I have firmly decided: If you do not tell me the dream, there is just one penalty for you. You have conspired to tell me misleading and wicked things, hoping the situation will change. So then, tell me the dream, and I will know that you can interpret it for me." The astrologers answered the king, "There is not a man on earth who can do what the king asks! No king, however great and mighty, has ever asked such a thing of any magician or enchanter or astrologer. What the king asks is too difficult. No one can reveal it to the king except the gods, and they do not live among men." This made the king so angry and furious that he ordered the execution of all the wise men of Babylon. So the decree was issued to put the wise men to death, and men were sent to look for Daniel and his friends to put them to death. When Arioch, the commander of the king's guard, had gone out to put to death the wise men of Babylon, Daniel spoke to him with wisdom and tact. He asked the king's officer, "Why did the king issue such a harsh decree?" Arioch then explained the matter to Daniel. At this, Daniel went in to the king and asked for time, so that he might interpret the dream for him. Then Daniel returned to his house and explained the matter to his friends Hananiah, Mishael and Azariah. He urged them to plead for mercy from the God of heaven concerning this mystery, so that he and his friends might not be executed with the rest of the wise men of Babylon. During the night the mystery was revealed to Daniel in a vision. Then Daniel praised the God of heaven and said: "Praise be to the name of God for ever and ever; wisdom and power are his. He changes times and seasons; he sets up kings and deposes them. He gives wisdom to the wise and knowledge to the discerning. He reveals deep and hidden things; he knows what lies in darkness, and light dwells with him. I thank and praise you, O God of my fathers: You have given me wisdom and power, you have made known to me what we asked of you, you have made known to us the dream of the king."

DANIEL INTERPRETS THE DREAM

Then Daniel went to Arioch, whom the king had appointed to execute the wise men of Babylon, and said to him, "Do not execute the wise men of Babylon. Take me to the king, and I will interpret his dream for him." Arioch took Daniel to the king at once and said, "I have found a man among the exiles from Judah who can tell the king what his dream means." The king asked Daniel (also called Belteshazzar), "Are you able to tell me what I saw in my dream and interpret it?" Daniel replied, "No wise man, enchanter, magician or diviner can explain to the king the mystery he has asked about, but there is a God in heaven who reveals mysteries. He has shown King Nebuchadnezzar what will happen in days to come. Your dream and the visions that passed through your mind as you lay on your bed are these: "As you were lying there, O king, your mind turned to things to come, and the revealer of mysteries showed you what is going to happen. As for me, this mystery has been revealed to me, not because I have greater wisdom than other living men, but so that you, O king, may know the interpretation and that you may understand what went through your mind. "You looked, O king, and there before you stood a large statue—an enormous, dazzling statue, awesome in appearance. The head of the statue was made of pure gold, its chest and arms of silver, its belly and thighs of bronze, its legs of iron, its feet partly of iron and partly of baked clay. While you were watching, a rock was cut out, but not by human hands. It struck the statue on its feet of iron and clay and smashed them. Then the iron, the clay, the bronze, the silver and the gold were broken to pieces at the same time and became like chaff on a threshing floor in the summer. The wind swept them away without leaving a trace. But the rock that struck the statue became a huge mountain and filled the whole earth. "This was the dream, and now we will interpret it to the king. You, O king, are the king of kings. The God of heaven has given you dominion and power and might and glory; in your hands he has placed mankind and the beasts of the field and the birds of the air. Wherever they live, he has made you ruler over them all. You are that head of gold. "After you, another kingdom will rise, inferior to yours. Next, a third kingdom, one of bronze, will rule over the whole earth. Finally, there will be a fourth kingdom, strong as iron—for iron breaks and smashes everything—and as iron breaks things to pieces, so it will crush and break all the others. Just as you saw that the feet and toes were partly of baked clay and partly of iron, so this will be a divided kingdom; yet it will have some of the strength of iron in it, even as you saw iron mixed with clay. As the toes were partly iron and partly clay, so this kingdom will be partly strong and partly brittle. And just as you saw the iron mixed with baked clay, so the people will be a mixture and will not remain united, any more than iron mixes with clay. "In the time of those kings, the God of heaven will set up a kingdom that will never be destroyed, nor will it be left to another people. It will crush all those kingdoms and bring them to an end, but it will itself endure forever. This is the meaning of the vision of the rock cut out of a mountain, but not by human hands—a rock that broke the iron, the bronze, the clay, the silver and the gold to pieces. "The great God has shown the king what will take place in the future. The dream is true and the interpretation is trustworthy." Then King Nebuchadnezzar fell prostrate before Daniel and paid him honor and ordered that an offering and incense be presented to him. The king said to Daniel, "Surely your God is the God of gods and the Lord of kings and a revealer of mysteries, for you were able to reveal this mystery." Then the king placed Daniel in a high position and lavished many gifts on him. He made him ruler over the entire province of Babylon and placed him in charge of all its wise men. Moreover, at Daniel's request the king appointed Shadrach, Meshach and Abednego administrators over the province of Babylon, while Daniel himself remained at the royal court."

By God's help in answer to their prayer, Nebuchadnezzar's forgotten dream, was revealed and interpreted by Daniel. The great image, as Daniel gave the interpretation to the king, symbolizes the entire period known in prophecy as, "The Times of The Gentiles." This is the long period of time when Jerusalem is in political subjection to to the nations, (The Goyim). This began with Judah's captivity to Babylon in 605 B.C., and will continue to extend until the second coming of Christ; who is The Rock; which was not cut out by human hands, and who will destroy The Gentile world system. Then, and only then, will The Rock who is Jesus, become a mountain, which symbolizes His Millennial Kingdom. This is **"The King Who was prophesied Who shall Live Forever, and The Kingdom Which Shall Never Be Destroyed, and Shall Last For All of Eternity."**

The four metals we see here symbolize four empires:

```
*** Gold=Babylon
*** Silver=Media-Persia
*** Brass=Macedonian-Greece
*** Iron=Rome
```

The Roman Empire which is the fourth kingdom, is seen by Daniel in a huge panorama, as it would be in the future. He would see it as being divided into two empires. The Eastern and Western Empires which occurred in 364 B.C.; which are represented by the two legs on The Colossus. Daniel sees these

11

two divisions being resurrected, in our day and time, and who will enjoy an endtime political revival in a ten-kingdom United States of Europe; which is NOT The European Common Market. The Eastern division which are the dictatorships, [which are the iron], and the Western division which are the democracies, [which are the baked clay]. Then, and only then, will The Rock of Ages, Who is Jesus, will strike and destroy Gentile world power and restore the kingdom to Israel. When we go to Rome today, we usually take our christian group to The Coliseum; and we look at the two maps that are there on the face of it. One map showing the old Roman Empire, and one map showing The Nations of The European Common Market. With just a few minor variances these two maps are identical. **The European Common Market IS NOT, and again I repeat IS NOT,** the ten kingdoms of the ten toes shown to Daniel; if it was, Jesus would have been here by now. This is still to happen. The ten kingdoms will be an outgrowth of the Kingdom of Alexander The Great; which eventually became The Roman Empire. In 538 B.C., Medo-Persia brought to an end Babylon, the first world-empire, and that part of Daniel's prophecy regarding the four great empires was fulfilled. At the close of the old testament canon the Persian rule had existed for about 100 years. This rule was tolerant. It allowed the high priest to exercise his religious functions and after Palestine was annexed to the Satrapy of Syria, the high priests, under the governors of Syria, enjoyed considerable political power in the government of the country. The ambitions and hopes of Philip of Macedon were realized by His son Alexander. With the rising of this mighty conqueror the sun of Persia was due to set. The weapon with which the Persian Empire was to be broken to pieces was now prepared. The mighty he-goat that had been seen 200 years earlier in Daniel's vision on the banks of the Ulai, was advancing from the west to overthrow the two-horned ram, the vast but now tottering Medo-Persian Empire. At the age of twenty in 336 B.C. Alexander came to the throne, and during the brief period of 13 years altered the course of world history. Thus arose the third world-empire represented in Daniel's vision by the body and thighs of brass. Within the remarkably brief period of his reign, Alexander became the master of Greece, Asia, Egypt and Syria. In the battle of Arbela; Persia; the second world-power, was crushed. In 333 B.C., Syria fell into Alexander's hands. After reducing Egypt he founded the city of Alexandria which became the meeting place of the East and the West. The ruling ambition of this king was not just that of conquering the world, but of leaving upon the nations of the world a Grecian civilization, and thus bring the East under western influences. As THE PUPIL of Aristotle he was trained by that master mind in the matters of philosophy. He gave the world a universal language of culture into which the Old Testament was later translated at Alexandria which paved the way for Christianity. Alexander appreciated the intelligence, industriousness and steadiness of the Hebrew people, and in placing them in Alexandria and other centers they were brought into world-wide contacts. Away from Jerusalem, from the sacrificial part of their worship, greater attention was given to the Law and the Prophets and the result was that in the countries of their dispersion the expectation of the coming Messiah was widely spread. This period of 116 years from 320-204 B.C. had an important bearing upon Hebrew interests. Daniel had predicted that the empire of Alexander would separate into four parts, that the great horn would be broken and in its place would arise four horns. Following Alexander's death his empire was divided between his four generals. Egypt, Libya, and later Palestine, fell to Ptolemy. Great numbers of Jews were settled in Egypt. Ptolemy Philadelphus treated them kindly and during his reign the sacred writings of the Hebrews was translated into the Greek. This version of the Old Testament is called The Septuagint and is known as the LXX; which means seventy, for the reason seventy Rabbis went down from Jerusalem to Alexandria and rewrote the entire Old Testament from Hebrew into Greek. This was done in 285 B.C. and was one of the great results for the spreading of the Gospel later on. The significance of the Septuagint can not be over estimated. Not only were the Scriptures translated into the language of the Greeks, but could be read and known by the whole Greek speaking world. The prophecies of The Coming Messiah would lead to a greater expectation of Him than just by the Hebrew people. The Syrian Monarchy now arose, Seleucus, another of Alexander's generals, founded Antioch which became the western capital of his kingdom, and nearly all of Asia came into his possession. This city became one of the great centers of Christianity. Because of their characteristics, Seleucus induced the Jews to settle in the new cities. In the conflicts between Syria and Egypt, Antiochus the Great was defeated by Ptolemy Philopator who took possession of Palestine. Under this rule the Jews were bitterly persecuted. This period lasted for 39 years, from 204-165 B.C. Ptolemy Philopator died and

Antiochus seized Palestine and Syria. At this time the land was divided into five provinces which all readers of The New Testament are familiar with: Judea, Samaria, Galilee, Trachonitis and Perea. Antiochus Epiphanes came to the throne and then began a bitter period for the Jews. He deposed the high priest Onias and placed the priesthood in the hands of his brother Jason; who was a compromiser with heathenism. It was reported that Antiochus died in Egypt which caused great rejoicing among the Jews. It was a false report and when he Antiochus, returned in 168 B.C., he slew 40,000 Jews and profaned the Temple of God by sacrificing a sow on the altar, and then erected an altar to Jupiter. "This desolation" is considered by some, as a picture prophecy of the final "abomination of desolation" spoken of by Jesus in Matthew 24:15. The people of Israel were forbidden to worship in the Temple and were compelled to eat the flesh of swine. A great massacre followed where 40,000 women were raped and then sold into slavery, plus an additional 40,000 children were sold into slavery. In terror the people of Israel fled from Jerusalem and for over three years Temple worship was abandoned. The Hebrew religion was forbidden and the Temple of God was devoted to the worship of the Grecian gods. This monster, Antiochus Epiphanes, who is considered by some, to be a picture type of the Anti-Christ, did everything in his power to wipe out the Jewish people. Upon the death of Alexander we see that his kingdom was divided by his four generals. The two most powerful Empires were the Seleucid and the Ptolemaic Empires. The Ptolemaic Empire was Libya and the Kingdom of Egypt on the Nile with Alexandria as its capital. It was ruled by a dynasty whose last representative was Cleopatra. The Seleucid Empire included these Middle Eastern Kingdoms. All of Asia Minor, Southern Turkey, Iran, Iraq, Lebanon, Syria, Jordan, Afghanistan, and Western Pakistan. The countdown to The Rapture will begin as soon as there is a confederacy of ten kings, meaning ten nations; and there is **a local war among themselves; and not a nuclear war**; where one them emerges as victor and subdues three of these kings or three of these nations. Syria, today is EMBARKING on one of the most "power plays" in modern history. Lebanon is already under her control. With Iraq and Iran engaged in a war for the last 8 years; the "Climate" is right for Syria to take over those two nations. For the Prophecy continues to show us that when this Occurs, all the other **Arab Nations** will now Delegate their combined authority to SYRIA to make peace with Israel. JESUS was nailed to a cross; but this LEADER of SYRIA who will MAKE the peace with ISRAEL will be hailed as the Greatest Peace Maker the world has ever seen."THE WORLD WILL RUN AFTER HIM TO WORSHIP HIM." Now remember my beloved Jesus told us no will know when The Rapture will take place; or when The Antichrist will be revealed: The Antichrist will come from one of these nations of the old Seleucid Empire according to God's Word as we see in Daniel 7:23-25. No one will know when these events will take place except "The Father In Heaven." But praise The Holy Name Of Jesus for He gave us these many signs of these end times; that "we may look up knowing His Redemption draweth nigh unto us."

THE IMAGE OF GOLD
AND THE FIERY FURNACE

DAN 3:1 King Nebuchadnezzar made an image of gold, ninety feet high and nine feet wide, and set it up on the plain of Dura in the province of Babylon. He then summoned the satraps, prefects, governors, advisers, treasurers, judges, magistrates and all the other provincial officials to come to the dedication of the image he had set up. So the satraps, prefects, governors, advisers, treasurers, judges, magistrates and all the other provincial officials assembled for the dedication of the image that King Nebuchadnezzar had set up, and they stood before it. Then the herald loudly proclaimed, "This is what you are commanded to do, O peoples, nations and men of every language: As soon as you hear the sound of the horn, flute, zither, lyre, harp, pipes and all kinds of music, you must fall down and worship the image of gold that King Nebuchadnezzar has set up. Whoever does not fall down and worship will immediately be thrown into a blazing furnace." Therefore, as soon as they heard the sound of the horn, flute, zither, lyre, harp and all kinds of music, all the peoples, nations and men of every language fell down and worshiped the image of gold that King Nebuchadnezzar had set up. At this time some astrologers came forward and denounced the Jews. They said to King Nebuchadnezzar, "O king, live forever! You have issued a decree, O king, that everyone who hears the sound of the horn, flute, zither, lyre, harp, pipes and all kinds of music must fall down and worship the image of gold, and that whoever does not fall down and worship will be thrown into a blazing furnace. But there are some Jews whom you have set over the affairs of the province of Babylon—Shadrach, Meshach and Abednego—who pay no attention to you, O king. They neither serve your gods nor worship the image of gold you have set up." Furious with rage, Nebuchadnezzar summoned Shadrach, Meshach and Abednego. So these men were brought before the king, and Nebuchadnezzar said to them, "Is it true, Shadrach, Meshach and Abednego, that you do not serve my gods or worship the image of gold I have set up? Now when you hear the sound of the horn, flute, zither, lyre, harp, pipes and all kinds of music, if you are ready to fall down and worship the image I made, very good. But if you do not worship it, you will be thrown immediately into a blazing furnace. Then what god will be able to rescue you from my hand?" Shadrach, Meshach and Abednego replied to the king, "O Nebuchadnezzar, we do not need to defend ourselves before you in this matter. If we are thrown into the blazing furnace, the God we serve is able to save us from it, and he will rescue us from your hand, O king. But even if he does not, we want you to know, O king, that we will not serve your gods or worship the image of gold you have set up." Then Nebuchadnezzar was furious with Shadrach, Meshach and Abednego, and his attitude toward them changed. He ordered the furnace heated seven times hotter than usual and commanded some of the strongest soldiers in his army to tie up Shadrach, Meshach and Abednego and throw them into the blazing furnace. So these men, wearing their robes, trousers, turbans and other clothes, were bound and thrown into the blazing furnace. The king's command was so urgent and the furnace so hot that the flames of the fire killed the soldiers who took up Shadrach, Meshach and Abednego, and these three men, firmly tied, fell into the blazing furnace. Then King Nebuchadnezzar leaped to his feet in amazement and asked his advisers, "Weren't there three men that we tied up and threw into the fire?" They replied, "Certainly, O king." He said, "Look! I see four men walking around in the fire, unbound and unharmed, and the fourth looks like a son of the gods." Nebuchadnezzar then approached the opening of the blazing furnace and shouted, "Shadrach, Meshach and Abednego, servants of the Most High God, come out! Come here!" So Shadrach, Meshach and Abednego came out of the fire, and the satraps, prefects, governors and royal advisers crowded around them. They saw that the fire had not harmed their bodies, nor was a hair of their heads singed; their robes were not scorched, and there was no smell of fire on them. Then Nebuchadnezzar said, "Praise be to the God of Shadrach,

Meshach and Abednego, who has sent his angel and rescued his servants! They trusted in him and defied the king's command and were willing to give up their lives rather than serve or worship any god except their own God. Therefore I decree that the people of any nation or language who say anything against the God of Shadrach, Meshach and Abednego be cut into pieces and their houses be turned into piles of rubble, for no other god can save in this way." Then the king promoted Shadrach, Meshach and Abednego in the province of Babylon. Nebuchadnezzar's arrogance and idolatry culminated and manifested itself in his making of The Image of Gold. The image was 90 feet high and 9 feet wide in the form of an obelisk, grotesque, as man's idolatry and self-deification, is being flaunted before God's Face. At the sound of the music; which was about the largest and longest **ROCK AND ROLL** concert ever held in the history of man; the people were to get involved in **BESTIALITY** by **COPULATING** with animals; having **ILLICIT SEX** one with another; Men with Men; Women with Women; The Worshiping of Satan and The Image. The spirit of Humanism, Idolatry, ILLICIT Sex, and the Deification of man are still with us till today; as we see that many of our LEADERS ARE TEACHING OUR PEOPLE IN OUR CHURCHES HOW TO BECOME "GODS." We are still living in The Age of The Gentile which will not come to an end until the second coming of Jesus The Christ. All the Pharoah's of Egypt declared themselves to be God's, and all the Dictators and Emperors after Nebuchadnezzar declared the same. Is it any wonder that Shadrach, Meshach, and Abednego refused to worship The Image; and get involved in **THE LICENTIOUSNESS** that most of the rest of the people were involved in. Webster's Dictionary explains to us what Licentiousness means. It means "unrestrained by law or morality, especially in sexual behavior; lasciviousness; lewd." Shadrach, Meshach and Abednego now make the statement to the king saying "O Nebuchadnezzar, we do not need to defend ourselves in this matter. If we are thrown into the blazing furnace, the God we serve is able to save us from it, and He will rescue us from your hand, O king. But even if He does not, we want you to know, O king, that we will not serve your gods or worship the image of gold you have set up." As they were thrown into the fire, they walked in the heart of the fire, praising God and blessing the Lord. Azariah, who's name was changed to Abednego, stood still among the flames and began to pray aloud: "Blessed art Thou, O Lord, the God of our fathers, Your Name is worthy of praise and glorious for ever: You are just in all Your deeds and true in all Your works; straight in all Your paths, and all Your judgments just. Just sentence You have passed in all that You have brought upon us and upon Jerusalem the holy city of our fathers: Yes, just sentence You have passed upon our sins. For indeed we sinned and broke Your law in rebellion against You, in all we did we sinned; we did not heed Your commandments, we did not keep them, we did not do what You had commanded us for our good. In all the punishments You have sent upon us Your judgments have been just. You have handed us over to our bitterest enemies, rebels against Your law, and to a wicked king, the vilest in the world. And so now we are speechless for shame: Contempt has fallen on your servants and your worshipers. For Your Honor's sake do not abandon us for ever; do not annul Your covenant. Do not withdraw Your mercy from us, for the sake of Abraham, your beloved, for the sake of Isaac, your servant and Israel, your holy one. You did promise to multiply their descendants as the stars in the sky and the sand on the seashore. But now, Lord, we have been made the smallest of all nations; for our sins we are today the most abject in the world. We have no ruler, no prophet, no leader now; there is no burnt offering, no sacrifice, no oblation, no incense, no place to make an offering before You and find mercy. But because we come with contrite heart and humbled spirit, accept us. As though we came with burnt offerings of rams and bullocks and with a thousand of fat lambs, so let our sacrifice be made before You this day. Accept our pledge of loyalty to You, for no shame shall come to those who put their trust in You. Now we will follow You with our whole heart and fear You. We seek Your presence; do not put us to shame, but deal with us in Your forbearance and in the greatness of Your mercy. Grant us again Your marvelous deliverance, and win glory for Your name, O Lord. Let all who do your servants harm be humbled; may they be put to shame and stripped of all their power, and may their strength be crushed; let them know that You alone are The Lord God, and glorious over all the world." The servants of the king who threw them in kept on feeding the furnace with naphtha, pitch, tow, faggots, and the flames poured out above it to a height of 75 feet. The flames spread out and burned to death those who were near the furnace. But The Angel of The Lord came down into the furnace to join Azariah, and his companions; and He scattered the flames out of the furnace and He made the heart of it as if a moist wind were whistling through.

The fire did not touch them at all and neither hurt nor distressed them. The fourth person who was seen walking in the fiery furnace with the three hebrew children; was non other than Jesus himself, The Angel of The Lord, The Pre-incarnate Christ, The Pre-existent Christ who appeared many times during The Old Testament Period!

He appeared to Moses in Exodus 3:2
He appeared to Joshua in Joshua 5:14
He appeared to The Children of Israel in Judges 2:1-5
He appeared to Gideon in Judges 6:11-24

He appeared to Samson's mother in Judges 13:3-25. Praise Jesus!!!!

EXO 3:1 Now Moses was tending the flock of Jethro his father-in-law, the priest of Midian, and he led the flock to the far side of the desert and came to Horeb, the mountain of God. There THE ANGEL OF THE LORD appeared to him in flames of fire from within a bush. Moses saw that though the bush was on fire it did not burn up. So Moses thought, "I will go over and see this strange sight—why the bush does not burn up." When the LORD saw that he had gone over to look, GOD called to him from within the bush, "Moses! Moses!" And Moses said, "Here I am."

JOS 5:13 Now when Joshua was near Jericho, he looked up and saw a man standing in front of him with a drawn sword in his hand. Joshua went up to him and asked, "Are you for us or for our enemies?" "Neither," he replied, "but as PRINCE OF THE ARMY OF THE LORD I have now come." Then Joshua fell facedown to the ground in reverence and worshiped Him, and asked him, "What message does my LORD have for his servant?"

JDG 2:1 The angel of the Lord went up from Gilgal to Bokim and said, "I brought you up out of Egypt and led you into the land that I swore to give to your forefathers. I said, 'I will never break my covenant with you, and you shall not make a covenant with the people of this land, but you shall break down their altars.' Yet you have disobeyed me. Why have you done this? When the angel of the Lord had spoken these things to all the Israelites, the people wept aloud, and they called that place Bokim. There they offered sacrifices to the Lord.

JDG 6:11 The angel of the Lord came and sat down under the oak in Ophrah that belonged to Joash the Abiezrite, where

19

his son Gideon was threshing wheat in a winepress to keep it
from the Midianites. When the angel of the Lord appeared to
Gideon, he said, "The Lord is with you, mighty warrior." "But
sir," Gideon replied, "if the Lord is with us, why has all this
happened to us? Where are all his wonders that our fathers
told us about when they said, 'Did not the Lord bring us up out
of Egypt?' But now the Lord has abandoned us and put us into
the hand of Midian." The Lord turned to him and said, "Go in
the strength you have and save Israel out of Midian's hand.
Am I not sending you?" "But Lord," Gideon asked, "how can I
save Israel? My clan is the weakest in Manasseh, and I am the
least in my family." The Lord answered, "I will be with you,
and you will strike down all the Midianites together." When
Gideon realized that it was the angel of the Lord, he ex-
claimed, "Ah, Sovereign Lord! I have seen the angel of the
Lord face to face!" But the Lord said to him, "Peace! Do not be
afraid. You are not going to die." So Gideon built an altar to
the Lord there and called it JEHOVAH SHALOM; The Lord is
Peace. To this day it stands in Ophrah of the Abiezrites. Then
the Spirit of the Lord came upon Gideon.

Chapter 3

Nebuchadnezzar's Insanity

DAN 4:1 King Nebuchadnezzar, To the peoples, nations and men of every language, who live in all the world: May you prosper greatly! It is my pleasure to tell you about the miraculous signs and wonders that the Most High God has performed for me. How great are his signs, how mighty his wonders! His kingdom is an eternal kingdom; his dominion endures from generation to generation. I, Nebuchadnezzar, was at home in my palace, contented and prosperous. I had a dream that made me afraid. As I was lying in my bed, the images and visions that passed through my mind terrified me. So I commanded that all the wise men of Babylon be brought before me to interpret the dream for me. When the magicians, enchanters, astrologers and diviners came, I told them the dream, but they could not interpret it for me. Finally, Daniel came into my presence and I told him the dream. (He is called Belteshazzar, after the name of my god, and the spirit of the holy gods is in him.) I said, "Belteshazzar, chief of the magicians, I know that the spirit of the holy gods is in you, and no mystery is too difficult for you. Here is my dream; interpret it for me. These are the visions I saw while lying in my bed: I looked, and there before me stood a tree in the middle of the land. Its height was enormous. The tree grew large and strong and its top touched the sky; it was visible to the ends of the earth. Its leaves were beautiful, its fruit abundant, and on it was food for all. Under it the beasts of the field found shelter, and the birds of the air lived in its branches; from it every creature was fed. "In the visions I saw while lying in my bed, I looked, and there before me was a messenger, a holy one, coming down from heaven. He called in a loud voice: 'Cut down the tree and trim off its branches; strip off its leaves and scatter its fruit. Let the animals flee from under it and the birds from its branches. But let the stump and its roots, bound with iron and bronze, remain in the ground, in the grass of the field. " 'Let him be drenched with the dew of heaven, and let him live with the animals among the plants of the earth. Let his mind be changed from that of a man and let him be given the mind of an animal, till seven times pass by for him. " 'The decision is announced by messengers, the holy ones declare the verdict, so that the living may know that the Most High is sovereign over the kingdoms of men and gives them to anyone he wishes and sets over them the lowliest of men.' "This is the dream that I, King Nebuchadnezzar, had. Now, Belteshazzar, tell me what it means, for none of the wise men in my kingdom can interpret it for me. But you can, because the spirit of the holy gods is in you." Then Daniel (also called Belteshazzar) was greatly perplexed for a time, and his thoughts terrified him. So the king said, "Belteshazzar, do not let the dream or its meaning alarm you." Belteshazzar answered, "My lord, if only the dream applied to your enemies and its meaning to your adversaries! The tree you saw, which grew large and strong, with its top touching the sky, visible to the whole earth, with beautiful leaves and abundant fruit, providing food for all, giving shelter to the beasts of the field, and having nesting places in its branches for the birds of the air—you, O king, are that tree! You have become great and strong; your greatness has grown until it reaches the sky, and your dominion extends to distant parts of the earth. "You, O king, saw a messenger, a holy one, coming down from heaven and saying, 'Cut down the tree and destroy it, but leave the stump, bound with iron and bronze, in the grass of the field, while its roots remain in the ground. Let him be drenched with the dew of heaven; let him live like the wild animals, until seven times pass by for him.' "This is the interpretation, O king, and this is the decree the Most High has issued against my lord the king: You will be driven away from people and will live with the wild animals; you will eat grass like cattle and be drenched with the dew of heaven. Seven times will pass by for you until you acknowledge that the Most High is sovereign over the kingdoms of men and gives them to anyone he wishes. The command to leave the stump of the tree with its roots means that your kingdom will be restored to you when you acknowledge that Heaven rules. Therefore, O king, be pleased to accept my advice: Renounce your sins by doing what is right, and your wickedness by being kind to the oppressed. It may be that then your prosperity will continue." All this happened to King Nebuchadnezzar. Twelve months later, as the king was walking on the roof of the royal palace of Babylon, he said, "Is not this the great Babylon I have built as the royal residence, by my mighty power and for the glory of my majesty?" The words were still on his lips when a voice came from heaven, "This is what is decreed for you, King Nebuchadnezzar: Your royal authority has been taken from you. You will be driven away from people and will live with the wild animals; you will eat grass like cattle. Seven times will pass by for you until you acknowledge that the Most High is sovereign over the kingdoms of men and gives them to anyone he wishes." Immediately what had been said about Nebuchadnezzar was fulfilled. He was driven away from people and ate grass like cattle. His body was drenched with the dew of heaven until his hair grew like the feathers of an eagle and his nails like the claws of a bird. At the end of that time, I, Nebuchadnezzar, raised my eyes toward heaven, and my sanity was restored. Then I praised the Most High; I honored and glorified him who lives forever. His dominion is an eternal dominion; his kingdom endures from generation to generation. All the peoples of the earth are regarded as nothing. He does as he pleases with the powers of heaven and the peoples of the earth. No one can hold back his hand or say to him: "What have you done?" At the same time that my sanity was restored, my honor and splendor were returned to me for the glory of my kingdom. My advisers and nobles sought me out, and I was restored to my throne and became even greater than before. Now I, Nebuchadnezzar, praise and exalt and glorify the King of heaven, because everything he does is right and all his ways are just. And those who walk in pride he is able to humble." The purpose of this chapter like the preceding one, is to teach that the GOD of ISRAEL is the God of the whole universe, and that the temporal power and greatness of all nations and monarchs are subject to His will. The episode which was just related illustrates the truth of the scripture found in 1st. Samuel 2:7, "The Lord sends poverty and wealth; He humbles and He exalts." There are, in addition, a number of subsidiary lessons which God through Daniel drives home to today's world, and society.

1. True wisdom is based upon the fear of God.
2. Pride, or as the word in Hebrew means, arrogance, comes before a fall.
3. Repentance is an effective means of winning back God's divine grace.

From the interpretation that Daniel gave the king, he could not mistake the meaning of his dream. Then Daniel, like the faithful prophet that he was, took advantage of the opportunity and counseled the king to forsake his sinful ways. But the king did not take Daniel's advice, and later had to make the humiliating confession that all that had been foretold about him had come to pass. But it did not come at once; God gave him a year of grace to repent. Because the sentence was not executed at once Nebuchadnezzar thought that Daniel was mistaken, or that God had forgotten. But at the end of twelve months, as the king was walking in his palace and beheld the great city of Babylon from his palace window; the "I" syndrome took over in his life as it does in many people's lives we see today. Everything in regards to progress, development, beauty he Nebuchadnezzar had done it; and God had nothing to do with it. The fatal moment was when Nebuchadnezzar said, "Is not this Great Babylon, that "I" have built for the House of the Kingdom by the might of "My" Power, and for the honor of "My" Majesty?" His time of probation was up. The sentence was immediately executed. Not another moment of grace was given to the king. His insanity came upon him right then and there; And he imagined himself to be an Ox. Our Jewish history reveals that he was not confined but he was allowed to roam in the fields close to the palace. He did eat grass as oxen, and his body was wet with the dew of heaven, and he went about on all fours. Nebuchadnezzar's insanity lasted for seven years. At the end of the seven years, Nebuchadnezzar lifted up his eyes to heaven. A beast does not do that. In, particular an ox, looks downward and not up to heaven. What Nebuchadnezzar is saying here, is that he looked up to heaven in prayer to God, and asked God to forgive him of his sin, and he also acknowledged God's Supremacy. What we also see here is that Nebuchadnezzar was not a mindless animal. He knew God's sentence was upon him; and we see at the end of the seven year period his understanding returned: He Glorified, and Praised God and he was restored; which was the fulfillment of the promise made to him, by God, through Daniel that he would be restored. We see that there are many miracles to be found in this Book of Daniel. The major miracle of The Captivity of Israel in Babylon was that Israel, who from the very beginning of its call by God had constantly and always lapsed into idolatry, was now finally convinced in The Captivity that their God was **THE TRUE GOD**. Israel has never relapsed into idolatry ever again. Our Rabbis and our Prophets have constantly reminded us that when Israel received "The Ten Commandments", all of Israel heard God's Majestic Voice out of Sinai. That particular generation and All Succeeding Generations of Israelites after them heard God's voice. That Revelation at Sinai was the most remarkable event in the history of humanity. It was the birth-hour of **THE RELIGION OF THE SPIRIT** destined to illumine the souls, and order the lives of all of mankind!

Chapter 4

Belshazzar's Feast

DAN 5:1 King Belshazzar gave a great banquet for a thousand of his nobles and drank wine with them. While Belshazzar was drinking his wine, he gave orders to bring in the gold and silver goblets that Nebuchadnezzar his father had taken from the temple in Jerusalem, so that the king and his nobles, his wives and his concubines might drink from them. So they brought in the gold goblets that had been taken from the temple of God in Jerusalem, and the king and his nobles, his wives and his concubines drank from them. As they drank the wine, they praised the gods of gold and silver, of bronze, iron, wood and stone. Suddenly the fingers of a human hand appeared and wrote on the plaster of the wall, near the lampstand in the royal palace. The king watched the hand as it wrote. His face turned pale and he was so frightened that his knees knocked together and his legs gave way. The king called out for the enchanters, astrologers and diviners to be brought and said to these wise men of Babylon, "Whoever reads this writing and tells me what it means will be clothed in purple and have a gold chain placed around his neck, and he will be made the third highest ruler in the kingdom." Then all the king's wise men came in, but they could not read the writing or tell the king what it meant. So King Belshazzar became even more terrified and his face grew more pale. His nobles were baffled. The queen, hearing the voices of the king and his nobles, came into the banquet hall. "O king, live forever!" she said. "Don't be alarmed! Don't look so pale! There is a man in your kingdom who has the spirit of the holy gods in him. In the time of your father he was found to have insight and intelligence and wisdom like that of the gods. King Nebuchadnezzar your father—your father the king, I say—appointed him chief of the magicians, enchanters, astrologers and diviners. This man Daniel, whom the king called Belteshazzar, was found to have a keen mind and knowledge and understanding, and also the ability to interpret dreams, explain riddles and solve difficult problems. Call for Daniel, and he will tell you what the writing means." So Daniel was brought before the king, and the king said to him, "Are you Daniel, one of the exiles my father the king brought from Judah? I have heard that the spirit of the gods is in you and that you have insight, intelligence and outstanding wisdom. The wise men and enchanters were brought before me to read this writing and tell me what it means, but they could not explain it. Now I have heard that you are able to give interpretations and to solve difficult problems. If you can read this writing and tell me what it means, you will be clothed in purple and have a gold chain placed around your neck, and you will be made the third highest ruler in the kingdom." Then Daniel answered the king, "You may keep your gifts for yourself and give your rewards to someone else. Nevertheless, I will read the writing for the king and tell him what it means. "O king, the Most High God gave your father Nebuchadnezzar sovereignty and greatness and glory and splendor. Because of the high position he gave him, all the peoples and nations and men of every language dreaded and feared him. Those the king wanted to put to death, he put to death; those he wanted to spare, he spared; those he wanted to promote, he promoted; and those he wanted to humble, he humbled. But when his heart became arrogant and hardened with pride, he was deposed from his royal throne and stripped of his glory. He was driven away from people and given the mind of an animal; he lived with the wild donkeys and ate grass like cattle; and his body was drenched with the dew of heaven, until he acknowledged that the Most High God is sovereign over the kingdoms of men and sets over them anyone he wishes. "But you his son, O Belshazzar, have not humbled yourself, though you knew all this. Instead, you have set yourself up against the Lord of heaven. You had the goblets from his temple brought to you, and you and your nobles, your wives and your concubines drank wine from them. You praised the gods of silver and gold, of bronze, iron, wood and stone, which cannot see or hear or understand. But you did not honor the God who holds in his hand your life and all your ways. Therefore he sent the hand that wrote the inscription. "This is the inscription that was written: MENE, MENE, TEKEL, PARSIN "This is what these words mean:

MENE: God has numbered the days of your reign
and brought it to an end.
TEKEL: You have been weighed on the scales and
found wanting.
PERES: Your kingdom is divided and given to the
Medes and Persians."

Then at Belshazzar's command, Daniel was clothed in purple, a gold chain was placed around his neck, and he was proclaimed the third highest ruler in the kingdom. That very night Belshazzar, king of the Babylonians, was slain, and Darius the Mede took over the kingdom, at the age of sixty-two." Belshazzar's feast took place on the night of the fall of Babylon. Until 1853 no mention of Belshazzar, grandson of Nebuchadnezzar was found in Babylonian records; and Nabonidas, was known to have been the last king of Babylon. But in 1853 an inscription was found in a cornerstone of a temple built by Nabonidas in Ur to a god which read: "May I, Nabonidas, King of Babylon, not sin against thee. And may reverence for thee dwell in the heart of Belshazzar, my first born, favorite son." From other inscriptions it has been learned that Nabonidas, for much of the time, was in retirement outside of Babylon, and that Belshazzar was in control of the army and the government, co-regent with his father, and that it was Nabonidas who surrendered to Cyrus. The last we read about Nebuchadnezzar was about his restoration, and in which he lived a year after his restoration, in which many great honors were heaped upon him, and in which he Glorified God. He died after a brief illness in 561 B.C., and was succeeded by his son Evil-Merodach; who at once liberated King Jehoiakim, of Judah, from prison and fed him at his own table. 2nd.Kings 25:27-30. Jeremiah 52:31-34. After a reign of 2 years Evil-Merodach was put to death by Neriglissar, his brother-in-law, who ascended the throne and reigned for about 4 years, being killed in battle in the year 556 B.C. His son, and successor, Laborosoarchod, an imbecile child, was king for less than a year, when he was beaten to death, and the throne was seized by Nabonidas, another son of Nebuchadnezzar, who reigned from 555 B.C. until its fall in 538 B.C. Belshazzar, at the time the incidents in this chapter took place, was reigning in conjunction with his father Nabonidas; who was first in the kingdom, and Belshazzar second in the kingdom, which will explain to us the offer of making Daniel third in the kingdom. The feast of Belshazzar was no common feast, in a city where feasts were not uncommon. There is no feast like it recorded in all of history. The only feast that approaches it is the feast given by Ahasuerus, King of Persia in 521 B.C., as we see recorded in the first chapter of The Book of Esther. Belshazzar's Feast was the turning point in the history of Babylon. It marked the transition from the "Head of Gold" to the "Arms and Breast of Silver" of the "Image," and from the "Lion" to the "Bear" phase of Gentile rule of Daniel 7:1-5. It took place in 538 B.C., 23 years after the death of Nebuchadnezzar. As these years were taken up with events that had no relation to the Jews in the captivity, the Bible passes over them in silence. Even Daniel drops out of sight; but he is not forgotten by God, who gives him "Visions" of coming events. The Feast of Belshazzar was given in a spirit of contempt and defiance. The city of Babylon was in a state of siege. The armies of the Medes and the Persians were encamped outside its walls. But Belshazzar felt secure, for the drawbridges had been drawn up, the brazen gates barred, and Belshazzar knew that the walls of the city were impregnable; and he was confident that his soldiers from their position on the high walls would be able to destroy any one who would attempt to batter down the gates. The city was also provisioned for several years' siege, and with the tillable ground within the city walls its capture could be put off indefinitely. So, Belshazzar to show his contempt of the besieging army gave this great feast. The character of the feast is seen in the conduct of all who were there. It was a feast of licentiousness, debauchery, drunkenness, and idolatry. In the middle of the Feast, the King, Belshazzar, his brain befuddled with wine, and with a great desire to do something unique and sensational, now surpassed all of his previous blasphemous and sacrileges acts by ordering the sacred vessels of gold and silver that his grandfather Nebuchadnezzar had taken from the Temple of God in Jerusalem 68 years earlier; to be brought to The Banqueting Hall. The debauchery and licentiousness consisted of fornication with animals, fornication of men with men, women with women, and other abominable practices. When The Holy Vessels were brought in these were the the people they were distributed to, and they drank wine from them to the gods of gold, silver, brass, iron, wood, and stone, and thus they desecrated The Holy Vessels of The Lord. That was the fatal moment, the turning point of the feast. It now filled Babylon's "CUP OF INIQUITY" to the brim; and her doom was sealed. In that night Belshazzar King of Babylon was slain; and Darius the Mede received the kingdom. Darius the Mede did not take Babylon. It was captured by Cyrus. But as an act of courtesy, and because Media was the older of the two kingdoms of Media and Persia, and because Cyrus had other military campaigns to finish, Cyrus committed the governorship to his Uncle Darius, the King of Media, who ruled for 2 years.

The fall of Babylon is related to us by Xenophon, and Herodotus. "Cyrus diverted the Euphrates into a new channel, and guided by 2 deserters, marched by the dry bed into the city while The Babylonians were carousing."

Chapter 5

Daniel in the Den of Lions

DAN 6:1 It pleased Darius to appoint 120 satraps to rule throughout the kingdom, with three administrators over them, one of whom was Daniel. The satraps were made accountable to them so that the king might not suffer loss. Now Daniel so distinguished himself among the administrators and the satraps by his exceptional qualities that the king planned to set him over the whole kingdom. At this, the administrators and the satraps tried to find grounds for charges against Daniel in his conduct of government affairs, but they were unable to do so. They could find no corruption in him, because he was trustworthy and neither corrupt nor negligent. Finally these men said, "We will never find any basis for charges against this man Daniel unless it has something to do with the law of his God." So the administrators and the satraps went as a group to the king and said: "O King Darius, live forever! The royal administrators, prefects, satraps, advisers and governors have all agreed that the king should issue an edict and enforce the decree that anyone who prays to any god or man during the next thirty days, except to you, O king, shall be thrown into the lions' den. Now, O king, issue the decree and put it in writing so that it cannot be altered—in accordance with the laws of the Medes and Persians, which cannot be repealed." So King Darius put the decree in writing. Now when Daniel learned that the decree had been published, he went home to his upstairs room where the windows opened toward Jerusalem. Three times a day he got down on his knees and prayed, giving thanks to his God, just as he had done before. Then these men went as a group and found Daniel praying and asking God for help. So they went to the king and spoke to him about his royal decree: "Did you not publish a decree that during the next thirty days anyone who prays to any god or man except to you, O king, would be thrown into the lions' den?" The king answered, "The decree stands—in accordance with the laws of the Medes and Persians, which cannot be repealed." Then they said to the king, "Daniel, who is one of the exiles from Judah, pays no attention to you, O king, or to the decree you put in writing. He still prays three times a day." When the king heard this, he was greatly distressed; he was determined to rescue Daniel and made every effort until sundown to save him. Then the men went as a group to the king and said to him, "Remember, O king, that according to the law of the Medes and Persians no decree or edict that the king issues can be changed." So the king gave the order, and they brought Daniel and threw him into the lions' den. The king said to Daniel, "May your God, whom you serve continually, rescue you!" A stone was brought and placed over the mouth of the den, and the king sealed it with his own signet ring and with the rings of his nobles, so that Daniel's situation might not be changed. Then the king returned to his palace and spent the night without eating and without any entertainment being brought to him. And he could not sleep. At the first light of dawn, the king got up and hurried to the lions' den. When he came near the den, he called to Daniel in an anguished voice, "Daniel, servant of the living God, has your God, whom you serve continually, been able to rescue you from the lions?" Daniel answered, "O king, live forever! My God sent his angel, and he shut the mouths of the lions. They have not hurt me, because I was found innocent in his sight. Nor have I ever done any wrong before you, O king." The king was overjoyed and gave orders to lift Daniel out of the den. And when Daniel was lifted from the den, no wound was found on him, because he had trusted in his God. At the king's command, the men who had falsely accused Daniel were brought in and thrown into the lions' den, along with their wives and children. And before they reached the floor of the den, the lions overpowered them and crushed all their bones. Then King Darius wrote to all the peoples, nations and men of every language throughout the land: "May you prosper greatly! "I issue a decree that in every part of my kingdom people must fear and reverence the God of Daniel. "For he is the living God and he endures forever; his kingdom will not be destroyed, his dominion will never end. He rescues and he saves; he performs signs and wonders in the heavens and on the earth. He has rescued Daniel from the power of the lions." So Daniel prospered during the reign of Darius and the reign of Cyrus the Persian."

There is a beautiful spiritual lesson in Daniel's deliverance. The "Den of Lions" is a picture prophecy of "The Tomb of Joseph of Arimathea" in which our Lord and Savior Jesus Christ was laid, and before which a stone was rolled, and sealed, and marked with the King's signet. Just as the lions could not harm Daniel, so Jesus who went into the "Jaws of Death" could not be "Held by Death." When Daniel was delivered from the lions' den, he could not be thrown in again, he was free from that "law," for he had paid its penalty. So when we accept Jesus as our Lord and personal Savior we are free from the "Law of Sin and Death," because Jesus our Savior paid its penalty on The Cross of Calvary, and His deliverance from the "Tomb" by resurrection shows and proves that He Jesus fulfilled "The Sentence" and the "Tomb" could no longer hold Him!

In the erection of the Golden Image on the Plain of Dura we saw the characteristic feature of the Babylonian Empire, was the "Deification of Man." And here in this chapter, in the decree that no one for thirty days could offer a petition to any god or man except King Darius, we see the same "Deification of Man," was present in the second kingdom, or The Medo-Persian Empire. So it was in the Grecian and Roman Empires, and so it will be until the end of "The Times of the Gentiles," when the last Great Gentile Ruler, The Beast, The Anti-Christ is revealed as we see in Revelation 13:4, 14–5. Daniel like the three Hebrew children is a picture type of the Jewish Remnant, that Jesus promised to save during the time of The Great Tribulation.

At this point let us see what God has to say about Babylon through Isaiah.

ISA 47:1 "Go down, sit in the dust, Virgin Daughter of Babylon; sit on the ground without a throne, Daughter of the Babylonians. No more will you be called tender or delicate. Take millstones and grind flour; take off your veil. Lift up your skirts, bare your legs, and wade through the streams. Your nakedness will be exposed and your shame uncovered. I will take vengeance; I will spare no one." Our Redeemer—the Lord Almighty is his name—is the Holy One of Israel. "Sit in silence, go into darkness, Daughter of the Babylonians; no more will you be called queen of kingdoms. I was angry with my people and desecrated my inheritance; I gave them into your hand, and you showed them no mercy. Even on the aged you laid a very heavy yoke. You said, 'I will continue forever—the eternal queen!' But you did not consider these things or reflect on what might happen. "Now then, listen, you wanton creature, lounging in your security and saying to yourself, 'I am, and there is none besides me. I will never be a widow or suffer the loss of children.' Both of these will overtake you in a moment, on a single day: loss of children and widowhood. They will come upon you in full measure, in spite of your many sorceries and all your potent spells. You have trusted in your wickedness and have said, 'No one sees me.' Your wisdom and knowledge mislead you when you say to yourself, 'I am, and there is none besides me.' Disaster will come upon you, and you will not know how to conjure it away. A calamity will fall upon you that you cannot ward off with a ransom; a catastrophe you cannot foresee will suddenly come upon you. "Keep on, then, with your magic spells and with your many sorceries, which you have labored at since childhood. There is not one that can save you."

Chapter 6

Daniel's Dream of Four Beasts

DAN 7:1 In the first year of Belshazzar king of Babylon, Daniel had a dream, and visions passed through his mind as he was lying on his bed. He wrote down the substance of his dream. Daniel said: "In my vision at night I looked, and there before me were the four winds of heaven churning up the great sea. Four great beasts, each different from the others, came up out of the sea. "The first was like a lion, and it had the wings of an eagle. I watched until its wings were torn off and it was lifted from the ground so that it stood on two feet like a man, and the heart of a man was given to it. "And there before me was a second beast, which looked like a bear. It was raised up on one of its sides, and it had three ribs in its mouth between its teeth. It was told, 'Get up and eat your fill of flesh!' "After that, I looked, and there before me was another beast, one that looked like a leopard. And on its back it had four wings like those of a bird. This beast had four heads, and it was given authority to rule. "After that, in my vision at night I looked, and there before me was a fourth beast—terrifying and frightening and very powerful. It had large iron teeth; it crushed and devoured its victims and trampled underfoot whatever was left. It was different from all the former beasts, and it had ten horns. "While I was thinking about the horns, there before me was another horn, a little one, which came up among them; and three of the first horns were uprooted before it. This horn had eyes like the eyes of a man and a mouth that spoke boastfully. "As I looked, "thrones were set in place, and the Ancient of Days took his seat. His clothing was as white as snow; the hair of his head was white like wool. His throne was flaming with fire, and its wheels were all ablaze. A river of fire was flowing, coming out from before him. Thousands upon thousands attended him; ten thousand times ten thousand stood before him. The court was seated, and the books were opened. "Then I continued to watch because of the boastful words the horn was speaking. I kept looking until the beast was slain and its body destroyed and thrown into the blazing fire. (The other beasts had been stripped of their authority, but were allowed to live for a period of time.) "In my vision at night I looked, and there before me was one like a son of man, coming with the clouds of heaven. He approached the Ancient of Days and was led into his presence. He was given authority, glory and sovereign power; all peoples, nations and men of every language worshiped him. His dominion is an everlasting dominion that will not pass away, and his kingdom is one that will never be destroyed."

THE INTERPRETATION OF THE DREAM

DAN 7:15 "I, Daniel, was troubled in spirit, and the visions that passed through my mind disturbed me. I approached one of those standing there and asked him the true meaning of all this. "So he told me and gave me the interpretation of these things: 'The four great beasts are four kingdoms that will rise from the earth. But the saints of the Most High will receive the kingdom and will possess it forever—yes, for ever and ever.' " Then I wanted to know the true meaning of the fourth beast, which was different from all the others and most terrifying, with its iron teeth and bronze claws—the beast that crushed and devoured its victims and trampled underfoot whatever was left. I also wanted to know about the ten horns on its head and about the other horn that came up, before which three of them fell—the horn that looked more imposing than the others and that had eyes and a mouth that spoke boastfully. As I watched, this horn was waging war

against the saints and defeating them, until the Ancient of Days came and pronounced judgment in favor of the saints of the Most High, and the time came when they possessed the kingdom. "He gave me this explanation: 'The fourth beast is a fourth kingdom that will appear on earth. It will be different from all the other kingdoms and will devour the whole earth, trampling it down and crushing it. The ten horns are ten kings who will come from this kingdom. After them another king will arise, different from the earlier ones; he will subdue three kings. He will speak against the Most High and oppress his saints and try to change the set times and the laws. The saints will be handed over to him for a time, times and half a time.
" 'But the court will sit, and his power will be taken away and completely destroyed forever. Then the sovereignty, power and greatness of the kingdoms under the whole heaven will be handed over to the saints, the people of the Most High. His kingdom will be an everlasting kingdom, and all rulers will worship and obey him.' "This is the end of the matter. I, Daniel, was deeply troubled by my thoughts, and my face turned pale, but I kept the matter to myself."

THE FIRST BEAST

This is a continuation of the prophecy of chapter two, which was revealed 60 years earlier: Two aspects of one revelation of history: Four world empires, and then the Kingdom of God. In chapter two these are represented by an Image with a Head of Gold, a Breast of Silver, Thighs of Brass, and Feet of Iron, broken in pieces by a Stone. In this chapter these same Four World Empires are represented as a Lion, a Bear, a Leopard and a Terrible Beast. The First Beast was like a Lion, and had eagle's wings which Daniel saw emerge from the churning foam of The Great Sea. Its appearance would recall to Daniel the colossal figures of lions, with the wings of an eagle, and the face of a man, that adorned the palaces of Nineveh and Babylon, and would remind him that The First Beast was a symbol of The Babylonian Empire, and its first king, Nebuchadnezzar, and that it corresponded to The Head of Gold of The Image. In this Eagle Winged Lion we see a combination of the king of beasts and the king of birds, typical of the Absolute Monarchy of Nebuchadnezzar's conquering of the nations. But as Daniel gazed upon the beast its wings were plucked. That is, that Nebuchadnezzar, satisfied with his conquests gave himself up to the building of palaces, and to the pursuits of peace; where we see from that time on the glory of the empire began to fade. Then Daniel saw it lifted up and caused to walk on two feet instead of four, like a man, and a man's heart was given to it, but otherwise it was still a beast. Which means, it no longer resorted to the use of its teeth and claws to overcome its enemies, but to its intellect. The plucking of the wings also refers to the insanity of Nebuchadnezzar, and the standing on two feet like a man, and the receiving of a man's heart, to his recovery from his beastly state, as he acknowledged and praised The Living God, and his humane conduct from then on.

THE SECOND BEAST

The second beast was like a Bear. The Bear is the strongest beast after the Lion, and is known for its voracity, but it has none of the agility and majesty of the Lion, is awkward in its movements, and effects its purpose with comparative slowness, and by brute force and sheer strength. These were the characteristics of The Medo-Persian Empire. It was ponderous in its movements, and gained its victories by hurling vast masses of troops upon its enemies. Xerxes' expedition against Greece was undertaken with 2,500,000 fighting men. Its easy to see that the deployment of such enormous numbers of men would "devour much flesh." The side of the Bear which raised up, prepared to attack, represented Persia, which of The Dual Empire was the stronger and the most aggressive. It corresponded to the "right shoulder and arm" of the Image. The three ribs stood for the Three Kingdoms of Libya, Babylon, and Egypt, that formed a Triple Alliance to check the Medo-Persian power, but they were destroyed by it. As the Bear is an inferior animal to the Lion, we see that the Medo-Persian Empire was inferior to the Babylonian; in wealth, in magnificence, in its form of government but not in "Power." Thus the four wild beasts correspond with the metals of the image, in that each succeeding beast is inferior to the one that preceded it.

THE THIRD BEAST

The Third Beast was like a Leopard, with this difference that it had four heads and four wings. The leopard is the most agile and graceful of wild beasts. Slight in its frame, but strong, swift, and fierce, its characteristics reveal it as a fitting symbol of the rapid conquests of the Greeks under Alexander the Great, who, followed by small and well equipped armies, moved with lightening speed, and in about ten years over-threw the massive forces of Persia, and subdued the entire civilized world. While the four wings of a bird would add to the rapidity of its progress, they were only the wings of a bird, and not those of an eagle, indicating that even though its progress was swift, it would not be as victorious as the armies of Nebuchadnezzar. The four heads represent the four kingdoms into which the empire of Alexander the Great was divided; Macedonia, Thrace, Syria, and Egypt. Daniel now understood that the leopard corresponded to the Abdomen and the Thigh parts of the Image. He was confused by the four heads of the leopard for there was no fourfold division of the lower part of the brass of the Image, indicating that the Grecian Empire was to be divided into four parts. That is why we read in the scripture that the Visions of His Head troubled him. Daniel had to wait another two full years, until his Vision of the Ram and the He Goat, which he had seen to be fulfilled, for a solution to his difficulty.

THE FOURTH BEAST

The Fourth Beast was like no other beast that had been ever seen on earth. It was hideous to behold, and had, what no natural beast has, Teeth of Iron, and Nails of Brass. The fact that the Fourth Beast had Iron Teeth and Ten Horns would cause Daniel to see that the Iron Teeth corresponded to the Iron Legs of the Image, and the Ten Horns to the Ten Toes, and therefore the Fourth Beast represented the Roman Empire. But what mystified Daniel was the Little Horn that came up among the Ten Horns, for he had not seen a Little Toe spring up among the Ten Toes of the Image. Daniel understood at once that the Little Horn with its Eyes of a Man and its Mouth speaking blasphemy, meant some new additional revelation that God did not see fit to reveal to Nebuchadnezzar; which was reserved for Daniel and his people Israel. Therefore as we examine the last six chapters of this book, we must not forget that Daniel's own Visions have to do with God's dealings with the Jewish People in the Latter Days. We should remember that Daniel's Fourth Wild Beast is descriptive of the Roman Empire in both of it's First and Last stages. Before Daniel could ask for an explanation of the Little Horn he had another Vision. It is important to see that the Fourth Beast, and the 10 kingdom confederation growing out of it, is The End Time revived Rome, since the whole context involves the Second Coming of Christ and His subsequent rule. The saints of The Most High who possess The Kingdom, are the saved Jewish remnant who pass through The Great Tribulation and inherit The Kingdom and The Covenants and all the promises made by God to Israel in connection with it. The Kingdom will be Eternal, THE MEDIATORIAL AND TEMPORAL aspects of it, The thousand year reign of Christ on earth, merge into The Eternal state when Christ, after His reign on earth, delivers up The Kingdom to God The Father . . . that God may be all in all. It is important that the designation of God as The Most High, is used when The Messiah comes to make good that title in His Kingdom Rule on earth. In the beginning was The Word, and The Word was with God, and The Word was God:

PRAISE GOD THAT JESUS IS LORD!

Chapter 7

Daniel's Vision of a Ram and a Goat

DAN 8:1 In the third year of King Belshazzar's reign, I, Daniel, had a vision, after the one that had already appeared to me. In my vision I saw myself in the citadel of Susa in the province of Elam; in the vision I was beside the Ulai Canal. I looked up, and there before me was a ram with two horns, standing beside the canal, and the horns were long. One of the horns was longer than the other but grew up later. I watched the ram as he charged toward the west and the north and the south. No animal could stand against him, and none could rescue from his power. He did as he pleased and became great. As I was thinking about this, suddenly a goat with a prominent horn between his eyes came from the west, crossing the whole earth without touching the ground. He came toward the two-horned ram I had seen standing beside the canal and charged at him in great rage. I saw him attack the ram furiously, striking the ram and shattering his two horns. The ram was powerless to stand against him; the goat knocked him to the ground and trampled on him, and none could rescue the ram from his power. The goat became very great, but at the height of his power his large horn was broken off, and in its place four prominent horns grew up toward the four winds of heaven. Out of one of them came another horn, which started small but grew in power to the south and to the east and toward the Beautiful Land. It grew until it reached the host of the heavens, and it threw some of the starry host down to the earth and trampled on them. It set itself up to be as great as the Prince of the host; it took away the daily sacrifice from him, and the place of his sanctuary was brought low. Because of rebellion, the host of the saints and the daily sacrifice were given over to it. It prospered in everything it did, and truth was thrown to the ground. Then I heard a holy one speaking, and another holy one said to him, "How long will it take for the vision to be fulfilled—the vision concerning the daily sacrifice, the rebellion that causes desolation, and the surrender of the sanctuary and of the host that will be trampled underfoot?" He said to me, "It will take 2,300 evenings and mornings; then the sanctuary will be reconsecrated." While I, Daniel, was watching the vision and trying to understand it, there before me stood one who looked like a man. And I heard a man's voice from the Ulai calling, "Gabriel, tell this man the meaning of the vision." As he came near the place where I was standing, I was terrified and fell prostrate. "Son of man," he said to me, "understand that the vision concerns the time of the end." While he was speaking to me, I was in a deep sleep, with my face to the ground. Then he touched me and raised me to my feet. He said: "I am going to tell you what will happen later in the time of wrath, because the vision concerns the appointed time of the end. The two-horned ram that you saw represents the kings of Media and Persia. The shaggy goat is the king of Greece, and the large horn between his eyes is the first king. The four horns that replaced the one that was broken off represent four kingdoms that will emerge from his nation but will not have the same power. "In the latter part of their reign, when rebels have become completely wicked, a stern-faced king, a master of intrigue, will arise. He will become very strong, but not by his own power. He will cause astounding devastation and will succeed in whatever he does. He will destroy the mighty men and the holy people. He will cause deceit to prosper, and he will consider himself superior. When they feel secure, he will destroy many and take his stand against the Prince of princes. Yet he will be destroyed, but not by human power. "The vision of the evenings and mornings that has been given you is true, but seal up the vision, for it concerns the distant future." I, Daniel, was exhausted and lay ill for several days. Then I got up and went about the king's business. I was appalled by the vision; it was beyond understanding."

While Daniel knew from Nebuchadnezzar's dream in 603 B.C. that there were to be four world empires that were to succeed each other, he was not told their names, except the first, Babylon. Neither in his vision of the four wild beasts, given to him 62 years later, were the names of of the Kingdoms that were to succeed Babylon given. But in this vision of the Ram and the He-Goat there were revealed to him the names of the Kingdoms represented by the silver and brass of the image, and their corresponding beasts, the Bear and the Leopard. In Daniel's vision of of the four wild beasts, Medo-Persia and Greece are represented by a Bear and a Leopard; in this vision they are also represented by Beasts, a Ram and a He-Goat. The national emblem of Persia was a Ram, and the national emblem of Macedonia was a Goat. When Daniel compared the Leopard and the He-Goat he saw that the four heads of the Leopard corresponded to the Four Horns that came up in the place of the Great Horn on the head of the He-Goat. So far everything was clear to Daniel. But what was meant by The Little Horn that came up on one of the four horns of the He-Goat was a mystery to him. We are told by the Angel Gabriel that The Great Horn that was between the eyes of the He-Goat represented The First King of Greece who was Alexander The Great. Alexander son of Philip of Macedon became King of Greece at the age of 20 in the year 336 B.C. Two years later in 334 B.C. in goat like fashion, he jumped over The Hellespont, and with an army of 30,000 infantry and 5,000 cavalry he defeated a Persian force on the banks of the Granicus. By advancing swiftly eastward, he, in the following year in 333 B.C. defeated at Issus a Persian army of 600,000 men, commanded by The Persian King Darius. After minor conquests in Phoenicia and Egypt he returned to Syria, where he defeated an enormous army of Persian's led by Darius on the banks of The Tigris River. This is known in history as The Battle of Arbela which took place in 331 B.C. From 330 B.C. to 327 B.C., Alexander was engaged in subjugating the outlying provinces of The Persian Empire. Later he returned to Babylon, where, at the climax of his glory, he died of Syphilis at the age of 33 in June 323 B.C. After the death of Alexander there was dissension as to who would be his successor, which ended as God's

Prophecy had foretold, in four of his generals dividing the territory of The Empire among themselves.

GASSANDER = Took Macedonia and The Western part.
LYSIMACHUS = Took Thrace and The Northern part.
SELEUCUS = Took Syria and The Eastern part.
PTOLEMY = Took Egypt and The Southern part.

The four horns we can now name; Macedonia, Thrace, Syria, and Egypt. These four kingdoms were in time absorbed by the fourth world wide empire, The Roman Empire. The last to lose its identity was Egypt in 30 B.C. Therefore we see that there was to be four world wide empires; The Babylonian, Medo-Persian, Grecian, and Roman during the times of The Gentiles, yet they were not to succeed each other without a break. This was not revealed on the Image, nor in The Vision of the Four Wild Beasts, but is first revealed in The Vision of The He-Goat. The break between The Grecian and Roman Empires is now proven by history; that God's Word is infallible without error, for we now see The Four Minor Kingdoms of Macedonia, Thrace, Syria, and Egypt. The Angel Gabriel having explained the meaning of The Ram, The He-Goat and The Four Horns that came up in place of The Great Horn now continues to explain The Little Horn. The Angel Gabriel tells us in verse 23 that The Little Horn is not to rise out of one of The Four Kingdoms "until the Latter Time of their kingdom, when transgressors are come to the full." So we see here a distinction between The Former and The Latter time of The Four Kingdoms into which Alexander's Empire was divided, which tells us that Those Four Kingdoms are to be resurrected.

Chapter 8

The Little Horn

In comparing the descriptions of The Little Horn in the different chapters in The Book of Daniel, we see that they are progressive, each successive description adding new details to the preceding one. Therefore the picture continues to be filled out for us until the portrait of The Little Horn, who is The Anti-Christ is complete. In chapter seven (verses 24 & 25) Daniel describes The Little Horn as plucking up three of the ten horns, and having eyes like the eyes of a man, and a mouth speaking great things. The Holy One who interprets the vision repeats that The Little Horn will subdue three kings and adds "He shall speak great words against The Most High, and shall wear out The Saints of The Most High, and think to change times and laws: and they shall be given into his hand until a time and times and half a time." Daniel describes The Little Horn of chapter eight (verses 9–12) as one, "which started small but grew in power to the south and to the east and toward The Beautiful Land (which is Palestine).It grew until it reached the host of the heavens, and it threw some of the starry host down to the earth and trampled on them. It set itself up to be as great as The Prince of The Host; it took away the daily sacrifice from Him, and the place of His sanctuary was brought low, (Christ's Sanctuary). Because of rebellion, The Host of The Saints, and the daily sacrifice were given over to it. It prospered in everything it did, and truth was thrown to the ground." In (verses 23–25) The Angel Gabriel in interpreting The Little Horn says, "In the latter part of their reign, when rebels have become completely wicked, a stern-faced king, a master of intrigue, will arise. He will become very strong, but not by his own power. (It will be super-human). He will cause astounding devastation and will succeed in whatever he does. He will destroy the mighty men and the holy people. (The Jews). And through his policy also he shall cause craft, (all kinds of business) to prosper in his hand: and he shall magnify himself in his heart, and by PEACE shall destroy many: He will take his stand against The Prince of princes. (Christ). Yet he will be destroyed, but not by human power." But these two descriptions of The Little Horn from chapters seven and eight, still do not complete the picture of The Little Horn; therefore let us anticipate and turn to the description of:

THE KING WHO EXALTS HIMSELF

in chapter 11: 36–39, which fills out, and completes the picture for us of The Little Horn. "The king will do as he pleases. He will exalt and magnify himself above every god, and will say unheard-of things against The God of gods. He will be successful until the time of wrath is completed, (The Great Tribulation), for what has been determined must take place. He will show no regard for The God of his fathers, nor the desire of women, nor will he regard any god, but will exalt himself above them all. Instead of them, he will honor a god of fortresses; a god unknown to his fathers he will honor with gold and silver, with precious stones and costly gifts. He will attack the mightiest fortresses with the help of a foreign god and will greatly honor those who acknowledge him. He will make them rulers over many people and will distribute the land at a price." This completes the picture of The Little Horn as far as it was revealed to the Prophet Daniel. From what has been revealed to us, its very clear that The Little Horn is to come up from the Ten Horns of the Fourth Wild Beast, and that of those ten horns or kingdoms, four will be The Four Kingdoms into which Alexander The Great's empire was divided.

1. Macedonia = Greece
2: Thrace = Asia Minor
3: Syria
4: Egypt,

and that out of one these four The Little Horn (The Anti-Christ) shall rise. We stated earlier that The Little Horn will rise out of The Seleucid Empire, and we will see very shortly in chapter 11 that he will come out of SYRIA. The reason and purpose that God had chosen us, The People of Israel, was for the sole purpose of bringing forth The Messiah, His Son, Jesus The Christ. With election comes responsibility. We were to preach the gospel of The Old Testament, and make believers out of the heathen that surrounded us. We failed in our mission, and instead the heathen converted us to their practices and so we were driven out of our land, and we became an abomination to all peoples as God had warned us in Deuteronomy Chapter 28.

DEU 28:1 If you fully obey the Lord your God and carefully follow all his commands I give you today, the Lord your God will set you high above all the nations on earth. All these blessings will come upon you and accompany you if you obey the Lord your God: You will be blessed in the city and blessed in the country. The fruit of your womb will be blessed, and the crops of your land and the young of your livestock—the calves of your herds and the lambs of your flocks. You will be blessed when you come in and blessed when you go out. The Lord will grant that the enemies who rise up against you will be defeated before you. They will come at you from one direction but flee from you in seven. The Lord will send a blessing on your barns and on everything you put your hand to. The Lord your God will bless you in the land he is giving you. The Lord will establish you as his holy people, as he promised you on oath, if you keep the commands of the Lord your God and walk in his ways. Then all the peoples on earth will see that you are called by the name of the Lord, and they will fear you. The Lord will grant you abundant prosperity—in the fruit of your womb, the young of your livestock and the crops of your ground—in the land he swore to your forefathers to give you. The Lord will open the heavens, the storehouse of His bounty, to send rain on your land in season and to bless all the work of your hands.

DEU 28:14 Do not turn aside from any of the commands I give you today, to the right or to the left, following other gods and serving them. However, if you do not obey the Lord your

God and do not carefully follow all his commands and decrees I am giving you today, all these curses will come upon you and overtake you: You will be cursed in the city and cursed in the country. Your basket and your kneading trough will be cursed. The fruit of your womb will be cursed, and the crops of your land, and the calves of your herds and the lambs of your flocks. You will be cursed when you come in and cursed when you go out. The Lord will send on you curses, confusion and rebuke in everything you put your hand to, until you are destroyed and come to sudden ruin because of the evil you have done in forsaking him. The Lord will plague you with diseases until he has destroyed you from the land you are entering to possess. The Lord will strike you with wasting disease, with fever and inflammation, with scorching heat and drought, with blight and mildew, which will plague you until you perish. The sky over your head will be bronze, the ground beneath you iron. The Lord will turn the rain of your country into dust and powder; it will come down from the skies until you are destroyed. The Lord will cause you to be defeated before your enemies." THE CURSE OF THE LAW THAT MAN BRINGS ON HIMSELF BY DISOBEDIENCE. By the same token, where the people of Israel brought forth The Messiah, the people of Israel could very well bring forth The Anti-Messiah. Chapter 11 of this book tells us very clearly that The Anti-Messiah will come out of Syria, so we will say of necessity that he will either be A Syrian Arab, A Syrian Jew, or Syrian Christian. He must be someone whom the government of the State of Israel will relate to, and likewise the governments of all the Arab States. They all must feel that this person is one who has lived among them and understands them both. Jesus Christ they nailed to a cross but this man will be hailed as the greatest hero the world has ever seen.

Chapter 9

Daniel's Prayer

DAN 9:1 In the first year of Darius son of Xerxes (a Mede by descent), who was made ruler over the Babylonian kingdom—in the first year of his reign, I, Daniel, understood from the Scriptures, according to the word of the Lord given to Jeremiah the prophet, that the desolation of Jerusalem would last seventy years. So I turned to the Lord God and pleaded with him in prayer and petition, in fasting, and in sackcloth and ashes. I prayed to the Lord my God and confessed: "O Lord, the great and awesome God, who keeps his covenant of love with all who love him and obey his commands, we have sinned and done wrong. We have been wicked and have rebelled; we have turned away from your commands and laws. We have not listened to your servants the prophets, who spoke in your name to our kings, our princes and our fathers, and to all the people of the land. "Lord, you are righteous, but this day we are covered with shame—the men of Judah and people of Jerusalem and all Israel, both near and far, in all the countries where you have scattered us because of our unfaithfulness to you. O Lord, we and our kings, our princes and our fathers are covered with shame because we have sinned against you. The Lord our God is merciful and forgiving, even though we have rebelled against him; we have not obeyed the Lord our God or kept the laws he gave us through his servants the prophets. All Israel has transgressed your law and turned away, refusing to obey you. "Therefore the curses and sworn judgments written in the Law of Moses, the servant of God, have been poured out on us, because we have sinned against you. You have fulfilled the words spoken against us and against our rulers by bringing upon us great disaster. Under the whole heaven nothing has ever been done like what has been done to Jerusalem. Just as it is written in the Law of Moses, all this disaster has come upon us, yet we have not sought the favor of the Lord our God by turning from our sins and giving attention to your truth. The Lord did not hesitate to bring the disaster upon us, for the Lord our God is righteous in everything he does; yet we have not obeyed him. "Now, O Lord our God, who brought your people out of Egypt with a mighty hand and who made for yourself a name that endures to this day, we have sinned, we have done wrong. O Lord, in keeping with all your righteous acts, turn away your anger and your wrath from Jerusalem, your city, your holy hill. Our sins and the iniquities of our fathers have made Jerusalem and your people an object of scorn to all those around us. "Now, our God, hear the prayers and petitions of your servant. For your sake, O Lord, look with favor on your desolate sanctuary. Give ear, O God, and hear; open your eyes and see the desolation of the city that bears your Name. We do not make requests of you because we are righteous, but because of your great mercy. O Lord, listen! O Lord, forgive! O Lord, hear and act! For your sake, O my God, do not delay, because your city and your people bear your Name."

Let us see how God speaks about sin and repentance through Ezekiel!

EZE 18:1 The word of the Lord came to me: "What do you people mean by quoting this proverb about the land of Israel: "'The fathers eat sour grapes, and the children's teeth are set on edge'? "As surely as I live, declares the Sovereign Lord, you will no longer quote this proverb in Israel. For every living soul belongs to me, the father as well as the son—both alike belong to me. THE SOUL WHO SINS IS THE ONE WHO WILL DIE. "Suppose there is a righteous man who does what is just and right. He does not eat at the mountain shrines or look to the idols of the house of Israel. He does not defile his neighbor's wife or lie with a woman during her period. He does not oppress anyone, but returns what he took in pledge for a loan. He does not commit robbery but gives his food to the hungry and provides clothing for the naked.

EZE 18:8 He does not lend at usury or take excessive interest. He withholds his hand from doing wrong and judges fairly between man and man. He follows my decrees and faithfully keeps my laws. That man is righteous; he will surely live, declares the Sovereign Lord. "Suppose he has a violent son, who sheds blood or does any of these other things (though the father has done none of them): "He eats at the mountain shrines. He defiles his neighbor's wife. He oppresses the poor and needy. He commits robbery. He does not return what he took in pledge. He looks to the idols. He does detestable things. He lends at usury and takes excessive interest. Will such a man live? He will not! Because he has done all these detestable things, he will surely be put to death and his blood will be on his own head. "But suppose this son has a son who sees all the sins his father commits, and though he sees them, he does not do such things: "He does not eat at the mountain shrines or look to the idols of the house of Israel. He does not defile his neighbor's wife. He does not oppress anyone or require a pledge for a loan. He does not commit robbery but gives his food to the hungry and provides clothing for the naked. He withholds his hand from sin and takes no usury or excessive interest. He keeps my laws and follows my decrees. He will not die for his father's sin; he will surely live. But his father will die for his own sin, because he practiced extortion, robbed his brother and did what was wrong among his people. "Yet you ask, 'Why does the son not share the guilt of his father?' Since the son has done what is just and right and has been careful to keep all my decrees, he will surely live. THE SOUL WHO SINS IS THE ONE WHO WILL DIE. The son will not share the guilt of the father, nor will the father share the guilt of the son. The righteousness of the righteous man will be credited to him, and the wickedness of the wicked will be charged against him. "But if a wicked man turns away from all the sins he has committed and keeps all my decrees and does what is just and right, he will surely live; he will not die. NONE OF THE OFFENSES HE HAS COMMITTED WILL BE REMEMBERED AGAINST HIM. Because of the righteous things he has done, he will live. Do I take any pleasure in the death of the wicked? declares the Sovereign Lord. Rather, am I not pleased when they turn from their ways and live? (REPENT) (REPENT) (REPENT)

EZE 18:24 "But if a righteous man turns from his righteousness and commits sin and does the same detestable things the wicked man does, will he live? None of the righteous things he has done will be remembered. Because of the unfaithfulness he is guilty of and because of the sins he has committed, he will die. "Yet you say, 'The way of the Lord is not just.' Hear, O house of Israel: Is my way unjust? Is it not your ways that are unjust? If a righteous man turns from his righteousness and commits sin, he will die for it; because of the sin he has committed he will die. But if a wicked man turns away from the wickedness he has committed and does what is just and right, he will save his life. Because he considers all the offenses he has committed and turns away from them, he will surely live; he will not die. Yet the house of Israel says, 'The way of the Lord is not just.' Are my ways unjust, O house of Israel? Is it not your ways that are unjust? "Therefore, O house of Israel, I will judge you, each one according to his ways, declares the Sovereign Lord. REPENT! Turn away from all your offenses; then sin will not be your downfall. Rid yourselves of all the offenses you have committed, and GET A NEW HEART AND A NEW SPIRIT. Why will you die, O house of Israel?

EZE 18:32 For I take no pleasure in the death of anyone, declares the Sovereign Lord. REPENT AND LIVE! Praise God for His never failing MERCY and GRACE; that He is just and faithful to forgive us of ALL OF OUR SIN; as soon as we come to Him and say; please forgive me Jesus; then we put our REPENTANCE into ACTION!

Chapter 10

The Seventy "Sevens"

DAN 9:20 While I was speaking and praying, confessing my sin and the sin of my people Israel and making my request to the Lord my God for his holy hill—while I was still in prayer, Gabriel, the man I had seen in the earlier vision, came to me in swift flight about the time of the evening sacrifice. He instructed me and said to me, "Daniel, I have now come to give you insight and understanding. As soon as you began to pray, an answer was given, which I have come to tell you, for you are highly esteemed. Therefore, consider the message and understand the vision: "Seventy 'sevens' are decreed for your people and your holy city to finish transgression, to put an end to sin, to atone for wickedness, to bring in everlasting righteousness, to seal up vision and prophecy and to anoint the most holy. "Know and understand this: From the issuing of the decree to restore and rebuild Jerusalem until the Anointed One, the ruler, comes, there will be seven 'sevens,' and sixty-two 'sevens.' It will be rebuilt with streets and a trench, but in times of trouble. After the sixty-two 'sevens,' the Anointed One will be cut off and will have nothing. The people of the ruler who will come will destroy the city and the sanctuary. The end will come like a flood: War will continue until the end, and desolations have been decreed. He will confirm a covenant with many for one 'seven.' In the middle of the 'seven' he will put an end to sacrifice and offering. And on a wing of the temple he will set up an abomination that causes desolation, until the end that is decreed is poured out on him. "The date of the prophecy of the seventy weeks is given to us as a result of Daniel's prayer; which we see to be in the first year of Darius, which was 538 B.C. Daniel was stirred to intercessory prayer for the restoration of Israel by reading Jeremiah's prophecy in regards to Israel being in captivity in Babylon for 70 years as we see in Jer 25:11–12; 29:10. Daniel receives an answer to his prayer, and it is The Prophecy of The Seventy Weeks. Jeremiah's prophecy of the 70 year Babylonian captivity is now made the basis of a panoramic prediction of the entire history of Daniel's people, the children of Israel, from the rebuilding of the walls of Jerusalem until the time of the establishment of The Messiah's earthly kingdom. The figure of 70 weeks is used. One week in Hebrew is called "Shabua", weeks are called "Shabuot". The weeks which in The Greek are called Heptads, or "sevens" are Heptads of years. The total given to Daniel is 70 Heptads, or 490 years. Daniel receives a complete answer to his prayer. And in the revelation given to him, he is shown when Israel's national chatisement will be ended, when prophetic vision will be sealed and closed; because it will be fulfilled, and everlasting righteousness brought to Israel when Israel accepts her Messiah at His Second Coming. The total of 70 weeks or "sevens" is first divided into 7 weeks or 49 years. At the beginning of this time the commandment to restore and rebuild Jerusalem was issued by the decree of Artaxerxes I to rebuild Jerusalem's walls in the Hebrew month of Nisan, which is March-April, 457 B.C., which we see in Nehemiah chapter 2. The next division is 62 weeks or 434 years, plus the first seven weeks or 49 years which now equals 483 years. The date from which the 70 weeks are to be counted is when the decree to rebuild Jerusalem was issued. There were three decrees issued for this purpose=536 B.C., 457 B.C., 444 B.C. The main decree was issued in 457 B.C. The 483 years is the period between the decree to rebuild Jerusalem and the coming "Anointed One"; which in Hebrew means, "The Messiah." Adding 483 years to 457 B.C. or to put it this way; + 483 to – 457 = 26 A.D.: This was the year that Jesus was baptized and began His public ministry. Apostolic History and Jewish history reveals to us that Jesus was born in the year 4 B.C., where we see that when He was baptized by John in 26 A.D.

He was 30 years old. We now see Daniel's prophecy being fulfilled by God as to the exact year, proving to all mankind, that
Jesus is The Real Messiah of Israel and of all of mankind.
Furthermore within the next 3 1/2 years Jesus was crucified at
the age of 33 in the year 30 A.D. which fulfilled verse 26 of
this ninth chapter which stated "the Anointed one will be cut
off and will have nothing." Verse 24 told us that "seventy sevens are decreed for your people and your holy city to finish
transgression, and to put an end to sin, to atone for wickedness, to bring in everlasting righteousness, to seal up vision
and prophecy and to anoint The Most Holy." We see that following the sixty-two weeks plus the seven that an unreckoned
period is prophesied. Israel would be rejected all over the world
in a time of Gentile power until the fulfillment of the 69th.
week. Jesus told us that the temple would be destroyed and
that Jerusalem would be ravished. In 70 A.D. Titus of Rome
came in to Israel and ravished and destroyed Jerusalem; and
in one afternoon crucified 1,500,000 Jews; and his army raped
and pillaged and butchered another 500,000 before they were
through that day; and we see that the Jews have been scattered ever since. In 1948 they were restored to the land of
Israel by the vote of the United Nations which fulfilled the
prophecy of Isaiah 66:8. "Who has ever heard of such a thing?
Who has ever seen such things? Can a country be born in a
day or a nation be brought forth in a moment? Yet no sooner is
Zion in labor than she gives birth to her children." * An inter-
esting sideline note is this! Of all the armies of the history of
the world, The Army of The United States of America is the
only Army that has never raped, pillaged, or butchered.* The
final seven years constitute the climax of Jewish history prior
to the Second Coming of Jesus, or the Messianic Kingdom.
The Messiah, The King will usher in The Messianic Kingdom,
not "The Church". The perfecting of "The Bride" will be accomplished by "The Bridegroom" and not by "The Bride". The
final week of seven years constitutes the climax of Jewish history before the establishment of The Messianic Kingdom . The
final Seven years are divided into two half periods of three and
a half years each. During the first half the world ruler, or the
prince, or the little horn who is called by all three names being
the Anti-Christ will make a covenant with the Jews who have
been restored in Palestine with the resumption of temple worship. In the middle of the week he breaks the covenant with
Israel and worship for the Jews stops once again and the time
of The Great Tribulation begins, as we see in 2nd. Thessalo-

nians 2:3–4. "Don't let anyone deceive you in any way, for that day will not come until the rebellion occurs and the man of lawlessness is revealed, the man doomed to destruction. He opposes and exalts himself over everything that is called God or is worshiped, and even sets himself up in God's Temple, proclaiming himself to be God!" The second coming of Jesus The Christ, The Messiah, consummates this period of desolation, bringing everlasting righteousness to Israel, and judgment upon "The Desolater" and his hosts as we see in Revelation 19:20. "But the beast was captured, and with him the false prophet who had performed the miraculous signs on his behalf. With these signs he had deluded those who had received the mark of the beast and worshiped his image. The two of them were thrown alive into the fiery lake of burning sulfur." In the second half of verse 26 of this 9th. chapter of The Book of Daniel, the scripture tells us "the people of the ruler who will come will destroy the city and the sanctuary." Without a temple and a sacrificial system restored in Israel we cannot enter and begin the seventieth week. We have been living in Daniel's 69th. week for the last 1987 years, and we are anticipating the "Seventieth Week" which I believe will be fulfilled during our lifetime. Praise God for Jesus Who is The Christ, Who died for our sins, Who healed us, delivered us, Who restored us in righteousness before God our Heavenly Father, Who constantly says "Father Forgive Them For They Know Not What They Do", and Who healed us in every area of our lives; Spiritually, Physically, Emotionally, and Financially!!!! Praise God for Jesus Who's promise is revealed to us in The Gospel According to John 16:1 "All this I have told you so that you will not go astray. They will put you out of the synagogue; in fact, a time is coming when anyone who kills you will think he is offering a service to God. They will do such things because they have not known the Father or me. I have told you this, so that when the time comes you will remember that I warned you. I did not tell you this at first because I was with you. "Now I am going to him who sent me, yet none of you asks me, 'Where are you going?' Because I have said these things, you are filled with grief. But I tell you the truth: It is for your good that I am going away. Unless I go away, the Counselor will not come to you; but if I go, I will send him to you. When he comes, he will convict the world of guilt in regard to sin and righteousness and judgment: in regard to sin, because men do not believe in me; in regard to righteousness,

56

because I am going to the Father, where you can see me no longer; and in regard to judgment, because the prince of this world now stands condemned. "I have much more to say to you, more than you can now bear. But when he, the Spirit of truth, comes, he will guide you into all truth. He will not speak on his own; he will speak only what he hears, and he will tell you what is yet to come. He will bring glory to me by taking from what is mine and making it known to you. All that belongs to the Father is mine. That is why I said the Spirit will take from what is mine and make it known to you. "In a little while you will see me no more, and then after a little while you will see me." Some of his disciples said to one another, "What does he mean by saying, 'In a little while you will see me no more, and then after a little while you will see me,' and 'Because I am going to the Father'?" They kept saying, We don't understand what he is saying." Jesus saw that they wanted to ask him about this, so he said to them, "Are you asking one another what I meant when I said, 'In a little while you will see me no more, and then after a little while you will see me'? I tell you the truth, you will weep and mourn while the world rejoices. You will grieve, but your grief will turn to joy. So with you: Now is your time of grief, but I will see you again and you will rejoice, and no one will take away your joy. In that day you will no longer ask me anything. I tell you the truth, my Father will give you whatever you ask in my name. Until now you have not asked for anything in my name. Ask and you will receive, and your joy will be complete. "Though I have been speaking figuratively, a time is coming when I will no longer use this kind of language but will tell you plainly about my Father. In that day you will ask in my name. I am not saying that I will ask the Father on your behalf. No, the Father himself loves you because you have loved me and have believed that I came from God. I came from the Father and entered the world; now I am leaving the world and going back to the Father." Then Jesus' disciples said, "Now you are speaking clearly and without figures of speech. Now we can see that you know all things and that you do not even need to have anyone ask you questions. This makes us believe that you came from God." "You believe at last!" Jesus answered. "But a time is coming, and has come, when you will be scattered, each to his own home. You will leave me all alone. Yet I am NOT ALONE, for my FATHER is with me. "I have told you these things, so that in me you may have peace. In

this world you will have trouble. But take heart! I have over-
come the world." PRAISE GOD that JESUS IS NOT on THE
CROSS nor in THE TOMB, but that both The Cross and The
Tomb ARE EMPTY, that Jesus is RESURRECTED, He is
RISEN, He is ALIVE, and Because He LIVES we LIVE! THE
ONE AND ONLY SAVIOR.

Chapter 11

Daniel's Vision of a Man

DAN 10:1 In the third year of Cyrus king of Persia, a revelation was given to Daniel (who was called Belteshazzar). Its message was true and it concerned a great war. The understanding of the message came to him in a vision. At that time I, Daniel, mourned for three weeks. I ate no choice food; no meat or wine touched my lips; and I used no lotions at all until the three weeks were over. On the twenty-fourth day of the first month, as I was standing on the bank of the great river, the Tigris, I looked up and there before me was a man dressed in linen, with a belt of the finest gold around his waist. His body was like chrysolite, his face like lightning, his eyes like flaming torches, his arms and legs like the gleam of burnished bronze, and his voice like the sound of a multitude. I, Daniel, was the only one who saw the vision; the men with me did not see it, but such terror overwhelmed them that they fled and hid themselves. So I was left alone, gazing at this great vision; I had no strength left, my face turned deathly pale and I was helpless. Then I heard him speaking, and as I listened to him,

I fell into a deep sleep, my face to the ground. A hand touched me and set me trembling on my hands and knees. He said, "Daniel, you who are highly esteemed, consider carefully the words I am about to speak to you, and stand up, for I have now been sent to you." And when he said this to me, I stood up trembling. Then he continued, "Do not be afraid, Daniel. Since the first day that you set your mind to gain understanding and to humble yourself before your God, your words were heard, and I have come in response to them. But the prince of the Persian kingdom resisted me twenty-one days. Then Michael, one of the chief princes, came to help me, because I was detained there with the king of Persia. Now I have come to explain to you what will happen to your people in the future, for the vision concerns a time yet to come." While he was saying this to me, I bowed with my face toward the ground and was speechless. Then one who looked like a man touched my lips, and I opened my mouth and began to speak. I said to the one standing before me, "I am overcome with anguish because of the vision, my lord, and I am helpless. How can I, your servant, talk with you, my lord? My strength is gone and I can hardly breathe." Again the one who looked like a man touched me and gave me strength. "Do not be afraid, O man highly esteemed," he said. "Peace! Be strong now; be strong." When he spoke to me, I was strengthened and said, "Speak, my lord, since you have given me strength." So he said, "Do you know why I have come to you? Soon I will return to fight against the prince of Persia, and when I go, the prince of Greece will come; but first I will tell you what is written in the Book of Truth. (No one supports me against them except Michael, your prince."

THE ROLE OF DEMONIC POWERS IN GOVERNMENTS OF THE WORLD

This chapter is the prologue for the vision given to Daniel in chapter 11, while we see that chapter 12 is the epilogue. The thing that was revealed to Daniel was true, and it concerned a great war. The battle involved a spiritual war with demon powers operating in the governments of the world system. Daniel's three weeks of prayer and fasting challenged these demons in the heavenlies. These were evil spirits that were connected with governmental administration operating through King Cyrus. The prince of the kingdom of Persia

(Iran) was the evil spirit of government working in and through Cyrus, to hinder him in his good intentions of letting The Jews return to Israel and Jerusalem. The Archangel Michael who is The Guardian Angel of The Jewish People, came to Daniel's assistance in the war which was brought on by Daniel's believing prayer.

The Meaning Of The Vision

The world governments during The Times of The Gentiles, of which we are still in, are operated by unseen evil spirits and demons in The Satanic world system. The scriptures clearly teach us that there is a "KINGDOM OF DARKNESS" over which Satan reigns as king which we see in Matt. 12:24–30, and that his kingdom is composed of Principalities, Powers, Age Rulers of Darkness, and Wicked Spirits which we see in Ephesians 6:12, where St. Paul says, "We wrestle not against flesh and blood, but against principalities, and powers, and rulers of the darkness of this world age, and against spiritual wickedness in the heavenlies." Satan is the prince of the power of the air, and the god of this world age, which we see in Ephesians 2:2. It was no false claim that Satan made when he offered to give to Jesus the kingdoms of this world, and the glory of them, which we see in Matt. 4:8–9. From this we see that Satan has his kingdom organized in a very orderly manner. It is divided into Kingdoms and Principalities. These divisions correspond to the different Nations on Planet Earth; and he has A Prince for every nation. Now remember my beloved, Satan has his limitations. He is not Omnipresent, neither is he Omnipotent or Omniscient. He has to depend upon his agents; and Jesus told us that in His Name Rebuke The Devil And He Shall Flee From You; every demon in hell knows Who Jesus Is; HE IS LORD! Webster's Dictionary tells us what these big and fancy words mean.

*OMNIPRESENT = Present everywhere
at the same time. JESUS
*OMNIPOTENT = All powerful, The Unlimited
Power of God. JESUS
*OMNISCIENT = All knowledge, The Faculty
of Knowing Everything. JESUS

These demons and evil spirits tried to hinder Daniel in his prayer for his people, whose ultimate restoration in The Kingdom will be preceded by the end of "The Times of The Gentiles"; and the imprisonment of Satan and his demons, his workers, his co-horts, and his spirits which we see in Revelation 20:1–3 which will make possible The Perfect Government of King Jesus in The Messianic Kingdom Age.

Chapter 12

The Kings of the South and the North

DAN 11:1 And in the first year of Darius the Mede, I took my stand to support and protect him.) "Now then, I tell you the truth: Three more kings will appear in Persia, and then a fourth, who will be far richer than all the others. When he has gained power by his wealth, he will stir up everyone against the kingdom of Greece. Then a mighty king will appear, who will rule with great power and do as he pleases. After he has appeared, his empire will be broken up and parceled out toward the four winds of heaven. It will not go to his descendants, nor will it have the power he exercised, because his empire will be uprooted and given to others. "The king of the South will become strong, but one of his commanders will become even stronger than he and will rule his own kingdom with great power. After some years, they will become allies. The daughter of the king of the South will go to the king of the North to make an alliance, but she will not retain her power, and he and his power will not last. In those days she will be handed over, together with her royal escort and her father and the one who supported her. "One from her family line will arise to take her place. He will attack the forces of the king of the North and enter his fortress; he will fight against them and be victorious. He will also seize their gods, their metal images and their valuable articles of silver and gold and carry them off to Egypt. For some years he will leave the king of the North alone. Then the king of the North will invade the realm of the king of the South but will retreat to his own country. His sons will prepare for war and assemble a great army, which will sweep on like an irresistible flood and carry the battle as far as his fortress. "Then the king of the South will march out in a rage and fight against the king of the North, who will raise a large army, but it will be defeated. When the army is carried off, the king of the South will be filled with pride and will slaughter many thousands, yet he will not remain triumphant. For the king of the North will muster another army, larger than the first; and after several years, he will advance with a huge army fully equipped. "In those times many will rise against the king of the South. The violent men among your own people will rebel in fulfillment of the vision, but without success. Then the king of the North will come and build up siege ramps and will capture a fortified city. The forces of the South will be powerless to resist; even their best troops will not have the strength to stand. The invader will do as he pleases; no one will be able to stand against him. He will establish himself in the Beautiful Land and will have the power to destroy it. He will determine to come with the might of his entire kingdom and will make an alliance with the king of the South. And he will give him a daughter in marriage in order to overthrow the kingdom, but his plans will not succeed or help him. Then he will turn his attention to the coastlands and will take many of them, but a commander will put an end to his insolence and will turn his insolence back upon him. After this, he will turn back toward the fortresses of his own country but will stumble and fall, to be seen no more. "His successor will send out a tax collector to maintain the royal splendor. In a few years, however, he will be destroyed, yet not in anger or in battle. "He will be succeeded by a contemptible person who has not been given the honor of royalty. He will invade the kingdom when its people feel secure, and he will seize it through intrigue. Then an overwhelming army will be swept away before him; both it and a prince of the covenant will be destroyed. After coming to an agreement with him, he will act deceitfully, and with only a few people he will rise to power. When the richest provinces feel secure, he will invade them and will achieve what neither his fathers nor his forefathers did. He will distribute plunder, loot and wealth among his followers. He will plot the overthrow of fortresses—but only for a time. "With a large army he will stir up his strength and courage against the king of the South. The king of the South will wage war with a large and very powerful army, but he will not be able to stand because of the plots devised against him. Those who eat from the king's provisions will try to destroy him; his army will be swept away, and many will fall in battle. The two kings, with their hearts bent on evil, will sit at the same table and lie to each other, but to no avail, because an end will still come at the appointed time. The king of the North will return to his own country with great wealth, but his heart will be set against the holy covenant. He will take action against it and then return to his own country. "At the appointed time he will invade the South again, but this time the outcome will be different from what it was before. Ships of the western coastlands will oppose him, and he will lose heart. Then he will turn back and vent his fury against the holy covenant. He will return and show favor to those who forsake the holy covenant. "His armed forces will rise up to desecrate the temple fortress and will abolish the daily sacrifice. Then they will set up the abomination that causes desolation. With flattery he will corrupt those who have violated the covenant, but the people who know their God will firmly resist him. "Those who are wise will instruct many, though for a time they will fall by the sword or be burned or captured or plundered. When they fall, they will receive a little help, and many who are not sincere will join them. Some of the wise will stumble, so that they may be refined, purified and made spotless until the time of the end, for it will still come at the appointed time. "The king will do as he pleases. He will exalt and magnify himself above every god and will say unheard-of things against the God of gods. He will be successful until the time of wrath is completed, for what has been determined must take place. He will show no regard for the gods of his fathers or for the one desired by women, nor will he regard any god, but will exalt himself above them all. Instead of them, he will honor a god of fortresses; a god unknown to his fathers he will honor with gold and silver, with precious stones and costly gifts. He will attack the mightiest fortresses with the help of a foreign god and will greatly honor those who acknowledge him. He will make them rulers over many people and will distribute the land at a price. "At the time of the end the king of the

South will engage him in battle, and the king of the North will storm out against him with chariots and cavalry and a great fleet of ships. He will invade many countries and sweep through them like a flood. He will also invade the Beautiful Land. Many countries will fall, but Edom, Moab and the leaders of Ammon will be delivered from his hand. He will extend his power over many countries; Egypt will not escape. He will gain control of the treasures of gold and silver and all the riches of Egypt, with the Libyans and Nubians in submission. But reports from the east and the north will alarm him, and he will set out in a great rage to destroy and annihilate many. He will pitch his royal tents between the seas at the beautiful holy mountain. Yet he will come to his end, and no one will help him."

In this chapter we have what the angel Gabriel calls the scripture of truth. It is a pre-written history of the wars of the Ptolemies of Egypt, the kings of the south; and the Seleucids of Syria, the kings of the north. Prophecy then is history written in advance. The relationship of history to prophecy is not that of interpretation, but of verification. The detailed accuracy of this prophecy is fantastic. The prophecy is not clothed in figures and symbols as in the previous visions. In fact this is not a vision, but a description in literal language of historical events concerning The Jewish People and The Holy Land, from Daniel's time down to The Second Coming of Christ. For the sake of clarity I will take the prophecy verse by verse, and where necessary several verses together. The prophecy begins with the second verse of chapter 11.

VERSE 2: Since the prophecy was given in the third year of Cyrus, the three kings that were to come up after him, were Ahasuerus, Artaxerxes, and Darius, who are known in history as Cambyses, Pseudo-Smerdis, and Darius Hystaspes. The fourth king was Xerxes, the son of Darius Hystaspes, whose wealth enabled him to put vast armies in the field. He stirred up Persia against Greece, which he invaded in 480 B.C., but failed to conquer it. The remaining kings of Persia are omitted, and the prophecy jumps ahead nearly 150 years to the time of Alexander the Great.

VERSES 3–4: These verses take us back to the vision of the Ram and the He-Goat, and we remember in this mighty king, the notable horn the He-Goat that was broken off, and in the 4 horns that came up in its place, the division of the kingdom toward the four winds. This mighty King was Alexander the Great, and the division of his kingdom toward the four winds of heaven was the division of his kingdom at his death by his four generals. Gassander took Macedonia and the western part; Lysimachus took Thrace and the northern part; Seleucus took Syria and the eastern part; and Ptolemy took Egypt and the southern part. None of Alexander the Great's children ever succeeded him, and within 15 years his entire family was extinct.

VERSE 5: The prophecy now narrows down to two of the four kingdoms into which Alexander the Great's Empire was divided. The angel Gabriel told Daniel that the prophecy belonged to Daniel's people; The Jews. And as the Glorious Land which is Palestine lay between Syria on the north and Egypt on the south, so the the prophecy narrows down to a description of the wars between the kings of the north and the kings of the south, whose battlefield would be Palestine, where for hundreds of years Daniel's people would be ground between Syria and Egypt. Because of the suffering that these wars would bring to Daniel's people, and the desolation they would cause the land of Israel, God revealed these wars to Daniel that he might see it would be "many days" before his people would ever become a nation again. Of the four kingdoms into which Alexander's Empire was divided, the kingdom of Egypt was the first to appear. It was founded by Ptolemy Soter, one of Alexander's generals. Another of Alexander's generals, Seleucus Nicator was appointed vice-regent of Babylon, but he was driven out by Antigonus and fled to Egypt, where he was favorably received by Ptolemy and was made one of his princes. With Ptolemy's assistance he recovered his province and enlarged it, until it extended to the Indus and included Syria, as well as Assyria, and he became stronger than Ptolemy, and his dominion became a great dominion.

VERSE 6: There was peace between Egypt and Syria during the reigns of Ptolemy Soter and Seleucus Nicator. But, after a period time, Ptolemy Soter abdicated in favor of his son Ptolemy Philadelphus, whose half brother Magas had married a daughter of Antiochus Soter, who had succeeded Seleucus Nicator as king of Syria. This marriage led to war between Egypt and Syria. For Magas induced his father-in-law, Antiochus Soter, to declare war on Egypt. Antiochus Soter, was succeeded by Antiochus Theus, who continued to war with Ptolemy. At length, at the end of years, Ptolemy offered Antiochus Theus, as a bribe for peace, his daughter Berenice with a large dowry, on the condition that the Syrian king would declare his former marriage to Laodice void, and her two sons

67

illegitimate. This compact of iniquity was carried out. But when Ptolemy Philadelphus died his daughter Berenice could no longer retain her power, for Antiochus Theus put her away, and took back his former wife Laodice. But neither he himself would stand for Laodice, distrusting his own motives; and Laodice eager to secure the crown for her own son, poisoned her husband, and so opened the succession to Seleucus Callinicus. Then Laodice persuaded Seleucus to have Berenice assassinated, and her child, who by the articles of her marriage had been made heir to the throne, was also killed, as well as all those who strengthened her in those times.

VERSES 7-8: Out of a branch of her roots meaning an offspring of Berenice's parents, and referring to her brother, Ptolemy Euergetus, who succeeded his father Ptolemy Philadelphus. And who, furious of the treatment of his sister, marched into Syria with a very large army, and, although he arrived to late save Berenice and her son, took revenge by putting Laodice to death, captured Seleucia, which was the fortress of the king of the north, and would have possessed for himself the entire kingdom had he not been recalled by an insurrection in Egypt. He did not return empty handed. He carried back many captives including the the Royalty, plus the spoil of 40,000 talents of silver, and 2,500 precious vessels of gold and Idols of the gods. 40,000 talents of silver equaling 48,000,000 ounces at $7.50 an ounce at todays price was worth $360,000,000.00. The vessels of gold weighing 3,000,000 ounces at todays price of $450.00 an ounce was worth $1,350,000,000.00. Among the images that he brought back from Syria were many that Cambyses had formerly taken from Egypt and carried into Persia. These were replaced in the temples of Egypt with very great ceremony, and in gratitude for their restoration the priests of Egypt bestowed upon Ptolemy his surname of Euergetes, or Benefactor.

VERSES 9-10: But his sons, not the sons of the king of south, but the sons of the king of the north shall be stirred up by the invasion of the king of the south, and shall assemble a multitude of great armies. We know that this actually happened. The sons of Seleucus Callinicus, Seleucus Ceraunus, and Antiochus who was later called Magnus The Great, assembled large armies. Seleucus Ceraunus who succeeded his father, assembled a large army to recover his father's dominions but being a weak and spoiled prince, was unable to discipline his army, was poisoned by two of his generals after an inglorious reign of about three years. He was succeeded by his brother Antiochus, who assembled a very large army and who took the field in person. He is the one which the scripture points to, "who should overflow and pass through." He directed his energies against the king of the south, Ptolemy Philopater, who had succeeded his father, Ptolemy Euergetes. He seized Tyre and Ptolemais, overflowed and passed through Palestine, and marched against Gaza, which was the fortress of the king of the south, and which was the limit set by The Prophecy. This occurred in 218 B.C.

VERSES 11-12: The very fat king of the south, Ptolemy Philopater, was thoroughly aroused by the invasion of his realm by the king of the north, Antiochus. He assembled a great army, and defeated the large and well appointed army of Antiochus, at Raphia, not far from Gaza, in 217 B.C. Ptolemy's heart was lifted up by his success, and he could of followed up his victory and grabbed the kingdom of Antiochus, but he was too anxious to return to his sensual pleasures, and so he lost his opportunity of gaining supremacy, and so we see that he was not strengthened at all by his great victory.

VERSE 13: The peace concluded between Ptolemy Philopater and Antiochus lasted thirteen years. In the meantime Antiochus strengthened himself in his kingdom. When his armies were many and well equipped, and riding high with many victories, and his treasuries filled to the brim with gold and silver; he now learned of the death of Ptolemy Philopater, and that he had been succeeded by his infant son Ptolemy Epiphanes. Antiochus feeling the time was ripe, marched against Egypt with a great army and much riches, expecting an easy victory.

VERSE 14: Among the many that stood up against the infant king of the south was Philip, king of Macedon, who entered into an alliance with Antiochus to divide the kingdom of Ptolemy Epiphanes between them. Egypt itself was a seething pot of sedition. There were also Jews, who were Jews by birth only, who were wicked, and who did not believe in the God of Abraham, Isaac, and Jacob, who lived in Palestine who hoped to gain the favor of Antiochus. They were called robbers because by their action and conduct, they made it very hard for their brethren of Israel, the true followers of God. They thus established the prophecy of suffering for Daniel's people during those times. Antiochus turned against these robbers and he slaughtered them one and all.

VERSES 15-19: I am putting these verses together because they cover the remainder of the wars of Antiochus the

Great, the King of the North. In considering these wars let us not forget that the Glorious Land, Palestine was under the dominion of the king of the south, who was at this time Ptolemy Epiphanes. Therefore to reach Egypt it was necessary for Antiochus to first conquer Palestine. Upon his entrance to Palestine he encountered Scopas, the General of Ptolemy's army, and forced him to seek refuge in the strongly fortified city of Sidon, which he besieged. Desperate attempts were made by the Egyptians to relieve the city, but everything failed, and Sidon was forced to surrender. Then Antiochus was able to do according to his own will, and none were able to stand before him. So he took possession of the Glorious Land. Then he set his face to enter Egypt with the whole strength of his kingdom. But he was forced to change his plans. The Egyptian regency had sought the help of the Romans, who were then rising in power, and their assistance had been promised. So Antiochus decided to resort to diplomacy. He proposed that his daughter Cleopatra be espoused to the infant king Ptolemy Epiphanes, who was then seven years old. Cleopatra herself was still very young and it was because she was of tender years, and still under the care of her mother and a nurse, that she was called the daughter of woman. The marriage was consummated some five years later. The words corrupting her, refer to Antiochus' scheme to get her to play into his hands, rather than into the hands of her husband. But the plan failed. Cleopatra not only took sides with her husband, but even joined him in sending congratulations to the Romans on their victories over her father. To avenge himself against the Romans, Antiochus fitted out a fleet of 300 ships and attacked the coasts and islands of Asia Minor. He was defeated at Magnesia, in 190 B.C. by Scipio Asiaticus, the prince mentioned in the prophecy given to Daniel. Antiochus then turned his face homeward. At Antioch he sent ambassadors to sue for peace. The terms were hard. He was not only to give up Europe, but also Asia on the European side of the Taurus, and pay 2,550 talents of gold as a down payment for the peace he was seeking, and 1,000 talents for the next twelve years; which in todays money amounted to $7,857,000,000.00. A few months later while traveling his eastern provinces to raise this tribute money he attempted to plunder the Temple of Bel in Elymais, but the people rose up and killed him. So as the scripture stated, he stumbled and fell, and was found no more.

VERSE 20: Antiochus the Great was succeeded by his eldest son, Seleucus Philopater. He was compelled to be a raiser of taxes to pay the heavy tribute which was imposed on his father. He reigned for about twelve years. Toward the end of that time, being hard pressed for money, he sent his treasurer, Heliodorus, to Jerusalem to confiscate the treasures of the Temple. Shortly after, within a few days, he was mysteriously poisoned. So he died "neither in anger nor in battle."

VERSES 21–31: The next King of the North was Antiochus Epiphanes, spoken of in the text as a vile person. He was the younger son of Antiochus the Great. He was involved in the most degraded and unnatural passions, he was unscrupulous, he was cruel, and of a savage nature, yet he did not lack courage and ability. The "honor of the kingdom" was not given to him because his nephew, Demetrius, was the rightful heir. He was aided by Eumenes, King of Pergamum, and his brother Attalus. With their help his enemies, as the "arms of a flood" were swept away, and the "prince of the covenant," the Jewish High Priest Onias III, was deposed. He broke the "covenant" he made with King Eumenes and his brother, Attalus, when he persuaded the Romans to recognize him, where in the meantime he was working "deceitfully," letting on that he just had a small following. But he soon became "strong with a small people," and entered "peaceably into the fattest places of the province." Unlike his predecessors, he was profuse and extravagant with his gifts, and "scattered the spoil" of his conquests among his friends, where the entire time he was "forecasting his devices against the strongholds" of Egypt, three of which, Pelusium, Naucratis, and Memphis, he later occupied, but he failed to take Alexandria. This he did, "even for a time," but he was finally checked by the Romans. When he was ready to invade Egypt, he marched against it with a very large army, and he was met by an equally large army, which, after great losses, dissolved and Ptolemy Philometer fell into the hands of Antiochus, betrayed by those that "fed of the portion of his meat." His brother Physcon was proclaimed King in his place. Antiochus received Ptolemy Philometer with much consideration, and concluded a peace treaty with him on favorable terms, and then, on the pretense of taking his part against his brother Physcon, laid siege against Alexandria, but without success. In the meantime, Philometer suspicious of Antiochus, and scheming for himself, made overtures to Physcon, on the basis of a joint sovereignty, and was received into Alexandria. Both brothers then declared themselves against Antiochus. And so the prophecy was fulfilled; "these kings' Antiochus and Philometer with hearts bent on evil against each other, will sit at the same table and lie to each other. Antiochus then returned toward Syria, loaded with the rich spoils of Egypt. On the march he heard, that, owing to a false report of his own death, Jason, who had been deprived of his High Priestly Office, had made an attack on Jerusalem, and had tried to recover his Office by force. Choosing, by his own choice, to regard this as a revolt of the Jews against him, and especially when he found that the news of his supposed death caused great joy among them, he attacked Jerusalem, slew 40,000 Jews, sold 40,000 more into slavery, and his men raped 40,000 or more of the Women of Israel. He then attacked The Holy Temple, and plundered The Temple, carrying off treasure to the tune of 1800 talents of gold. A talent is 75 pounds; therefore 1800 x 75 x 16 = 2,160,000 ounces of gold. Multiplying that figure at todays price of gold at $450.00 an ounce, he carried off $972,000,000.00 from The Temple of God. Thus venting his anger against the "Holy Covenant," he continued his march toward Antioch. In the spring of 168 B.C., Antiochus again led his troops to Egypt in order to subjugate the two brothers, Ptolemy Philometer and Ptolemy Physcon. But the same success no longer awaited him, for the Ptolemies had appealed to Rome. Along the well known route the Syrian King passed, no one dared hinder his progress, until he was within four miles of Alexandria. A Roman fleet lay at anchor in the bay, and Antiochus was met by Cpopilius Laenas, who put into his hand a letter from the Roman Senate commanding him to leave the friends of the Roman people unmolested, and to be content with his Kingdom. Having read this letter, Antiochus remarked that he would call his advisers and consult with them as to what was to be done. Whereupon Popilius drew a circle around him in the sand with his staff, and said "Before you step out of that circle give such an answer as I may report to the Senate." King Antiochus being backed down by the Roman, replied "If it so please the Senate, we will depart." Antiochus then withdrew his army from Egypt and vented his fury upon the Jews of The Holy Land, in the fearful massacres, persecutions, and desecration of the Temple. Also in doing this he repaired the massive walls and towers of the Citadel of David, and he garrisoned them with Syrian soldiers. He commanded that all of his subjects should be one people, with one religion, and with the same laws. And, in order to enforce this upon the Jews, the Sanctuary of God was profaned, the offerings and sacrifices prohibited, and an "Idol-Altar" built over the "Altar of God," upon which swine's flesh was sacrificed, to an image placed over it. This was the "Abomination that maketh desolate," spoken of in the text, but not the "Abomination of Desolation", spoken of by Jesus in Matthew 24:15. That is still in the future, which I believe will come to pass in our generation. Antiochus' tough measures for the Hellenization of Judea caused the Maccabean revolt. In the mean time Antiochus had gone with an army into Persia, gaining many victories everywhere. Later he was forced to retire to Babylon. Heart broken at the news of the Maccabean revolt in Palestine, he died a natural death at Tabae in 164 B.C. It is very important right here to note that all that has been recorded from verses 21–31, inclusive, has reference to Antiochus Epiphanes, and not to the Anti-Christ, or to any other person, and was literally and completely fulfilled by Antiochus Epiphanes as the scripture had foretold. So there is absolutely nothing in these verses left for the future. There is no intimation that Antiochus Epiphanes is even to be regarded as a type of Anti-Christ. All of the people we are reading about are distinct historical personages, each one of them dealt with in his own place, and in his own time, and though many of them resemble each other in some respects, on account of their conduct, and their treatment of the Jewish People, they must not be confounded with one another. This Prophetic and Pre-Written historical account recorded in verses 21–31, of the wars of the Persian and Grecian Empires, and yet more in detail of the Syrian and Egyptian Divisions of the Grecian Empire, extending from 536 B.C. to 164 B.C., a period of 372 years, is the most fantastic "Prophetic Foreview" in the entire Bible, because it goes into details that only the Omniscience of God could reveal.

VERSES 32–33: The behavior of the Jews under the oppression of Antiochus Epiphanes we see in verse 32. The scripture says some of them did wickedly, and forsook the covenant, and the faith of their fathers, and worshiped idols, and they were led into this by flatteries. But there were some who knew their God, The God of Abraham, Isaac, and Jacob, who knew that He was able to deliver, and so they were made strong, and did many exploits. This refers to Mattathias, an aged High Priest, and his sons, who are known as The Maccabees, who from 166 B.C. to 47 B.C., fought to restore the national life of Israel as had been known under the reigns of King David and his son Solomon. Mattathias, driven to desperation by the cruelty and brutality of Antiochus, raised a revolt against him,

and escaped to the mountains with quite a number of followers, who were zealous for the faith, and The God of Israel.
Two years later Mattathias died and he was succeeded by his
third son, Judas, who was known as "The Hammer", who by
avoiding direct battles, and by his implementation of guerrilla
warfare, defeated, and routed every Syrian army sent against
him, and in 165 B.C. retook Jerusalem. He purified The Temple, and restored the daily sacrifice. He was killed in battle in
160 B.C., and was succeeded by his younger brother Jonathan,
a High Priest. During the leadership of Jonathan the Syrians
were engaged in a civil war, so Judea was left in peace. Jonathan then strengthened his position by entering into a treaty
with the Romans and the Spartans. Jonathan was treacherously murdered by a Syrian General in 143 B.C., and was succeeded by his brother Simon, the last remaining son of
Mattathias. Simon and two of his sons were treacherously
murdered by his own son-in-law in 135 B.C. His son John,
known as John Hyrcanus, who had escaped, succeeded his father Simon, and had a long and prosperous reign. Others in
the same line followed, with varying success, until The Maccabean's, fell into disfavor, with their own people, and were succeeded by The Idumaen, Antipater in 47 B.C.. a descendent of
Esau. After the murder of Antipater in 43 B.C., Marc Anthony
visited Syria, and appointed two of Antipater's sons, Pha-
saelus and Herod, who afterwards would be known as "Herod
The Great" who ruled the Jews under Roman Authority from
37 B.C.to 4 B.C. Herod the Great was still King when Jesus
was born in 4 B.C. From this we see that The Maccabees
bridged the greater part of history from Antiochus Epiphanes
up to the birth of Jesus. During the latter part of this period a
new class of spiritual leaders arose who understood The Prophetic Scriptures, and who knew how to teach the people
about their coming Messiah and Deliverer, they were people
like Simeon and Anna, who waited for "The Consolation of
Israel".

VERSES 36–45: The sudden appearance of the King in
verse 36 implies that he is the one of whom we have heard
about before, and that he is not a new character. Notice that
the scripture does not say a king, but "The King". The fact
that this willful King appears on the seen now, identifies him
with the "Prince That Shall Come" of Daniel 9:26–27, and he
is therefore the Little Horn of Daniel's fourth wild beast.
Again in verse 40 of this chapter this wilful King is called the
King of the North. We know from our study of chapter 8, that

the Four Kingdoms into which Alexander the Great's Empire was divided are to be revived, and that in the latter time of their kingdom a king of fierce countenance shall stand up; which we saw in Daniel 8:21–23. We now know that one of the Four Kingdoms was Syria, known as the Kingdom of the North, and also known as the Little Horn of chapter 8 which appeared on the "Syrian Horn", then therefore the King of Fierce Countenance of chapter 8 must be the King of the North of the revived "Syrian Kingdom", and The Wilful King, and The King of The North of chapter 11. "The king will do as he pleases. He will exalt and magnify himself above every god and will say unheard-of things against the God of gods. He will be successful until the time of wrath, meaning the tribulation is completed, for what has been determined must take place. He will show no regard for the God of his fathers, The God of Abraham, Isaac, and Jacob." This means The Anti-Christ COULD be a Syrian Jew, a Sephardic Jew, one who speaks Hebrew and Arabic, or he COULD be a Syrian Christian, or he COULD be a Syrian Moslem, but the fact is He Will Be A Syrian, one who speaks Hebrew and Arabic, and one who will be able to sit at the table and negotiate the peace between the Arabs and the Jews. Jesus was nailed to a cross by mankind, a death that only the most fiendish minds in Rome could conceive of, but this Anti-Christ will be hailed as the greatest hero the world has ever seen. He will show no regard for the one desired by women, for every Jewish woman till today desires to be the mother of "The Messiah"; and every Arab woman till today desires to be the mother of "The Mahdi Of Islam, for to the Arab and Jewish people The Messiah has not come as yet; nor will he regard any god, but will exalt himself above them all. Instead of them, he will honor a god of fortresses; that is, he shall depend on the "god" that can secure for him the Kingdoms of This World, and that is the God of This World Age, SATAN, who offered the Kingdoms of The World to Jesus, which we see in Matthew 4:8–9. Jesus refused the Kingdoms from the hand of Satan, for He knew He would receive the Kingdoms from "The Hand of The Father." The Anti-Christ will accept Satan's offer, which we read about in Revelation 13:2. The Dragon, who is Satan, shall give him, The Beast, his Power, and his seat, which is Satan's Throne, and he will also give him his great authority. A god unknown to his fathers he will honor with gold and silver, with precious stones and costly gifts. He will attack the mightiest fortresses with the help of a foreign god and will greatly honor those who acknowledge him. By the help of this "strange god" the "Wilful King shall secure the Fortresses, or the fortified cities, of The Ten Federated Kingdoms, and he will garrison them with his Imperial troops on the pretext of maintaining peace. Thus he shall distribute the land for "graft", for a price. At this time the King of the South, which is Egypt re-appears. Who this King or President of Egypt will be I do not know. But he will be one of the Ten Federated Kings, who is to appear after the Four Kingdoms into which Alexander's Empire was divided. He will be a future King of Egypt who will oppose the claims and military success of the Wilful King, the King of the North; who is the King or President of Syria. The King of the North will lose no time in opposing the King of the South, and he will swoop down on him like a whirlwind, with chariots and cavalry, and a great fleet of ships, and he He will invade many countries and sweep through them like a flood. He will also invade the Beautiful Land, which is called Palestine, or in todays terminology is called "The State of Israel". Many countries will fall, but Edom, Moab and the leaders of Ammon will be delivered from his hand. He will extend his power over many countries; Egypt will not escape. He will gain control of the treasures of gold and silver and all the riches of Egypt, with the Libyans and Ethiopians in submission. But in the midst of his conquest of Egypt bad news shall come to him from the east, from Babylon, his Capital City, and from the north. These will fill him with rage, and he will depart from Egypt with great fury; and he will pitch the Royal Tents of his palace which he lived in while he was in the field; between the Mediterranean Sea and the Dead Sea, on that Glorious Holy Mountain, which is called Zion. And there with no one, and nothing to help him, yet he will come to his end.

HIS END WHICH WE SEE IS IN HELL FOREVER.

Chapter 13

The End Times

DAN 12:1 "At that time Michael, the great prince who protects your people, will arise. There will be a time of distress such as has not happened from the beginning of nations until then. But at that time your people—everyone whose name is found written in the book—will be delivered. Multitudes who sleep in the dust of the earth will awake: some to everlasting life, others to shame and everlasting contempt. Those who are wise will shine like the brightness of the heavens, and those who lead many to righteousness, like the stars for ever and ever. But you, Daniel, close up and seal the words of the scroll until the time of the end. Many will go here and there to increase knowledge." Then I, Daniel, looked, and there before me stood two others, one on this bank of the river and one on the opposite bank. One of them said to the man clothed in linen, who was above the waters of the river, "How long will it be before these astonishing things are fulfilled?" The man clothed in linen, who was above the waters of the river, lifted his right hand and his left hand toward heaven, and I heard him swear by him who lives forever, saying, "It will be for a time, times and half a time. When the power of the holy people has been finally broken, all these things will be completed." I heard, but I did not understand. So I asked, "My lord, what will the outcome of all this be?" He replied, "Go your way, Daniel, because the words are closed up and sealed until the time of the end. Many will be purified, made spotless and refined, but the wicked will continue to be wicked. None of the wicked will understand, but those who are wise will understand. "From the time that the daily sacrifice is abolished and the abomination that causes desolation is set up, there will be 1,290 days. Blessed is the one who waits for and reaches the end of the 1,335 days. "As for you, go your way till the end. You will rest, and then at the end of the days you will rise to receive your allotted inheritance."

MICHAEL THE PRINCE

VERSE 12:1 The time of the Wilful King, which we have seen is the Time of The End. At that time Michael will arise, and take the part of Daniel's People. Who is Michael? He is mentioned three times in the book of Daniel, where he is called a "Prince" who stands for Daniel's People-The Jews. He is called in Jude 9 "The Archangel". He has his angels, and in Rev 12:7 he is seen in command of the Angelic Army of Heaven. His work is to deliver God's People, including the Jews, from the power of Satan, and finally to oust Satan and his angels from The Heavenlies, and cast them down to the earth; which we see in Rev 12:7-9. The Archangel Michael also has something to do with the resurrection of the dead, for he is associated with "The Resurrection" mentioned in this chapter Daniel 12:1-2, and he contested with The Devil the resurrection of Moses which we see in Jude 9, and The Voice of The Archangel that will be heard when The Dead in Christ shall rise, according to 1st. Thess 4:16 will be the voice of Michael, for he is The Only Archangel mentioned in The Scriptures.

THE GREAT TRIBULATION

VERSE 12:1 There will be a time of distress such as has not happened from the beginning of nations until then. But at that time your people—everyone whose name is found written in the book—will be delivered. Multitudes who sleep in the dust of the earth will awake: some to everlasting life, others to shame and everlasting contempt. The Scriptures speak about "A Great Tribulation" that is coming on the earth. Jesus in

His Discourse which He gave on The Mount of Olives, on the Tuesday evening before His Crucifixion, said, which we see in Matt 24:21-22, "For then shall be Great Tribulation, such as was NOT since the beginning of the world to this time, NO, nor ever shall be. And except those days should be shortened, there should no flesh, Human or Animal be saved: But for the Elects Sake, meaning the elect of Israel, those days shall be shortened." That The Great Tribulation spoken of by Jesus was NOT the terrible sufferings that befell The Jewish People at the time of the destruction of Jerusalem in 70 A.D. is very clear. That horror was local, and fell upon The Jews Only, while The Tribulation foretold is to come upon the whole world, and is to be immediately followed by great physical changes, and the return of THE SON OF MAN IN THE CLOUDS OF HEAVEN WITH POWER AND GREAT GLORY.

MATT 24:29-30 "Immediately after the distress of those days " 'the sun will be darkened, and the moon will not give its light; the stars will fall from the sky, and the heavenly bodies will be shaken.' "At that time the sign of the Son of Man will appear in the sky, and all the nations of the earth will mourn. They will see the Son of Man coming on the clouds of the sky, with power and great glory."

None of these things happened immediately after The Destruction of Jerusalem, nor have they happened as yet. It will not do to say as some of our modern Theologians have said, as they try to do away with the Words and Deity of Jesus The Christ, that the physical changes, such as the darkening of the sun, etc., are figurative, and represent the downfall of rulers, governments, and authorities from the Political scene, for such physical changes have happened before, and they will happen again. YES, they happened in the days of Moses, when there was Darkness in Egypt for three days, which we see in Exodus 10:21-23, and they shall happen again when the "BOWLS" of the Book of Revelation are poured out, as they will be during the Great Tribulation, which we see in Revelation 16:1-21; for four of the Bowl Plagues are repetitions of four of the Plagues of Egypt.

REV 16:1 Then I heard a loud voice from the temple saying to the seven angels, "Go, pour out the seven bowls of God's wrath on the earth." The first angel went and poured out his bowl on the land, and ugly and painful sores broke out on the people who had the mark of the beast and worshiped his image. The second angel poured out his bowl on the sea, and it turned into blood like that of a dead man, and every living

79

thing in the sea died. The third angel poured out his bowl on the rivers and springs of water, and they became blood. Then I heard the angel in charge of the waters say: "You are just in these judgments, you who are and who were, the Holy One, because you have so judged; for they have shed the blood of your saints and prophets, and you have given them blood to drink as they deserve." And I heard the altar respond: "Yes, Lord God Almighty, true and just are your judgments." The fourth angel poured out his bowl on the sun, and the sun was given power to scorch people with fire. They were seared by the intense heat and they cursed the name of God, who had control over these plagues, but they refused to repent and glorify him. The fifth angel poured out his bowl on the throne of the beast, and his kingdom was plunged into darkness. Men gnawed their tongues in agony and cursed the God of heaven because of their pains and their sores, but they refused to repent of what they had done. The sixth angel poured out his bowl on the great river Euphrates, and its water was dried up to prepare the way for the kings from the East. Then I saw three evil spirits that looked like frogs; they came out of the mouth of the dragon, out of the mouth of the beast and out of the mouth of the false prophet. They are spirits of demons performing miraculous signs, and they go out to the kings of the whole world, to gather them for the battle on the great day of God Almighty. "Behold, I come like a thief! Blessed is he who stays awake and keeps his clothes with him, so that he may not go naked and be shamefully exposed." Then they gathered the kings together to the place that in Hebrew is called Armageddon. The seventh angel poured out his bowl into the air, and out of the temple came a loud voice from the throne, saying, "It is done!" Then there came flashes of lightning, rumblings, peals of thunder and a severe earthquake. No earthquake like it has ever occurred since man has been on earth, so tremendous was the quake. The great city split into three parts, and the cities of the nations collapsed. God remembered Babylon the Great and gave her the cup filled with the wine of the fury of his wrath. Every island fled away and the mountains could not be found. From the sky huge hailstones of about a hundred pounds each fell upon men. And they cursed God on account of the plague of hail, because the plague was so terrible."

The Plagues of Egypt were literal, and much to the dismay of the un-saved so shall the Bowl Plagues be. Jesus also said at that time, the time of, The Great Tribulation, that the "Powers of the Heavens shall be shaken." Now these Powers of the

Heavenlies, the Principalities and Powers of Evil, of which the Apostle Paul warns us about in Ephesians 6:12, have not been shaken as of yet, but in the middle of Daniel's Seventieth Week, when The Great Tribulation begins, there will be War in Heaven, and Satan, who is the Prince of these Evil Powers of the Air, will not only be shaken with them, but he will shaken out of the Heavenlies onto the earth, and it will be Satan's presence, incarnate in the Anti-Christ, that will cause The Great Tribulation. Once more, immediately after The Great Tribulation the Sign of the Son of Man will be seen in the heavens. That Sign is a Cloud. Jesus ascended in a cloud and He is to return in The Clouds; which we see in Matt 24:30. But as The Son of Man, Jesus DID NOT return immediately after the destruction of Jerusalem in 70 A.D., which means that the destruction of Jerusalem WAS NOT The Great Tribulation spoken of by Matthew. Many other prophets in the Old Testament spoke about the time of "Jacob's Trouble", and compared its sufferings to the "Birth-Pangs" of a woman. The Prophet Ezekiel speaks of this time as the time when Israel shall "Pass under the Rod" and when God shall gather Israel into the midst of Jerusalem and cast them into His "Melting Pot", where they are to be refined as silver is refined. While the Old Testament Prophets, and Jesus, foretell of this "TIME OF TROUBLE", it is the Apostle John in the book of Revelation who gives us the complete details as he receives them from Christ. From these references we see that The Great Tribulation will be a time of JUDGMENT for the Jews, through which, as a refining process, they will be made fit to once again be God's Chosen People. The Great Tribulation is not, and I repeat, IS NOT for the perfecting of the Saints. The Great Tribulation has nothing to with the Church. The Book of Revelation is written in chronological order, and the Church is "CAUGHT UP", or as commonly accepted Raptured, through "The Open Door" in chapter 4:1, before The Tribulation Period begins. The Church is not seen again until She re-appears with Christ at His Second Coming as the "Lambs Wife" in Revelation 19:6–9. If the Church is to pass through The Great Tribulation, then the Church should be watching and waiting for the Tribulation, and not watching and waiting for the Son of God from Heaven, whom He raised from the dead-Jesus, who rescues us from the coming wrath which we see in 1st. Thess.1:10. Then those in the Church who want to go through The Great Tribulation, really need to be watching and waiting for The Great Tribulation, but My Jesus speaks to me and to you in Luke 21:28 saying "And when these things begin to come to pass, then look up, and lift up your heads; for your redemption draweth nigh." Praise God!

VERSE 12:3: "Those who are wise will shine like the brightness of the heavens, and those who lead many to righteousness, like the stars for ever and ever." There is "ANOTHER GOSPEL", which is not another gospel, and which St. Paul repudiated. It is a perversion of the TRUE GOSPEL, and has many seductive forms, and it mainly teaches that "FAITH IS NOT SUFFICIENT TO SALVATION", nor able to keep and perfect, and therefore this other gospel emphasizes "GOOD WORKS". The Apostle Paul pronounces a fearful "ANATHEMA" upon its preachers and teachers which we see in Galatians 1:8–9. The WISE teachers of these END TIMES will be like the children of Issachar which we see in 1st. Chronicles 12:32, who were men that had understanding of the times. These wise teachers of these END TIMES, will be ones who understand the scriptures, and being mostly Born-Again, and Spirit-Filled Jews, who are Scholars in the Old Testament; in particular to the prophecies relating to Israel in these END TIMES. So prominent and noted will they be, they will shine as the brightness of the firmament on a clear winter's night, and as stars in the Prophetic Heavens, and they will be like the great prophets of old, Moses, Isaiah, Ezekiel, and Daniel, that they shall shine forever. So true and clear and forceful will be their exposition of the Word of God, that it will convict the hearers, and they shall turn many to righteousness.

VERSES 4–13: Daniel closes this book with the events of world history, past, present and future clear to the end. God through Daniel shows us there shall be trouble such as never was, followed by the Resurrection of the Dead, and the Everlasting Glory of the Saints. A time of trouble, such as never was, I believe, applies to our own generation today. We are seeing terrorism, torture, suffering, and death, of whole populations, by demon dictators, more intense than the atrocities perpetrated by Antiochus, Titus, the Roman Emperors, and the Popes during the time of the Inquisition. In these END TIMES we have had men out of the pit of Hell like Hitler and his 1000 year Reich, Mussolini, Stalin and the rest of the leaders of Russia that followed him, Khomeini the madman who is the head of Iran, which is the old Persian Empire, car bombings, the murdering of women and children, and the taking of hostages. After Lenin's death on January 21, 1924, there resulted an internal power struggle from which Joseph Stalin emerged the absolute ruler of Russia. Stalin secured his position at first by exiling his opponents, but from 1930 to 1953, he resorted to purge trials and mass executions. These measures resulted in over 30 million deaths, according to most estimates. The second World War brought 20th Century cruelty to its peak. Nazi murder camps systematically killed 6 1/2 million Jews, 7 million Christians, Gypsies, political opponents, sick and retarded people, and many others considered undesirable were murdered by the Nazis. By the end of World War II some 45 million people lost their lives in the war. By the end of April 1969 the United States Armed Forces peaked at 543,000 men in VietNam. The communist victory in Vietnam, Cambodia, and Laos by May 1975 did not bring peace. Attempts at radical social reorganization left over 1 million people dead in Cambodia during 1975–1978.

Daniel tells us that many shall run to and fro, and that knowledge shall be increased which is characteristic of the time of the end. All the accumulated knowledge of man from Adam until 1956 remained Status Quo, where it doubled in 1956. In 1966 it doubled again, and we have been seeing knowledge double every two years since then. LATEST NEWS FLASH! MANS KNOWLEDGE IS NOW DOUBLING EVERY 30 DAYS! This, also, applies to our own generation, as it has to no other: Trains, Automobiles, Ships, Airplanes, Books, Newspapers, Radios, Televisions, Satellites, Computers; as a means of travel and dissemination of knowledge, on a scale never before dreamed of in the history of man. And now, on top of all this has come the nuclear bomb, the Hydrogen bomb, the Neutron bomb, and the deadliest of all THE MX MISSILE which has struck terror to the hearts of men to such a degree, that makes us realize that we are living in the age, and the generation, and THE TIME PERIOD that Jesus spoke of as The Setting for His Return!

**DON'T PANIC CHRISTIAN
LOOK UP, AND LIFT UP YOUR HEADS; FOR YOUR
REDEMPTION DRAWETH NIGH.**

PART II

THE REVELATION ACCORDING TO SAINT JOHN

J
E
S
U
S

IS   LORD

P
R
A
I
S
E

H
I
S

H
O
L
Y

N
A
M
E

Chapter 14

How the Message was Given to John

This is the Revelation of Jesus Christ. It is His revelation given to Him by God the Father to be made known to His servants. Both internal and external evidence places the book towards the end of Emperor Domitian's reign in 96 A.D. It was Domitian who had the apostle John banished to the isle of Patmos in the Aegean Sea. There are four views as we told you, in our earlier statement, Preterist, Historical, Futurist, and Spiritualist. Preterist interpretation regards the book as referring to its own day. Historical interpretation is that the book was designed to Forecast a general view of the whole period of church history, from John's time to the end of the world. Futurist interpretation centers the book largely around the time of the coming of Jesus and the end of the world. Spiritualist interpretation separates the imagery of the book entirely from any reference to historical events-those of John's day, or those at the time of the end. To me, in taking the Hebrew, Greek, and Aramaic languages in their most apparent meaning, we will make our study a combination of the Historical and Futurist interpretations. It is the Revelation, God

Himself being the author. God Himself dictated it, through Christ, by an Angel, to John, who wrote it down, and sent the completed book to the seven churches. Chapters 1–3: are things which were in John's day: Seven letters to Seven Churches, dealing with the situation as it was then.

REV 1:1 The revelation of Jesus Christ, which God gave him to show his servants what must soon take place. He made it known by sending his angel to his servant John, who testifies to everything he saw—that is, the word of God and the testimony of Jesus Christ. Blessed is the one who reads the words of this prophecy, and blessed are those who hear it and take to heart what is written in it, because the time is near. John, To the seven churches in the province of Asia: Grace and peace to you from him who is, and who was, and who is to come, and from the seven spirits before his throne, and from Jesus Christ, who is the faithful witness, the first-born from the dead, and the ruler of the kings of the earth. To him who loves us and has freed us from our sins by his blood, and has made us to be a kingdom and priests to serve his God and Father—to him be glory and power for ever and ever! Amen. Look, he is coming with the clouds, and every eye will see him, even those who pierced him; and all the peoples of the earth will mourn because of him. So shall it be! Amen. "I am the Alpha and the Omega," says the Lord God, "who is, and who was, and who is to come, the Almighty." I, John, your brother and companion in the suffering and kingdom and patient endurance that are ours in Jesus, was on the island of Patmos because of the word of God and the testimony of Jesus. On the Lord's Day I was in the Spirit, and I heard behind me a loud voice like a trumpet, which said: "Write on a scroll what you see and send it to the seven churches: to Ephesus, Smyrna, Pergamum, Thyatira, Sardis, Philadelphia and Laodicea." I turned around to see the voice that was speaking to me. And when I turned I saw seven golden lampstands, and among the lampstands was someone "like a son of man," dressed in a robe reaching down to his feet and with a golden sash around his chest. His head and hair were white like wool, as white as snow, and his eyes were like blazing fire. His feet were like bronze glowing in a furnace, and his voice was like the sound of rushing waters. In his right hand he held seven stars, and out of his mouth came a sharp double-edged sword. His face was like the sun shining in all its brilliance. When I saw him, I fell at his feet as though dead. Then he placed his right hand on me and said: "Do not be afraid. I am the First and the Last.

I am the Living One; I was dead, and behold I am alive for ever and ever! And I hold the keys of death and Hades. "Write, therefore, what you have seen, what is now and what will take place later. The mystery of the seven stars that you saw in my right hand and of the seven golden lampstands is this: The seven stars are the angels of the seven churches, and the seven lampstands are the seven churches."

REV 2:1 "To the angel of the church in Ephesus write: These are the words of him who holds the seven stars in his right hand and walks among the seven golden lampstands: I know your deeds, your hard work and your perseverance. I know that you cannot tolerate wicked men, that you have tested those who claim to be apostles but are not, and have found them false. You have persevered and have endured hardships for my name, and have not grown weary. Yet I hold this against you: You have forsaken your first love. Remember the height from which you have fallen! Repent and do the things you did at first. If you do not repent, I will come to you and remove your lampstand from its place. But you have this in your favor: You hate the practices of the Nicolaitans, which I also hate. He who has an ear, let him hear what the Spirit says to the churches. To him who overcomes, I will give the right to eat from the tree of life, which is in the paradise of God. "To the angel of the church in Smyrna write: These are the words of him who is the First and the Last, who died and came to life again. I know your afflictions and your poverty—yet you are rich! I know the slander of those who say they are Jews and are not, but are a synagogue of Satan. Do not be afraid of what you are about to suffer. I tell you, the devil will put some of you in prison to test you, and you will suffer persecution for ten days. Be faithful, even to the point of death, and I will give you the crown of life. He who has an ear, let him hear what the Spirit says to the churches. He who overcomes will not be hurt at all by the second death. "To the angel of the church in Pergamum write: These are the words of him who has the sharp, double-edged sword. I know where you live—where Satan has his throne. Yet you remain true to my name. You did not renounce your faith in me, even in the days of Antipas, my faithful witness, who was put to death in your city—where Satan lives. Nevertheless, I have a few things against you: You have people there who hold to the teaching of Balaam, who taught Balak to entice the Israelites to sin by eating food sacrificed to idols and by committing sexual immorality. Likewise you also have those who hold to the teaching of the Nicolaitans. Repent therefore! Otherwise, I will soon come to you and will fight against them with the sword of my mouth. He who has an ear, let him hear what the Spirit says to the churches. To him who overcomes, I will give some of the hidden manna. I will also give him a white stone with a new name written on it, known only to him who receives it. "To the angel of the church in Thyatira write: These are the words of the Son of God, whose eyes are like blazing fire and whose feet are like burnished bronze. I know your deeds, your love and faith, your service and perseverance, and that you are now doing more than you did at first. Nevertheless, I have this against you: You tolerate that woman Jezebel, who calls herself a prophetess. By her teaching she misleads my servants into sexual immorality and the eating of food sacrificed to idols. I have given her time to repent of her immorality, but she is unwilling. So I will cast her on a bed of suffering, and I will make those who commit adultery with her suffer intensely, unless they repent of her ways. I will strike her children dead. Then all the churches will know that I am He who searches hearts and minds, and I will repay each of you according to your deeds. Now I say to the rest of you in Thyatira, to you who do not hold to her teaching and have not learned Satan's so-called deep secrets (I will not impose any other burden on you): Only hold on to what you have until I come. To him who overcomes and does my will to the end, I will give authority over the nations— 'He will rule them with an iron scepter; he will dash them to pieces like pottery'—just as I have received authority from my Father. I will also give him the morning star. He who has an ear, let him hear what the Spirit says to the churches."

REV 3:1 "To the angel of the church in Sardis write: These are the words of him who holds the seven spirits of God and the seven stars. I know your deeds; you have a reputation of being alive, but you are dead. Wake up! Strengthen what remains and is about to die, for I have not found your deeds complete in the sight of my God. Remember, therefore, what you have received and heard; obey it, and repent. But if you do not wake up, I will come like a thief, and you will not know at what time I will come to you. Yet you have a few people in Sardis who have not soiled their clothes. They will walk with me, dressed in white, for they are worthy. He who overcomes will, like them, be dressed in white. I will never blot out his name from the book of life, but will acknowledge his name before my Father and his angels. He who has an ear, let him hear what the Spirit says to the churches. "To the angel of the church in Philadelphia write: These are the words of him who is holy and true, who holds the key of David. What he opens no one can shut, and what he shuts no one can open. I know your deeds. See, I have placed before you an open door that no one can shut. I know that you have little strength, yet you have kept my word and have not denied my name. I will make those who are of the synagogue of Satan, who claim to be Jews though they are not, but are liars—I will make them come and fall down at your feet and acknowledge that I have loved you. Since you have kept my command to endure patiently, I will also keep you from the hour of trial that is going to come upon the whole world to test those who live on the earth. I am coming soon. Hold on to what you have, so that no one will take your crown. Him who overcomes I will make a pillar in the temple of my God. Never again will he leave it. I will write on him the name of my God and the name of the city of my God, the new Jerusalem, which is coming down out of heaven from my God; and I will also write on him my new name. He who has an ear, let him hear what the Spirit says to the churches. "To the angel of the church in Laodicea write: These are the words of the Amen, the faithful and true witness, the ruler of God's creation. I know your deeds, that you are neither cold nor hot. I wish you were either one or the other! So, because you are lukewarm—neither hot nor cold—I am about to spit you out of my mouth. You say, 'I am rich; I have acquired wealth and do not need a thing.' But you do not realize that you are wretched, pitiful, poor, blind and naked. I counsel you to buy from me gold refined in the fire, so you can become rich; and white clothes to wear, so you can cover your shameful nakedness; and salve to put on your eyes, so you can see. Those whom I love I rebuke and discipline. So be earnest, and repent. Here I am! I stand at the door and knock. If anyone hears my voice and opens the door, I will come in and eat with him, and he with me. To him who overcomes, I will give the right to sit with me on my throne, just as I overcame and sat down with my Father on his throne. He who has an ear, let him hear what the Spirit says to the churches."

Man from the very beginning of his creation has been under the impression that he can buy God. Man is under the impression that God delights in man's gold and silver. God does not need your money or my money. He owns the cattle on a thousand hills. The reason God asks you and me to give to His Work is that He might bless us abundantly as we exercise our faith and trust in Him. The church in Ephesus would bring the sacrifice of their tithe and their offering to the Lord; and then they would worship and praise God for His goodness. They then went to the house of prostitution which stood right next to the church. They thought they had bought God off by their gold and silver and their praise. God still says, OBEDIENCE IS BETTER THAN SACRIFICE.

Chapter 15

The Seven Churches

Revelation 2:1 Through 3:22

* Ephesus-The Loveless Church, a great and powerful church, which was losing its zeal.

* Smyrna-The Persecuted Church, a poor, suffering church, facing martyrdom.

* Pergamum-The Worldly Church, tolerating teachers of immorality: I now quote Jesus out of Revelation 2:14 "Nevertheless, I have a few things against you: You have people there who hold to the teaching of Balaam, who taught Balak to entice the Israelites to sin by eating food sacrificed to idols and by committing sexual immorality. Likewise you also have those who hold to the teaching of the Nicolaitans." The Nicolaitans were the ones in that church who followed the practices that Balaam taught the Moabites, which was the worship of Baal-Peor to cause Israel to sin against God. The abominable practice of Baal-Peor was Sodomy, copulating with animals, and the worship of the female sex opening. This abomination persisted clear down to The New Testament Church, and has been recently revived by Satan in our day and age. Have you ever wondered where A.I.D.S. came from? Straight out of the

HEART OF GOD and **ALLOWED BY GOD** for these practices of Baal-Peor.

* Thyatira-The Paganized Church, growing in zeal, but tolerating Jezebel. I now quote Revelation 2:20 "Nevertheless, I have this against you: You tolerate that woman Jezebel, who calls herself a prophetess. By her teaching she misleads my servants into sexual immorality and the eating of food sacrificed to idols." The abominable worship and sin of Jezebel was the building and erecting of a pole called an Asherah, which was made in the image of a male sex organ which was worshiped.

* Sardis-The Lifeless Church, the church with the reputation that it was alive, but in reality it was dead.

* Philadelphia-The Missionary Church, a nobody church in the city, but faithful to the Lord.

* Laodicea-The Lukewarm Church, neither cold nor hot. Chapters 4–22: Cover the time from then, on to the end. The visions were given to John, and the book was written, in the gruesome light of burning Christians. They had suffered, and were suffering, terrific persecutions. The First Imperial Persecution of Christians, thirty years before this Revelation was written, was by Nero, in 64–67 A.D. In that persecution multitudes of Christians were crucified, or thrown to wild animals, or wrapped in combustible garments and were burned to death while Nero laughed at the shrieks of burning men and women. Paul and Peter were put to death during Nero's persecution of the church. The Second Imperial persecution was instituted by Emperor Domitian in 85–86 A.D. It was short, but extremely severe. Over 40,000 Christians were tortured and killed. This was the persecution in which John was banished to the Isle of Patmos. The Third Imperial persecution, was that of Trajan, which was soon to begin in 98 A.D. John had lived through the first two and was now about to enter the third, where we see Rome's efforts to wipe out the Christian faith. Those were dark days for the church. There were darker days still ahead; there was not only persecution from without, but within the church itself which was beginning to show signs of corruption and apostasy. The book is built around a system of Sevens. Seven Letters to Seven Churches. Seven Seals and Seven Trumpets. Seven Vials. Seven Candlesticks. Seven Stars. Seven Angels. Seven Spirits. A Lamb with Seven Horns and Seven Eyes. Seven Lamps. Seven Thunders. A Red Dragon with Seven Heads and Seven Crowns. A Leopard like Beast with Seven Heads. A Scarlet Colored Beast with Seven Heads. Seven

Mountains. Seven Kings. The Sabbath is the Seventh day. The Levitical System of the Old Testament is built on a cycle of Sevens. Jericho fell after Seven Priests, with Seven Trumpets, for Seven days, marched around it's walls, and blew their Trumpets Seven times on the Seventh day. Naaman dipped in the Jordan Seven times. The bible begins with Seven Days of Creation, and ends with a Book of Sevens about the Ultimate Destiny of Creation. There are Seven days in a week. There are Seven notes in music. There are Seven colors in the rainbow.

There are Seven Beatitudes in The Revelation.

* Blessed is he that reads this prophecy.	1:3
* Blessed are the dead who die in the Lord.	14:13
* Blessed is he that watches for the Lord's coming.	16:15
* Blessed are those bidden to the Lamb's marriage supper.	19:9
* Blessed is he that has part in the first resurrection.	20:6
* Blessed is he that keeps the words of this book.	22:7
* Blessed are they that wash their robes.	22:14

CHAPTER 16

"The Signs of the End Times"

BEFORE WE START THE FUTURIST ASPECT OF THE BOOK BEGINNING WITH CHAPTER 4 LET US LOOK AT "THE SIGNS OF THE END TIMES" THAT JESUS HAS GIVEN US; JESUS SAID"

MATT. 24:7   NATION SHALL RISE AGAINST NATION, KINGDOM AGAINST KINGDOM

Since mans fall in the garden of Eden; Lamech descendent of Cain said to his wives, Adah and Zillah, "hear my voice you wives of Lamech, listen to what I say: I have slain a man for merely wounding me, and I killed another man for just striking me." Cain and his descendants were the inventors of weapons; and ever since it has been nation against nation; kingdom against kingdom; with the unleashing of hatred directed towards one another!

MATT. 24:7   EARTHQUAKES,   FAMINES,   AND PESTILENCE

Since the founding of this great nation of ours, 212 years ago, we formerly had an earthquake once a day somewhere in the world: We now have an earthquake every 1/2 minute of every hour of every day!

Famines are prevalent in our generation and they are going to get worse: 30,000 children died of starvation somewhere in the world today!

5,000 babies were murdered by ABORTION TODAY, as they are everyday!

Pestilence means pollution and disease; we have polluted our waters, our air, our soil, our minds, our bodies; everything that man has touched in his sinful state with out Christ he has corrupted! The most pronounced form of Pestilence is AIDS:

Aids is: Acquired Immune Deficiency Syndrome which is the breakdown of the NORMAL IMMUNE SYSTEM; which GOD gave man to protect him. THIS IMMUNE SYSTEM was given to man BY GOD AS A DIVINE PROTECTION; and did not evolve as many would have us believe. This is why most of The Leaders of The World predict that by the year 1991; 50,000,000 people of the world's population would die of A.I.D.S.! There would be 23,000,000 Americans in THESE UNITED STATES OF AMERICA infected with A.I.D.S. by the years 1991–1992. This is a plague, this is GOD'S JUDGMENT upon all mankind for his disobedience to GOD, his IMMORALITY, his hatred of GOD and of his fellow man. This why it's going to be most difficult to come up with a vaccine against this appalling disease. THERE IS A WAY! HIS NAME IS JESUS! God speaking to ALL OF MANKIND, as we see in 2nd. Chronicles 7: 13–14, ". . . or if I send pestilence among My people, and My people who are called by MY Name humble themselves and pray, and seek My face and turn from their wicked ways, then I will hear from heaven, will forgive their sin, and will heal their land!

Aids was originally spread primarily by male Homosexual intercourse which is anal intercourse. It was also spread by IV drug users sharing the same hypodermic needle. Dirty NEEDLES, dirty MINDS, dirty THOUGHTS, ANTI GOD! Aids can be caught by a woman through heterosexual intercourse which is vaginal intercourse. This can happen if intercourse is during the woman's menstrual period, or if she has open sores in her vagina. If the male has the Aids Virus, the virus will be secreted by his semen into the woman's blood system through her sores or the blood vessels that are open during menstruation. The U.S. Department of Health gives us these statistics: AIDS: 73% in active HOMOSEXUAL and BISEXUAL men! AIDS: 17% in present or past users of intravenous drugs!

GOD WILL NOT BE MOCKED

I have news for the Yo Yo's out there playing the game of religion, and church. Without the spirit of Holiness and Repentance in everyone who has professed to be a Christian, they are not going to make it when the Rapture takes place; and they are going to find that eternity is a very long time to spend in Hell for a fleeting moment of Lust. If God destroyed SODOM and GOMORRAH, and 6 of the cities of the plains; which we see in Genesis chapter 19 for Homosexuality, Cruelty, Criticism, how do you think He Looks Upon what is taking place today? These people who rejoice when a great T.V. Ministry or some other ministry falls through their manipulations, and who call themselves "Christian Activists, Christian Watchdogs, Christian Crusaders" are the worst of all. They play the game of hiding behind a mask which they call Jesus; and cause one ministry after another to topple: They rationalize their continued sin by saying to themselves that God died and left them His World, and His People, to JUDGE and CRITICIZE and to find fault with. Usually the sin they think they spot in someone else; is the very sin that they themselves are hung with; and they start spreading rumors and insinuations, innuendoes, and by casting aspersions upon any ministry!!!

DAN.12:4   MEN SHALL RUN TO AND FRO

The leaders of the world will run around like chickens with their heads cut off trying to make a decision of either right or wrong.

DAN. 12:4   KNOWLEDGE SHALL BE INCREASED

Since the very beginning of God's creation of Adam; all the accumulated knowledge of man remained status quo until 1956: In 1956 man's knowledge doubled, then it doubled again in 1966. Since 1968 until now man's knowledge has doubled every two years; TODAY IN 1988, MAN'S KNOWLEDGE IS DOUBLING EVERY 30 DAYS! Man today without God has the ability to blow himself and planet earth out of the universe!

Germany, suffering from British blockade, declared almost unrestricted submarine warfare January 31, 1917. U.S. cut diplomatic ties with Germany February 3, 1917, and formally declared war April 6, 1917. About 1,000 marines landed in China March 5, 1927 to protect property in their Civil war. U.S. and British consulates looted by nationalists March 24, 1927. Japan attacked Pearl Harbor, Hawaii, 7:55 AM December 7th. 1941, 19 ships were sunk or damaged, and 2,300 were dead. The U.S. declared war on Japan December 8, 1941 and on Germany and Italy December 11, 1941 after those countries declared war on The United States of America.

The U.S. Federal Government forcibly moved 110,000 Japanese-Americans including 75,000 U.S. citizens to detention camps. The exclusion, separation, and detention lasted for 3 years.

President Truman asked Congress for aid to Greece and Turkey to combat Communist terrorism March 12, 1947.

The Berlin Airlift: Russia began a land blockade of Berlin's Allied sectors April 1, 1948. This blockade and western counter-blockade were canceled September 30, 1949, after British and U.S. planes had airlifted over 2,343,315 tons of food and coal into the city.

Mrs. I. Toguri D'Aquino (Tokyo Rose) was sentenced October 7, 1949 to ten years in prison for treason. She was paroled in 1956 and then later pardoned in 1977. I WONDER WHO PAID WHOM, HOW MUCH TO GET HER OUT!

January 14, 1950 the U.S. recalled all consular officials from China after the latter seized the American Consulate General in Peking.

President Truman ordered The U.S. Air Force and Navy to Korea June 27, 1950 after North Korea invaded South Korea. President Truman approved ground forces, and air strikes against North Korea June 30, 1950. U.S. forces landed at Inchon September 15, 1950; U.N. forces took Pyongyang October 20, 1950 and reached China's border November 20, 1950, China then sent troops across the border on November 26, 1950.

President Eisenhower announced that on May 8, 1953 the U.S. had given France $60,000,000.00 for the war in Indochina. More aid was announced in September, 1954 and it was also reported at that time that 3/4ths. of the war's costs in Indochina (Viet Nam) were being financed by the U.S.

Five members of Congress were wounded in The House of Representatives in Washington D.C. March 1st.1954 by 4 Puerto Rican independence supporters who fired at random from the spectators gallery.

5,000 U. S. Marines were sent into Lebanon to protect the elected government and officials from overthrow during the months of July through October 1958.

A U-2 reconnaissance plane of the U. S. was shot down in Russia May 1st.1960.

Mobs attacked The U. S. Embassy in Panama September 17,1960

The U. S. announced on December 15, 1960 that it had backed the rightist group in Laos, which took power the next day.

The U. S. severed diplomatic relations with Cuba, January 3,1961.

The invasion of Cuba's Bay of Pigs, took place on April 17,1961 by Cuban Exiles, who were trained, armed, and directed by the U. S; attempting to overthrow the regime of Fidel Castro. The U. S. forces were repulsed! President Kennedy said on February 14,1962 that the U. S. military advisers in Viet Nam would return fire if fired upon.

A Soviet offensive missile build-up in Cuba was revealed by President Kennedy on October 22,1962, who ordered a naval and air quarantine on all shipments of offensive military equipment to the island.

The U. S. troops in Viet Nam totaled over 15,000 by years end; and aid to South Viet Nam by the end of 1963 totaled $500,000,000.00.

Panama suspended relations with The U.S. January 9, 1964 after riots.

President Johnson in February 1965 ordered continuous bombing of North Viet Nam below the 20th. Parallel.

14,000 U.S. troops were sent to the Dominican Republic during their Civil War on April 28, 1965.

U.S. forces began firing into Cambodia on May 1, 1966.

The bombing of the Hanoi area of North Viet Nam by U.S. plane's began June 29, 1966. By December 31, 1966 385,000 U.S. troops were stationed in South Viet Nam, plus another 60,000 offshore and 33,000 in Thailand.

The USS Pueblo and an 83 man crew were seized in the sea of Japan by North Koreans on January 23, 1968.

U.S. and South Vietnamese forces crossed Cambodian borders on April 30, 1970.

Illegal C.I.A. operations, including records on 300,000 persons and groups, and infiltration of agents into black, anti-war and political movements, were described by a blue ribbon panel headed by Vice president Rockefeller.

Some 90 people, including 63 Americans were taken Hostage, November 3, 1979 at the American Embassy in Teheran, Iran.

8 Americans were killed and 5 wounded on April 24, 1980 in an ill-fated attempt to rescue the hostages held by Iranian militants.

Minutes after the Inauguration of President Ronald Reagan, January 20, 1981 the 52 Americans who had been held hostage in Iran for 444 days were flown to freedom following an agreement in which the U.S. agreed to return to Iran 8 billion dollars in frozen assets.

The Soviet Union shot down a South Korean air liner out of the sky on September 1,1983 killing all 269 people on board.

On October 23,1983, 24 U.S. Marines and sailors, members of the multinational peacekeeping force in Lebanon, were killed when a TNT laden suicide terrorist blew up Marine headquarters at the Beirut International Airport. At the same time, a second truck bomb blew up a French paratroop barracks 2 miles away, killing more than 40.

U.S. Marines and Rangers and a small force from 6 Caribbean nations invaded the island of Grenada on October 25, 1983.

Indria Gandhi, the Prime Minister of India, was slain by 2 of her own bodyguards in New Delhi on October 31, 1984.

DID JESUS SAY SOMETHING ABOUT WARS AND RUMORS OF WARS?

2nd.TIM. 3:13   EVIL MEN SHALL WAX WORSE AND WORSE

MATT. 24:37   CONDITIONS WOULD BE AS THEY WERE IN THE DAYS OF NOAH

What were the conditions in Noah's day? The same as today! Drunkenness, sex, immorality, homosexuality, lesbianism, the killing of babies, drugs, man's inhumanity to man, sexual intercourse with animals; etc.

In Genesis chapter 6 we see God making the statement that it "regretted Him that He had made man, for every inclination of the thoughts of man was evil all the time; and God's heart was grieved and filled with pain."

MATT. 24:49	RESTAURANTS AND TAVERNS

MARK. 13:22 and MATT. 24:5 FALSE CHRIST'S

1st.TIM. 4:1–2	A FALLING AWAY FROM THE FAITH, AND PAYING ATTENTION TO DELUDING, SEDUCING SPIRITS
2nd.TIM 4:3,4	PEOPLE WILL NOT ENDURE SOUND DOCTRINE, NOT WANTING TO HEAR THE TRUTH, BUT HAVING ITCHING EARS
2nd.PET. 3:3,4	SCOFFERS WHO DON'T CARE TO HEAR OF THE SECOND COMING OF JESUS THE CHRIST
1st.THESS 5:3	THEY WILL SAY ALL IS WELL, THERE IS PEACE AND SAFETY, BUT THERE WILL BE NO ESCAPE
JUDE. 16–18	MEN WALKING AFTER THEIR OWN LUSTS
JAMES. 5:3–6	HEAPING UP TREASURES FOR THE LAST DAYS
MATT. 24:11	FALSE PREACHERS WILL LEAD MANY INTO ERROR
ZECH. 8:10	MEN AND HORSES OUT OF WORK

We have seen horses out of work for almost 100 years now; and yet Russia has the largest horse army in the world! Why? Every General since the days of Napoleon who have gone to the Holy Land and HAVE STOOD in The Valley of Jezreel; which is Israel's most fertile valley; have made the same statement that it is an ideal place for a battle. The Valley of Jezreel is also known by the name of The Valley of Meggido. It is surrounded on the one side by "Har Carmel and the other side by Har Meggido" where we get the Greek name "Armageddon" from. This valley is approximately 45 miles wide and 130 to 140 miles long; with very small entry ways at either end into the valley; into which only horses can enter. *Russia; not believing in God, or His Word, or prophecy;* is prepared for battle in this valley; by having the largest horse army in the world, *just in case God's Word turns out to be true.*

NAHUM. 2:3,4	AUTOMOBILES RUSHING MADLY IN THE STREETS
ISAIAH. 60:8	AIRSHIPS
2nd.TIM 3:1	THERE WILL BE PERILOUS TIMES, GREAT STRESS, TROUBLE, HARD TO DEAL WITH AND TO BEAR
2nd.TIM :2	LOVERS OF SELF, MONEY, ARROGANT, ABUSIVE, DISOBEDIENT TO PARENTS
2nd.TIM 3:4,5	LOVERS OF SENSUAL PLEASURES MORE THAN LOVERS OF GOD, HAVING A FORM OF GODLINESS, BUT DENYING THE POWER THEREOF, THEIR CONDUCT BELIES THE GENUINENESS OF THEIR PROFESSION OF CHRIST
JER. 32:36–42	THE JEWISH PEOPLE RETURNING TO PALESTINE

2nd.THESS 2:1–4 and REV. 13 COMING WORLD DICTATOR

REV. 13:5	LENGTH OF HIS RULE: FORTY TWO MONTHS
REV13:8	SOME WILL WORSHIP HIM
REV. 14:9–11	DOOM TO THOSE WHO WORSHIP THE BEAST
MATT. 24:21	THE TRIBULATION
MATT. 24:33	WHEN YOU SEE ALL THESE SIGNS TAKEN TOGETHER IN ONE GENERATION, KNOW THAT WILL BE THE LAST GENERATION!
MATT. 24:14	THIS GOSPEL OF THE KINGDOM WILL BE PREACHED IN THE WORLD AS A TESTIMONY TO ALL NATIONS, THEN THE END WILL COME.

LUKE. 21:25–27	SIGNS IN THE SUN, MOON, STARS, DISTRESS OF NATIONS WITHOUT RESOURCES, MEN'S HEARTS FAILING THEM WITH FEAR
LUKE. 21:36	ALL THESE THINGS ARE THE BEGINNING OF SORROWS. THE END OF ALL THINGS IS AT HAND. WATCH YOU, THEREFORE, AND PRAY ALWAYS THAT YOU BE ACCOUNTED WORTHY TO ESCAPE ALL THESE THINGS THAT SHALL COME TO PASS AND TO STAND BEFORE THE SON OF MAN
LUKE. 21:28	WHEN THESE THINGS BEGIN TO HAPPEN, LOOK UP AND LIFT UP YOUR HEADS, FOR YOUR REDEMPTION DRAWETH NIGH UNTO THEE!
1st.THESS 4:16–17	THE RAPTURE: THE LORD HIMSELF WILL DESCEND WITH A LOUD SUMMONS: THE SHOUT OF AN ARCHANGEL: THE BLAST OF THE TRUMPET OF GOD:

1st.THESS 4:13 Brothers, we do not want you to be ignorant about those who fall asleep, or to grieve like the rest of men, who have no hope. We believe that Jesus died and rose again and so we believe that God will bring with Jesus those who have fallen asleep in him. According to the Lord's own word, we tell you that we who are still alive, who are left till the coming of the Lord, will certainly not precede those who have fallen asleep. For the Lord himself will come down from heaven, with a loud command, with the voice of the archangel and with the trumpet call of God, and the dead in Christ will rise first. After that, we who are still alive and are left will be caught up together with them in the clouds to meet the Lord in the air. And so we will be with the Lord forever. Therefore encourage each other with these words. Concerning the coming of our Lord Jesus Christ and our being gathered to him, we ask you, brothers, not to become easily unsettled or alarmed by some prophecy, report or letter supposed to have come from us, saying that the day of the Lord has already come. Don't let anyone deceive you in any way, for that day will not come until the rebellion occurs and the man of lawlessness is revealed, the man doomed to destruction. He will oppose and will exalt himself over everything that is called God or is worshiped, so that he sets himself up in God's temple, proclaiming himself to be God. Don't you remember that when I was with you I used to tell you these things? And now you know what is holding him back, so that he may be revealed at the proper time. For the secret power of lawlessness is already at work; but the one who now holds it back will continue to do so till he is taken out of the way. And then the lawless one will be revealed, whom the Lord Jesus will overthrow with the breath of his mouth and destroy by the splendor of his coming. The coming of the lawless one will be in accordance with the work of Satan displayed in all kinds of counterfeit miracles, signs and wonders, and in every sort of evil that deceives those who are perishing. They perish because they refused to love the truth and so be saved. For this reason God sends them a powerful delusion so that they will believe the lie so that all will be condemned who have not believed the truth but have delighted in wickedness.

HEB. 9:22   WITHOUT THE SHEDDING OF BLOOD, THERE IS NO REMISSON OF SIN

HEB 9:1 Now the first covenant had regulations for worship and also an earthly sanctuary. A tabernacle was set up. In its first room were the lampstand, the table and the consecrated bread; this was called the Holy Place. Behind the second curtain was a room called the Most Holy Place, which had the golden altar of incense and the gold-covered ark of the covenant. This ark contained the gold jar of manna, Aaron's staff that had budded, and the stone tablets of the covenant. Above the ark were the cherubim of the Glory, overshadowing the atonement cover. But we cannot discuss these things in detail now. When everything had been arranged like this, the priests entered regularly into the outer room to carry on their ministry. But only the high priest entered the inner room, and that only once a year, and never without blood, which he offered for himself and for the sins the people had committed in ignorance. The Holy Spirit was showing by this that the way into the Most Holy Place had not yet been disclosed as long as the first tabernacle was still standing. This is an illustration for the present time, indicating that the gifts and sacrifices being offered were not able to clear the conscience of the worshiper. They are only a matter of food and drink and various ceremonial washings—external regulations applying until the time of the new order. When Christ came as high priest of the good things that are already here, he went through the greater and more perfect tabernacle that is not man-made, that is to say, not a part of this creation. He did not enter by means of the blood of goats and calves; but he entered the Most Holy Place once for all by his own blood, having obtained eternal redemption. The blood of goats and bulls and the ashes of a heifer sprinkled on those who are ceremonially unclean sanctify them so that they are outwardly clean. How much more, then, will the blood of Christ, who through the eternal Spirit offered himself unblemished to God, cleanse our consciences from acts that lead to death, so that we may serve the living God! For this reason Christ is the mediator of a new covenant, that those who are called may receive the promised eternal inheritance—now that he has died as a ransom to set them free from the sins committed under the first covenant. In the case of a will, it is necessary to prove the death of the one who made it, because a will is in force only when somebody has died; it never takes effect while the one who made it is living. This is why even the first covenant was not put into effect without blood. When Moses had proclaimed every commandment of the law to all the people, he took the blood of calves, together with water, scarlet wool and branches of hyssop, and sprinkled the scroll and all the people. He said, "This is the blood of the covenant, which God has commanded you to keep." In the same way, he sprinkled with the blood both the tabernacle and everything used in its ceremonies. In fact, the law requires that nearly everything be cleansed with blood, and without the shedding of blood there is no forgiveness. It was necessary, then, for the copies of the heavenly things to be purified with these sacrifices, but the heavenly things themselves with better sacrifices than these. For Christ did not enter a man-made sanctuary that was only a copy of the true one; he entered heaven itself, now to appear for us in God's presence. Nor did he enter heaven to offer himself again and again, the way the high priest enters the Most Holy Place every year with blood that is not his own. Then Christ would have had to suffer many times since the creation of the world. But now he has appeared once for all at the end of the ages to do away with sin by the sacrifice of himself. Just as man is destined to die once, and after that to face judgment, so Christ was sacrificed once to take away the sins of many people; and he will appear a second time, not to bear sin, but to bring salvation to those who are waiting for him.

JOHN. 3:16   ONLY ONE WAY TO ESCAPE

JOHN 3:1 Now there was a man of the Pharisees named Nicodemus, a member of the Jewish ruling council. He came to Jesus at night and said, "Rabbi, we know you are a teacher who has come from God. For no one could perform the miraculous signs you are doing if God were not with him." In reply Jesus declared, "I tell you the truth, no one can see the Kingdom of God unless he is born again." "How can a man be born when he is old?" Nicodemus asked. "Surely he cannot enter a second time into his mother's womb to be born!"

Jesus answered, "I tell you the truth, no one can enter the kingdom of God unless he is born of water and the Spirit. Flesh gives birth to flesh, but the Spirit gives birth to spirit. You should not be surprised at my saying, 'You must be born again.' The wind blows wherever it pleases. You hear its sound, but you cannot tell where it comes from or where it is going. So it is with everyone born of the Spirit." "How can this be?" Nicodemus asked. "You are Israel's teacher," said Jesus, "and do you not understand these things? I tell you the truth, we speak of what we know, and we testify to what we have seen, but still you people do not accept our testimony. I have spoken to you of earthly things and you do not believe; how then will you believe if I speak of heavenly things? No one has ever gone into heaven except the one who came from heaven—the Son of Man. Just as Moses lifted up the snake in the desert, so the Son of Man must be lifted up, that everyone who believes in him may have eternal life.

JOHN 3:16 "For God so loved the world that he gave his one and only Son, that whoever believes in him shall not perish but have eternal life. For God did not send his Son into the world to condemn the world, but to save the world through him. Whoever believes in him is not condemned, but whoever does not believe stands condemned already because he has not believed in the name of God's one and only Son. This is the verdict: Light has come into the world, but men loved darkness instead of light because their deeds were evil. Everyone who does evil hates the light, and will not come into the light for fear that his deeds will be exposed. But whoever lives by the truth comes into the light, so that it may be seen plainly that what he has done has been done through God." After this,

Jesus and his disciples went out into the Judean countryside, where he spent some time with them, and baptized. They came to John and said to him, "Rabbi, that man who was with you on the other side of the Jordan—the one you testified about—well, he is baptizing, and everyone is going to him." To this John replied, "A man can receive only what is given him from heaven. You yourselves can testify that I said, 'I am not the Christ but am sent ahead of him.' The bride belongs to the bridegroom. The friend who attends the bridegroom waits and listens for him, and is full of joy when he hears the bridegroom's voice. That joy is mine, and it is now complete. He must become greater; I must become less. "The one who comes from above is above all; the one who is from the earth belongs to the earth, and speaks as one from the earth. The one who comes from heaven is above all. He testifies to what he has seen and heard, but no one accepts his testimony. The man who has accepted it has certified that God is truthful. For the one whom God has sent speaks the words of God, for God gives the Spirit without limit.

The Father loves the Son and has placed everything in his hands. Whoever believes in the Son has eternal life, but whoever rejects the Son will not see life, for God's wrath remains on him." **JESUS THE NAME ABOVE ALL NAMES**

Chapter 17

The Divine Throne, the Twenty-four Elders, the Four Living Creatures

REV 4:1 After this I looked, and there before me was a door standing open in heaven. And the voice I had first heard speaking to me like a trumpet said, "Come up here, and I will show you what must take place after this. "At once I was in the Spirit, and there before me was a throne in heaven with someone sitting on it. And the one who sat there had the appearance of jasper and carnelian. A rainbow, resembling an emerald, encircled the throne. Surrounding the throne were twenty-four other thrones, and seated on them were twenty-four elders. They were dressed in white and had crowns of gold on their heads. From the throne came flashes of lightning, rumblings and peals of thunder. Before the throne, seven lamps were blazing. These are the seven spirits of God. Also before the throne there was what looked like a sea of glass, clear as crystal. In the center, around the throne, were four living creatures, and they were covered with eyes, in front and in back. The first living creature was like a lion, the second was like an ox, the third had a face like a man, the fourth was like a flying eagle. Each of the four living creatures had six wings and was covered with eyes all around, even under his wings. Day and night they never stop saying: "Holy, holy, holy is the Lord God Almighty, who was, and is, and is to come." Whenever the living creatures give glory, honor and thanks to him who sits on the throne and who lives for ever and ever, the twenty-four elders fall down before him who sits on the throne, and worship him who lives for ever and ever. They lay their crowns before the throne and say: "You are worthy, our Lord and God, to receive glory and honor and power, for you created all things, and by your will they were created and have their being."

ALL HEAVEN AND ALL HELL KNOW WHO JESUS IS; LORD OF LORDS AND KING OF KINGS!

Revelation 4:1-11

The four living creatures are a special order of created beings associated with the throne of God. Their appearance was the likeness of a man. Everyone of them had four faces. Each of the four living creatures had the face of a man in front, of a lion on the right side, of an ox on the left side, and of an eagle behind. According to the Revelation given to the prophet Ezekiel there were four faces in each direction, so that each creature had sixteen faces, and each of the faces had four wings. Thus all together they had sixty-four faces and two hundred and fifty-six wings. Their feet were straight feet meaning they had no joints. Joints were not necessary since the throne-bearers did not have to lie down or turn around. The sole of their feet was like the sole of a calf's foot; and they sparkled like the color of burnished brass. The reason for the calf's foot was that they were rounded, for turning smoothly in every direction. Under their wings on their four sides they had the hands of a man. All four of them had faces and wings, and their wings touched one another. Each one went straight ahead; they did not turn as they moved. Wherever the Holy Spirit would go, they would go, without turning as they went. Each of them was covered with eyes all around, even under their wings. So we see that this special order of created beings, the four living creatures combine characteristics both of the Cherubim, concerned with the public governmental glory of

God, and the Seraphim, concerned with the holiness of God. They adore the Lord God Almighty and they are joined in worship by the twenty-four elders as they praise God day and night, they never stop saying: Holy, Holy, Holy is the Lord God Almighty, who was, and is, and is to come.

* NOTE : The heavenly Sanhedrin of twenty-four Elders is composed of the twelve Apostles of Jesus Christ; and the other twelve Elders are composed of the twelve Princes of the tribes of Israel.

REV 5:1 Then I saw in the right hand of him who sat on the throne a scroll with writing on both sides and sealed with seven seals. And I saw a mighty angel proclaiming in a loud voice, "Who is worthy to break the seals and open the scroll?" But no one in heaven or on earth or under the earth could open the scroll or even look inside it. I wept because no one was found who was worthy to open the scroll or look inside. Then one of the elders said to me, "Do not weep! See, the Lion of the tribe of Judah, the Root of David, has triumphed. He is able to open the scroll and its seven seals." Then I saw a Lamb, looking as if it had been slain, standing in the center of the throne, encircled by the four living creatures and the elders. He had seven horns and seven eyes, which are the seven spirits of God sent out into all the earth. He came and took the scroll from the right hand of him who sat on the throne. And when he had taken it, the four living creatures and the twenty-four elders fell down before the Lamb. Each one had a harp and they were holding golden bowls full of incense, which are the prayers of the saints. And they sang a new song: "You are worthy to take the scroll and to open its seals, because you were slain, and with your blood you purchased men for God from every tribe and language and people and nation. You have made them to be a kingdom and priests to serve our God, and they will reign on the earth." Then I looked and heard the voice of many angels, numbering thousands upon thousands, and ten thousand times ten thousand. They encircled the throne and the living creatures and the elders. In a loud voice they sang: "Worthy is the Lamb, who was slain, to receive power and wealth and wisdom and strength and honor and glory and praise!" Then I heard every creature in heaven and on earth and under the earth and on the sea, and all that is in them, singing: "To him who sits on the throne and to the Lamb be praise and honor and glory and power, for ever and ever!" The four living creatures said, "Amen," and the elders fell down and worshiped."

Chapter 18

The Seven-sealed Book

Revelation 5:1 Through 8:5

The seven sealed book is the title deed to the forfeited inheritance of the earth lost by Adam when he fell. This legal document, guaranteeing the dispossession of Satan which was provided for by Christ's atoning death, is seen lying opened upon the right hand of the One sitting on the throne who is God the Father. The scroll or ancient book written within and on the back according to Hebrew Law shows the completeness of legal provision for dispossession. Being sealed with seven seals according to Hebrew Law shows the completeness of the sealing until one who is legally qualified to open the tightly closed legal document should appear. A mighty angel now proclaims in a loud voice, "Who is worthy to break the seals and open the scroll?" But no one in heaven or on earth or under the earth could open the scroll or even look inside it. No one was able to open it. Not angelic beings, because the inheritance was lost by a human being and a man must therefore open it. Not any of Adam's descendants, because they are all sinners. Then one of the Elders said to me, John, do not weep! See, the Lion of the tribe of Judah, the Root of David, has triumphed. He is able to open the scroll and it's seven seals. The death of Jesus the Christ is the basis of redemption not only of sinners but of all the earth. "Then I saw a Lamb, looking as if it had been slain, standing in the center of the throne, encircled by the four living creatures and the elders. He had seven horns and seven eyes, which are the seven spirits of God sent out into all the earth. The seven spirits of God is the seven manifold spirit of the Holy Spirit which we see rested on only one man, He being Jesus, as we see in Isaiah 11:1–3.

THE SEVEN MANIFOLD SPIRIT OF GOD'S HOLY SPIRIT

1. The spirit of wisdom.
2. The spirit of understanding.
3. The spirit of counsel.
4. The spirit of might.
5. The spirit of knowledge.
6. The spirit of reverential fear of the Lord.
7. The spirit of obedient fear of the Lord.

Jesus was and is the only One who ever came to planet earth to have THE SEVEN MANIFOLD SPIRIT OF GOD upon Him, and who moved in that Spirit. He came and took the scroll from the right hand of him, God , who sat on the throne. And when he had taken it, the four living creatures and the twenty-four elders fell down before the Lamb. It was the case of The God-Man, Jesus, being able to do what no one else could do, the redemptive price being Christ's own blood. As Jesus takes the seven-sealed book to claim possession of the earth, this now evokes the praise and worship of myriads of angels, the living creatures and all of the redeemed humanity in heaven. All of creation worships and praises the Lamb. Their great theme is worthy is the Lamb. "Worthy is the Lamb, who was slain, to receive power and wealth and wisdom and strength and honor and glory and praise!"

REV 6:1 I watched as the Lamb opened the first of the seven seals. Then I heard one of the four living creatures say in a voice like thunder, "Come!" I looked, and there before me was a white horse! Its rider held a bow, and he was given a crown, and he rode out as a conqueror bent on conquest. When the Lamb opened the second seal, I heard the second living creature say, "Come!" Then another horse came out, a fiery red one. Its rider was given power to take peace from the earth and to make men slay each other. To him was given a large sword. When the Lamb opened the third seal, I heard the third living creature say, "Come!" I looked, and there before me was a black horse! Its rider was holding a pair of scales in his hand. Then I heard what sounded like a voice among the four living creatures, saying, "A quart of wheat for a day's wages, and three quarts of barley for a day's wages, and do not damage the oil and the wine!" When the Lamb opened the fourth seal, I heard the voice of the fourth living creature say, "Come!" I looked, and there before me was a pale horse! Its rider was named Death, and Hades was following close behind him. They were given power over a fourth of the earth to kill by sword, famine and plague, and by the wild beasts of the earth. When he opened the fifth seal, I saw under the altar the souls of those who had been slain because of the word of God and the testimony they had maintained. They called out in a loud voice, "How long, Sovereign Lord, holy and true, until you judge the inhabitants of the earth and avenge our blood?" Then each of them was given a white robe, and they were told to wait a little longer, until the number of their fellow servants and brothers who were to be killed as they had been was completed. I watched as he opened the sixth seal. There was a great earthquake. The sun turned black like sackcloth made of goat hair, the whole moon turned blood red, and the stars in the sky fell to earth, as late figs drop from a fig tree when shaken by a strong wind. The sky receded like a scroll, rolling up, and every mountain and island was removed from its place. Then the kings of the earth, the princes, the generals, the rich, the mighty, and every slave and every free man hid in caves and among the rocks of the mountains. They called to the mountains and the rocks, "Fall on us and hide us from the face of him who sits on the throne and from the wrath of the Lamb! For the great day of their wrath has come, and who can stand?"

THE SEVEN-SEALED BOOK OPENED

Revelation 6:1–8:5

SEALS ONE AND TWO:

The opening of the seals hastens the occurrence of the Day of the Lord and the period of tribulation on the earth to dispossess Satan and wicked men and women. The rider on the White Horse, is the Anti-Christ who imitates Christ, the bow and the crown symbolizing his great conquests. The empty bow and no arrows to fool the world into thinking he is a great peace maker. The rider on the Red Horse symbolizes war and carnage.

SEALS THREE AND FOUR:

The rider on the Black Horse symbolizes famine, which follows war. Bread is rationed: One quart of wheat for a day's wages, and three quarts of barley for a day's wages. The rider on the Pale Horse represents pestilence and is called Death. With each of the first four seals, one of the living creatures associated with God's judicial government toward the earth cries, "Come." Thus they call forth the first judgments, symbolized by the four horsemen.

SEAL FIVE:

The first four seals had to do with happenings on earth. Now we are transported to heaven. This time there is no one living to say come. But the opening of the seal ushers in the vision. John saw the souls of the martyrs under the altar. The situation under the altar is unusual. It is a place of privilege and safety in God's keeping. The souls under the altar; which is the altar of sacrifice where the sacrificial blood of Jesus was poured out, represent the martyrs who died for Jesus as He died for them. They died for the word of God and their blood now cries for vengeance. Each of them is given a white robe which indicates their redemption. They are to rest for a little season while The Great Tribulation is still going on planet earth. They are to wait a little longer, until the number of their fellow servants and their brothers who were to be killed as they had been, is completed.

SEAL SIX:

This seal represents governmental anarchy under the figures of earthquake, the darkening of the sun and the moon, and the falling of the stars. The collapse of all human government brings forth awful terror as "the great day of God's wrath arrives on planet earth.

REV 7:1 After this I saw four angels standing at the four corners of the earth, holding back the four winds of the earth to prevent any wind from blowing on the land or on the sea or on any tree. Then I saw another angel coming up from the east, having the seal of the living God. He called out in a loud voice to the four angels who had been given power to harm the land and the sea: "Do not harm the land or the sea or the trees until we put a seal on the foreheads of the servants of our God." Then I heard the number of those who were sealed: 144,000 from all the tribes of Israel. From the tribe of Judah 12,000 were sealed, from the tribe of Reuben 12,000, from the tribe of Gad 12,000, from the tribe of Asher 12,000, from the tribe of Naphtali 12,000, from the tribe of Manasseh 12,000, from the tribe of Simeon 12,000, from the tribe of Levi 12,000, from the tribe of Issachar 12,000, from the tribe of Zebulun 12,000, from the tribe of Joseph 12,000, from the tribe of Benjamin 12,000. After this I looked and there before me was a great multitude that no one could count, from every nation, tribe, people and language, standing before the throne and in front of the Lamb. They were wearing white robes and were holding palm branches in their hands. And they cried out in a loud voice: "Salvation belongs to our God, who sits on the throne, and to the Lamb." All the angels were standing around the throne and around the elders and the four living creatures. They fell down on their faces before the throne and worshiped God, saying: "Amen! Praise and glory and wisdom and thanks and honor and power and strength be to our God for ever and ever. Amen!" Then one of the elders asked me, "These in white robes—who are they, and where did they come from?" I answered, "Sir, you know." And he said, "These are they who have come out of the great tribulation; they have washed their robes and made them white in the blood of the Lamb. Therefore, "they are before the throne of God and serve him day and night in his temple; and he who sits on the throne will spread his tent over them. Never again will they hunger; never again will they thirst. The sun will not beat upon them, nor any scorching heat. For the Lamb at the center of the throne will be their shepherd; he will lead them to springs of living water. And God will wipe away every tear from their eyes."

THE SEALING OF THE ISRAELITES

Revelation 7:1–8

A remnant of Israel is preserved exactly as Jesus said he would do. These elect of Israel are preserved from the end time Tribulation judgments which befall the earth. It's a public preservation, for "the servants of our God" are to be sealed upon their foreheads, involving no secret discipleship. These are earthly Israelites living in the time of "Jacob's trouble." Even though all tribal genealogies have ceased, God knows who the tribes of Israel are and where they are. He preserves an elect remnant, returning them to the restored kingdom. This event will occur when the "times of the Gentiles" has been fulfilled and the full number of Gentiles have been gathered in. In the enumeration of the tribes of Israel, the tribes of Dan, and Ephraim are deliberately left out by Jesus. Let us see why.

GEN 49:1 Then Jacob called for his sons and said: "Gather around so I can tell you what will happen to you in days to come. "Assemble and listen, sons of Jacob; listen to your father Israel. "Reuben, you are my firstborn, my might, the first sign of my strength, excelling in honor, excelling in power. Turbulent as the waters, you will no longer excel, for you went up onto your father's bed, onto my couch and defiled it. "Simeon and Levi are brothers— their swords are weapons of violence. Let me not enter their council, let me not join their assembly, for they have killed men in their anger and hamstrung oxen as they pleased. Cursed be their anger, so fierce, and their fury, so cruel! I will scatter them in Jacob and disperse them in Israel. "Judah, your brothers will praise you; your hand will be on the neck of your enemies; your father's sons will bow down to you. You are a lion's cub, O Judah; you return from the prey, my son. Like a lion he crouches and lies down, like a lioness—who dares to rouse him? The scepter will not depart from Judah, nor the ruler's staff from between his feet, until he comes to whom it belongs and the obedience of the nations is his.

THIS SCRIPTURE IN REGARDS TO THE TRIBE OF JUDAH IS REFERRING TO JESUS

He will tether his donkey to a vine, his colt to the choicest branch; he will wash his garments in wine, his robes in the blood of grapes. His eyes will be darker than wine, his teeth whiter than milk. "Zebulun will live by the seashore and become a haven for ships; his border will extend toward Sidon. "Issachar is a rawboned donkey lying down between two saddlebags. When he sees how good is his resting place and how pleasant is his land, he will bend his shoulder to the burden and submit to forced labor. "Dan will provide justice for his people as one of the tribes of Israel. Dan will be a serpent by the roadside, a viper along the path, that bites the horse's heels so that its rider tumbles backward. "I look for your deliverance, O Lord. "Gad will be attacked by a band of raiders, but he will attack them at their heels. "Asher's food will be rich; he will provide delicacies fit for a king. "Naphtali is a doe set free that bears beautiful fawns. "Joseph is a fruitful vine, a fruitful vine near a spring, whose branches climb over a wall. With bitterness archers attacked him; they shot at him with hostility. But his bow remained steady, his strong arms stayed limber, because of the hand of the Mighty One of Jacob, because of the Shepherd, the Rock of Israel, because of your father's God, who helps you, because of the Almighty, who blesses you with blessings of the heavens above, blessings of the deep that lies below, blessings of the breast and womb. Your father's blessings are greater than the blessings of the ancient mountains, than the bounty of the age-old hills. Let all these rest on the head of Joseph, on the brow of the prince among his brothers. "Benjamin is a ravenous wolf; in the morning he devours the prey, in the evening he divides the plunder." All these are the twelve tribes of Israel, and this is what their father said to them when he blessed them, giving each the blessing appropriate to him; and what would befall them in the TIME OF JESUS

* NOTE : In this chapter of Genesis the scripture tells us that Jacob called onto his sons, and said: Gather yourselves together, that I may tell you that which shall befall you in the end of days. In verses sixteen and seventeen the Holy Spirit tells us about the tribe of Dan: "Dan shall judge his people, as one of the tribes of Israel. Dan shall be a serpent in the path, that bites the horse's heels, so that his rider falls off backwards." Samson descended from the tribe of Dan who did judge Israel, and who was the worst judge ever seen by Israel, and who needed to be judged himself. Judas Iscariot descended from the tribe of Dan who did betray Jesus, and whom Jesus called the Son of Hell. The tribe of Ephraim are left out by Jesus because of their idolatry. ALL 19 KINGS OF THE NORTHERN KINGDOM OF ISRAEL WITH IT'S CAPITAL AT SAMARIA; ALL DESCENDED FROM THE TRIBE OF EPHRAIM AND EACH AND EVERY KING SUCCESSIVELY WAS MORE NOTORIOUS FOR HIS IDOLATRY!!!!!!!!

1KI 12:1 Rehoboam went to Shechem, for all the Israelites had gone there to make him king. When Jeroboam son of Nebat heard this (he was still in Egypt, where he had fled from King Solomon), he returned from Egypt. So they sent for Jeroboam, and he and the whole assembly of Israel went to Rehoboam and said to him: "Your father put a heavy yoke on us, but now lighten the harsh labor and the heavy yoke he put on us, and we will serve you." Rehoboam answered, "Go away for three days and then come back to me." So the people went away. Then King Rehoboam consulted the elders who had served his father Solomon during his lifetime. "How would you advise me to answer these people?" he asked. They replied, "If today you will be a servant to these people and serve them and give them a favorable answer, they will always be your servants." But Rehoboam rejected the advice the elders gave him and consulted the young men who had grown up with him and were serving him. He asked them, "What is your advice? How should we answer these people who say to me, 'Lighten the yoke your father put on us'?" The young men who had grown up with him replied, "Tell these people who have said to you, 'Your father put a heavy yoke on us, but make our yoke lighter'—tell them, 'My little finger is thicker than my father's waist. My father laid on you a heavy yoke; I will make it even heavier. My father scourged you with whips; I will scourge you with scorpions.'" Three days later Jeroboam and all the people returned to Rehoboam, as the king had said, "Come back to me in three days." The king answered the people harshly. Rejecting the advice given him by the elders, he followed the advice of the young men and said, "My father made your yoke heavy; I will make it even heavier. My father scourged you with whips; I will scourge you with scorpions." So the king did not listen to the people, for this turn of events was from the Lord, to fulfill the word the Lord had spoken to Jeroboam son of Nebat through Ahijah the Shilonite. When all Israel saw that the king refused to listen to them, they answered the king: "What share do we have in David, what part in Jesse's son? To your tents, O Israel! Look after your own house, O David!" So the Israelites went home. But as for the Israelites who were living in the towns of Judah, Rehoboam still ruled over them. King Rehoboam sent out Adoniram, who was in charge of forced labor, but all Israel stoned him to death. King Rehoboam, however, managed to get into his chariot and escape to Jerusalem. So Israel has been in rebellion against the house of David to this day. When all the Israelites heard that Jeroboam had returned, they sent and called him to the assembly and made him king over all Israel. Only the tribe of Judah remained loyal to the house of David. When Rehoboam arrived in Jerusalem, he mustered the whole house of Judah and the tribe of Benjamin—a hundred and eighty thousand fighting men—to make war against the house of Israel and to regain the kingdom for Rehoboam son of Solomon. But this word of God came to Shemaiah the man of God: "Say to Rehoboam son of Solomon king of Judah, to the whole house of Judah and Benjamin, and to the rest of the people, 'This is what the Lord says: Do not go up to fight against your brothers, the Israelites. Go home, every one of you, for this is my doing.' " So they obeyed the word of the Lord and went home again, as the Lord had ordered. Then Jeroboam fortified Shechem in the hill country of Ephraim and lived there. From there he went out and built up Peniel. Jeroboam thought to himself, "The kingdom will now likely revert to the house of David. If these people go up to offer sacrifices at the temple of the Lord in Jerusalem, they will again give their allegiance to their lord, Rehoboam king of Judah. They will kill me and return to King Rehoboam." After seeking advice, the king made two golden calves. He said to the people, "It is too much for you to go up to Jerusalem. Here are your gods, O Israel, who brought you up out of Egypt." One he set up in Bethel, and the other in Dan. And this thing became a sin; the people went even as far as Dan to worship the one there. Jeroboam built shrines on high places and appointed priests from all sorts of people, even though they were not Levites. He instituted a festival on the fifteenth day of the eighth month, like the festival held in Judah, and offered sacrifices on the altar. This he did in Bethel, sacrificing to the calves he had made. And at Bethel he also installed priests at the high places he had made. On the fifteenth day of the eighth month, a month of his own choosing, he offered sacrifices on the altar he had built at Bethel. So he instituted the festival for the Israelites and went up to the altar to make offerings.

IT'S TIME O'CHURCH TO WAKE UP
AND COME BACK TO GOD IN JESUS
IN HOLINESS

John now says I looked and there was before me a great multitude that no one could count, from every nation, tribe, people and language, standing before the throne and in front of the Lamb. The first scene of the sealing of the 144,000 are the elect of Israel which we see takes place on earth. The second scene is the sealing of the great multitude which takes place in heaven. The first group was sealed against a coming

Tribulation, the second group the Tribulation is past. The second group are the elect body of Gentiles, like the first group were the elect body of Jews. This second group have experienced unparalleled suffering in the great Tribulation, having been brought to salvation by dying a martyr's death.

SEAL SEVEN:

This concludes the complete opening of the seven-sealed book so that it's full contents, the trumpets and the bowls might be released upon the earth and its wicked inhabitants. The half hour of silence is the lull after the preceding storm and the prelude to a more terrible one.

REV 8:1 When he opened the seventh seal, there was silence in heaven for about half an hour. And I saw the seven angels who stand before God, and to them were given seven trumpets. Another angel, who had a golden censer, came and stood at the altar. He was given much incense to offer, with the prayers of all the saints, on the golden altar before the throne. The smoke of the incense, together with the prayers of the saints, went up before God from the angel's hand. Then the angel took the censer, filled it with fire from the altar, and hurled it on the earth; and there came peals of thunder, rumblings, flashes of lightning and an earthquake. Then the seven angels who had the seven trumpets prepared to sound them. The first angel sounded his trumpet, and there came hail and fire mixed with blood, and it was hurled down upon the earth. A third of the earth was burned up, a third of the trees were burned up, and all the green grass was burned up. The second angel sounded his trumpet, and something like a huge mountain, all ablaze, was thrown into the sea. A third of the sea turned into blood, a third of the living creatures in the sea died, and a third of the ships were destroyed. The third angel sounded his trumpet, and a great star, blazing like a torch, fell from the sky on a third of the rivers and on the springs of water—the name of the star is Wormwood. A third of the waters turned bitter, and many people died from the waters that had become bitter. The fourth angel sounded his trumpet, and a third of the sun was struck, a third of the moon, and a third of the stars, so that a third of them turned dark. A third of the day was without light, and also a third of the night. As I watched, I heard an eagle that was flying in midair call out in a loud voice: "Woe! Woe! Woe to the inhabitants of the earth, because of the trumpet blasts about to be sounded by the other three angels!"

Chapter 19

The Seven Trumpets Blown and the Tribulation Temple

Revelation 8:6–11:19

The first six trumpets now introduce more severe judgments. The first trumpet is blown resulting in hail and fire being thrown to the earth, which effects vegetation and brings forth severe drought. The second trumpet results in judgment upon the sea, affecting the sea food supply and the ocean transportation lines. The blowing of the third trumpet affects the fresh water supply, a third of which is made deadly bitter by the drug "wormwood". The heavens themselves are affected by the judgment resulting from the blowing of the fourth trumpet. Creation is reversed as a third of the light of heaven are touched and darkened. Three calamities are announced which are terrible judgments falling directly on mankind. These three woes constitute the final three trumpet judgments.

The Fifth Trumpet—The First Woe:

John sees a star fallen from heaven. This star is the angel custodian of the pit of Hell, a prison house of the demons. That he cannot be Satan, or even an evil angel, is shown by the fact that he is the same angelic personage who once again opens the pit of Hell to bind and imprison Satan prior to the Millennium. He is an angel fallen from heaven, not a fallen angel, the past participle "fallen" describing the swiftness of the angels descent and the suddenness with which this first woe comes upon mankind. We see the sun and the sky are darkened by the smoke from the Abyss. And out of the smoke locusts came down upon the earth and were given power like that of scorpions of the earth. The locusts represent demons and the way they will possess, drive, and torment men in the end time. While multitudes of demons have been free to torment the human race during previous ages many of them are so viciously depraved and harmful that God has imprisoned them in the Abyss. These are the terrible demons let loose under the first woe. The name of the king of the demons in hebrew is Abaddon, also Tehom, meaning "absolute destruction," and The King of The Bottomless Pit, The King of The Abyss. In the greek his name is Apollyon meaning "destroyer," or Chaos, destruction, or "chaotic destruction."

REV 9:1 The fifth angel sounded his trumpet, and I saw a star that had fallen from the sky to the earth. The star was given the key to the shaft of the Abyss. When he opened the Abyss, smoke rose from it like the smoke from a gigantic furnace. The sun and sky were darkened by the smoke from the Abyss. And out of the smoke locusts came down upon the earth and were given power like that of scorpions of the earth. They were told not to harm the grass of the earth or any plant or tree, but only those people who did not have the seal of God on their foreheads. They were not given power to kill them, but only to torture them for five months. And the agony they suffered was like that of the sting of a scorpion when it strikes a man. During those days men will seek death, but will not find it; they will long to die, but death will elude them. The locusts looked like horses prepared for battle. On their heads they wore something like crowns of gold, and their faces resembled human faces. Their hair was like women's hair, and their teeth were like lions' teeth. They had breastplates like breastplates of iron, and the sound of their wings was like the thundering of many horses and chariots rushing into battle. They had tails and stings like scorpions, and in their tails they had power to torment people for five months. They had as king over them the angel of the Abyss, whose name in Hebrew is Abaddon, and in Greek, Apollyon. The first woe is past; two other woes are yet to come. The sixth angel sounded his trumpet, and I heard a voice coming from the horns of the golden altar that is before God. It said to the sixth angel who had the trumpet, "Release the four angels who are bound at the great river Euphrates." And the four angels who had been kept ready for this very hour and day and month and year were released to kill a third of mankind. The number of the mounted troops was two hundred million. I heard their number. The horses and riders I saw in my vision looked like this: Their breastplates were fiery red, dark blue, and yellow as sulfur. The heads of the horses resembled the heads of lions, and out of their mouths came fire, smoke and sulfur. A third of mankind was killed by the three plagues of fire, smoke and sulfur that came out of their mouths. The power of the horses was in their mouths and in their tails; for their tails were like snakes, having heads with which they inflict injury. The rest of mankind that were not killed by these plagues still did not repent of the work of their hands; they did not stop worshiping demons, and idols of gold, silver, bronze, stone and wood—idols that cannot see or hear or walk. Nor did they repent of their murders, their magic arts, their sexual immorality or their thefts." From the altar of intercession, which is The Golden Altar of Incense, God answers the prayers of His martyred saints. Toward The Golden Altar their prayers ascend; and from it God's answer goes forth. The loosing of the armies is brought about by the release of the four angels; who are the ministers of the judgment of God under His Divine control. The place of their loosing, The Euphrates, was the location of ancient Babylon. The very hour of their release, the extent of their destruction, has already been determined by God. The number of the cavalrymen is 200,000,000 which we believe to be THE SOLDIERS OF RED CHINA. CHINA today boasts of a population of over 1,100,000,000 (one billion) people. 500,000,000 (500 MILLION) are under the age of 25. SHE also boasts that SHE HAS A STANDING ARMY OF 200,000,000 (200 MILLION) THAT ARE EXPENDABLE. We saw what these soldiers of Red China were like during the Korean Conflict, half starved, half crazed with DRUGS, and following THE DEVIL.

THE SIXTH TRUMPET—THE SECOND WOE

Revelation 9:13–21

The purpose of the second woe in God's design is twofold, punishment and reformation. A third of mankind was killed by the three plagues of fire, smoke, and sulfur. But those who survive this dreadful calamity do not repent of their works and idolatry. They did not stop worshiping demons, and idols of gold, silver , bronze, stone and wood-idols that cannot see or hear or walk. Nor did they repent of their murders, their magic arts, their idolatry, their sexual immorality or their thefts.

REV 10:1 Then I saw another mighty angel coming down from heaven. He was robed in a cloud, with a rainbow above his head; his face was like the sun, and his legs were like fiery pillars. He was holding a little scroll, which lay open in his hand. He planted his right foot on the sea and his left foot on the land, and he gave a loud shout like the roar of a lion. When he shouted, the voices of the seven thunders spoke. And when the seven thunders spoke, I was about to write; but I heard a voice from heaven say, "Seal up what the seven thunders have said and do not write it down." Then the angel I had seen standing on the sea and on the land raised his right hand to heaven. And he swore by him who lives for ever and ever, who created the heavens and all that is in them, the earth and all that is in it, and the sea and all that is in it, and said, "There will be no more delay! But in the days when the seventh angel is about to sound his trumpet, the mystery of God will be accomplished, just as he announced to his servants the prophets." Then the voice that I had heard from heaven spoke to me once more: "Go, take the scroll that lies open in the hand of the angel who is standing on the sea and on the land." So I went to the angel and asked him to give me the little scroll. He said to me, "Take it and eat it. It will turn your stomach sour, but in your mouth it will be as sweet as honey." I took the little scroll from the angel's hand and ate it. It tasted as sweet as honey in my mouth, but when I had eaten it, my stomach turned sour. Then I was told, "You must prophesy again about many peoples, nations, languages and kings."

THE ANGEL AND THE LITTLE BOOK

Revelation 10:1–11

This angel is an actual angel who symbolizes Christ. As representative of Christ, this angel reflects His glory and bears the insignia attributed to Jesus Himself. His stupendous act of setting his foot on land and sea shows Jesus' right to claim the earth as His own. The angel's loud cry and the seven thunders give full testimony to Jesus' authority over the earth. His oath that "there should be no more delay" shows Jesus' divine sovereignty in these matters of judgment. The mystery of God is the theme of "The Little Scroll," and concerns Jesus as the Incarnate Redeemer of the earth. It is a previously hidden truth, which is now fully revealed. This truth is The Grand Theme of the rest of The Revelation where the "mystery of God" is finished and completed. It will be as God has declared to, and by His servants The Prophets, who preached The Good News of Christ's redemption, and His Kingdom.

JOHN AND THE LITTLE SCROLL

Revelation 10:8–11

The little scroll is not only the record of the fulfillment of the mystery of God, and distinguished from the seven-sealed book, but it is also in part, the book Daniel was told to seal up till the time of the end. The reason the scroll was as sweet as honey when first eaten, but when digested bitter, was that the bright deliverance for Daniel and John's people, Israel were preluded by terrible suffering and judgment.

REV 11:1 I was given a reed like a measuring rod and was told, "Go and measure the temple of God and the altar, and count the worshipers there. But exclude the outer court; do not measure it, because it has been given to the Gentiles. They will trample on the holy city for 42 months. And I will give power to my two witnesses, and they will prophesy for 1,260 days, clothed in sackcloth." These are the two olive trees and the two lampstands that stand before the Lord of the earth. If anyone tries to harm them, fire comes from their mouths and devours their enemies. This is how anyone who wants to harm them must die. These men have power to shut up the sky so that it will not rain during the time they are prophesying; and they have power to turn the waters into blood and to strike the earth with every kind of plague as often as they want. Now when they have finished their testimony, the beast that comes up from the Abyss will attack them, and overpower and kill them. Their bodies will lie in the street of the great city, which is figuratively called Sodom and Egypt, where also their Lord was crucified. For three and a half days men from every people, tribe, language and nation will gaze on their bodies and refuse them burial. The inhabitants of the earth will gloat over them and will celebrate by sending each other gifts, because these two prophets had tormented those who live on the earth. But after the three and a half days a breath of life from God entered them, and they stood on their feet, and terror struck those who saw them. Then they heard a loud voice from heaven saying to them, "Come up here." And they went up to heaven in a cloud, while their enemies looked on. At that very hour there was a severe earthquake and a tenth of the city collapsed. Seven thousand people were killed in the earthquake, and the survivors were terrified and gave glory to the God of heaven. The second woe has passed; the third woe is coming soon. The seventh angel sounded his trumpet, and there were loud voices in heaven, which said: "The kingdom of the world has become the kingdom of our Lord and of his Christ, and he will reign for ever and ever." And the twenty-four elders, who were seated on their thrones before God, fell on their faces and worshiped God, saying: "We give thanks to you, Lord God Almighty, the One who is and who was, because you have taken your great power and have begun to reign. The nations were angry; and your wrath has come. The time has come for judging the dead, and for rewarding your servants the prophets and your saints and those who reverence your name, both small and great—and for destroying those who destroy the earth." Then God's temple in heaven was opened, and within his temple was seen the ark of his covenant. And there came flashes of lightning, rumblings, peals of thunder, an earthquake and a great hailstorm.

THE END OF THE TIMES
OF THE GENTILES

Revelation 11:1–2

This point marks the Lord's dealing with Israel again and its worship in a restored temple in The Holy City. This is symbolized by John's measuring of the temple, the altar, and those who worship therein. John did the measuring of the temple with a reed, which is about ten feet long. We see that Jesus accepts the true worshipers, the Godly remnant of Israel He promised to save, whereas the apostate Jews who linked themselves with the Gentiles, which is symbolized by the outer court, He now rejects.

THE TWO WITNESSES

Revelation 11:3-13

Although many people commonly identify the two witnesses as Moses and Enoch, or Moses and Elijah, I believe I have the answer: They are Starsky and Hutch, do you see how ludicrous that is? The identifications of all these are scarcely tenable since both of the witnesses are killed and resurrected, something which could not be true of these Old Testament Prophets as **Glorified Men.** These witnesses are evidently members of the end times remnant. They are Christ's witnesses and they preach in sackcloth; which in Israel is a sign of mourning, because they identify themselves with Israel's grievous sin and Jerusalem's wickedness. Their message is Jesus' Lordship over all the earth, proclaiming the soon coming King of kings and Lord of lords to take possession of the earth. The two olive trees and the two lamp stands connect the two witnesses to the testimony of Jesus the Messiah as fulfilling the two offices as King-Priest who will shortly reign as the light of the world over the restored Israel and which we also see in Zechariah 4:2-3. The two witnesses have miraculous powers like Moses and Elijah. Fire comes out of their mouth and they command drought like Elijah did, they also turn the water into blood and to strike the earth with every kind of plague as often as they want, as Moses did in Egypt. They are killed by the beast who comes up from the Abyss, but not until they have completed their testimony. Their corpses are dishonored in Jerusalem, but after three and a half days God resurrects them and translates them in a cloud up to heaven while their enemies look on. God now punishes their enemies and there is a severe earthquake where a tenth of the city of Jerusalem is destroyed and seven thousand die in the earthquake. The survivors are now terrified and they give glory to the God of heaven because of His power, and not because of their repentance. The second woe has passed; the third woe is coming soon.

THE SEVENTH TRUMPET—THE THIRD WOE

Revelation 11:14-19

The seventh angel sounded his trumpet, and there were loud voices in heaven, which said: "The kingdoms of the world has become the kingdom of our Lord and of his Christ, and he will reign for ever and ever." The third woe is still to come. This woe is said to come "quickly," and includes all the remaining judgments prior to the establishment of the kingdom. We are given a panorama of the rest of the book, future events being seen as already present. They envision the establishment of Christ's worldwide kingdom and reign, the judgment of the raging nations at Armageddon, the judgment of the dead when the destroyers of the earth will be destroyed, and the rewarding of the prophets and the saints in millennial positions of rule and dominion. Then God's temple in heaven was opened, and within His temple was seen the ark of the covenant. And there came flashes of lighting, rumblings, peals of thunder, an earthquake and a great hail storm. No man today will ever find the Ark of the Covenant because we have just seen it in heaven. Jesus is the Covenant. You hear many glorious stories from Israel that someone, somewhere, just found, or is about to find the ark of the covenant. "Popycock!" This story put out by The Ministry of Tourism of Israel is excellent for bringing many tourists to Israel.

REV 12:1 A great and wondrous sign appeared in heaven: a woman clothed with the sun, with the moon under her feet and a crown of twelve stars on her head. She was pregnant and cried out in pain as she was about to give birth. Then another sign appeared in heaven: an enormous red dragon with seven heads and ten horns and seven crowns on his heads. His tail swept a third of the stars out of the sky and flung them to the earth. The dragon stood in front of the woman who was about to give birth, so that he might devour her child the moment it was born. She gave birth to a son, a male child, who will rule all the nations with an iron scepter. And her child was snatched up to God and to his throne. The woman fled into the desert to a place prepared for her by God, where she might be taken care of for 1,260 days. And there was war in heaven. Michael and his angels fought against the dragon, and the dragon and his angels fought back. But he was not strong enough, and they lost their place in heaven. The great dragon was hurled down—that ancient serpent called the devil, or Satan, who leads the whole world astray. He was hurled to the earth, and his angels with him. Then I heard a loud voice in heaven say: "Now have come the salvation and the power and the kingdom of our God, and the authority of his Christ. For the accuser of our brothers, who accuses them before our God day and night, has been hurled down. They overcame him by the blood of the Lamb and by the word of their testimony; they did not love their lives so much as to shrink from death. Therefore rejoice, you heavens and you who dwell in them! But woe to the earth and the sea, because the devil has gone down to you! He is filled with fury, because he knows that his time is short." When the dragon saw that he had been hurled to the earth, he pursued the woman who had given birth to the male child. The woman was given the two wings of a great eagle, so that she might fly to the place prepared for her in the desert, where she would be taken care of for a time, times and half a time, out of the serpent's reach. Then from his mouth the serpent spewed water like a river, to overtake the woman and sweep her away with the torrent. But the earth helped the woman by opening its mouth and swallowing the river that the dragon had spewed out of his mouth. Then the dragon was enraged at the woman and went off to make war against the rest of her offspring—those who obey God's commandments and hold to the testimony of Jesus."

THE TRIBULATION TEMPLE

There appeared a news paper article in The Jerusalem Post in the summer of 1974 which also included most of the leading newspapers of the world!

Jerusalem, Israel 1974:

Construction is scheduled to be begin this summer on the first large, central Jewish house of worship in the Holy City since the destruction of the Temple 1904 years ago. Restoring the Jewish Temple here is a longed for dream, a Messianic sign for the Jews and a prophetic milestone for Christians. No one is suggesting that this means the restoration of the Temple, "Rabbi Dr. Maurice A. Jaffee told Ap Religion Writer George Cornell. "But," the President of the Union of Israel's Synagogues added, "There are parallels." Called the "Jerusalem Great Synagogue," The sanctuary will be a central, representative sanctuary to which Jewish pilgrims from all over the world may come to pray just as they did to the Temple of old. Also, every Jew in the world is encouraged to contribute something to the expense of building the structure, just as were the Jews of old to build the original Temple. Furthermore, The Great Jerusalem Synagogue is being constructed of radiant stone, like that of the Temple of Bible times and is to be situated next to the headquarters of Israel's Rabbinical authority, just as the historic Temple was. The first Temple, built in Solomon's time about 1,000 B.C. was destroyed by invading Babylonians in 586 B.C. but rebuilt afterwards. The second Temple was burned by Roman troops in crushing a Jewish revolt in 70 A.D., which marked the end of the Jewish state until it's modern restoration.

By: David F. Webber

The above news story that appeared in the leading newspapers of the world should have shaken the sleeping churches out of their lethargy. However, in as much as the majority of the larger denominations have departed from God's Word to give heed to the vain imaginations of men, most Church members today have no idea why the Jews are returning to Israel, much less the importance of the rebuilding of the Temple.

There are seven events that begin the restoration of David's Tabernacle. God's calendar for Israel leading up to this event is as follows:

1. The return of Israel after the Babylonian captivity was the result of a decree (Ezra 5). The decree that permitted the return of the Jews in these latter days was the decree in England, which we know as the Balfour Declaration, November, 1917.

2. After 30 years which is the Jewish age of maturity, Israel once again became a nation in one day by the decree of the United Nations. This fulfilled the prophecy of Isaiah 66:8 "Who has heard such a thing? Who has seen such things? Shall a land be born in one day? Or shall a nation be brought forth in a moment? For as soon as Zion was in labor she brought forth her children.

3. The new nation would be ruled by governors and not a king and Israel's army would win miraculous battles over their enemies to the east which is Syria, and to the west which is Egypt, which fulfilled the prophecy of Zechariah 12:6"In that day will I make the governors of Judah like an hearth of fire among the wood, and like a torch of fire in a sheaf; and they shall devour all the people round about, on the right hand and on the left."

131

4. The Old Jerusalem with the Temple site would be restored. "... Jerusalem shall be inhabited again by her own place, even in Jerusalem..." which fulfilled the prophecy of Zechariah 12:6. In 1967 which was fifty years after the Balfour Declaration; Jerusalem was restored to the nation of Israel. In Leviticus 25:8–13 we see that every 50th. year in Israel is God's year of the Jubilee, which is the year of restoration.

The Year of the Jubilee:

"Count off seven sabbaths of years—seven times seven years—so that the seven sabbaths of years amount to a period of forty-nine years. Then have the trumpet sounded everywhere on the tenth day of the seventh month; on the Day of Atonement sound the trumpet throughout your land. Consecrate the Fiftieth year and proclaim liberty throughout the land to all its inhabitants. It shall be a Jubilee for you; each one of you is to return to his family property and each to his own tribe. The Fiftieth year shall be a Jubilee for you; do not sow and do not reap what grows of itself or harvest the untended vines. For it is a Jubilee and is to be Holy for you; eat only what is taken directly from the fields. In this year of Jubilee everyone is to return to his own property. If you sell land to one of your countrymen or buy any from him, do not take advantage of each other. You are to buy from your countryman on the basis of the number of years since the Jubilee. And he is to sell you on the basis of the number of years left for harvesting crops. When the years are many, you are to increase the price, and when the years are few, you are to decrease the price, because what he is really selling you is the number of crops. Do not take advantage of each other, but fear your God. I am the Lord your God."

In the Fiftieth year, the Hebrew slaves with their families are emancipated, and all property, except house property in a walled city, reverts to its original owner. The Jubilee institution was a marvelous safeguard against deadening poverty. By the Jubilee, houses and lands were kept from accumulating in the hands of the few, and pauperism was prevented, and a race of independent freeholders was assured. The Jubilee represented such a rare and striking introduction of MORALS into ECONOMICS, that many heathen have been inclined to question whether this wonderful institution was ever in actual force. According to our Jewish history, the law of the Jubilee was observed as long as the entire territory of the Holy Land was inhabited by the children of Israel. When a portion of the Tribes went into exile, the law lapsed. The prophet Ezekiel speaks of its non-observance as one of the signs that "the end has come" upon Israel for its misdoings; and he even mentions "the year of liberty", when even a gift of land must return to its original owner.

For the first time in 6,000 YEARS; man on his knees with Jesus AND THE POWER OF PRAYER behind him, can put into office a man of God, TO BE THE NEXT PRESIDENT OF THESE UNITED STATES. With prayer and supplication we can vote into office A MAN WHO IS BORN AGAIN AND SPIRIT FILLED. If we do; I believe God is extending us A TIME OF GRACE FOR ANOTHER 8 TO 10 YEARS. If we don't we are going to have a president who will BE a very close ally of THE ANTICHRIST. This year of 1988 is very significant, it is now 40 YEARS, one generation from the restoration of THE JEWISH PEOPLE to THE LAND OF ISRAEL on May 14,1948. This is the year we elect a president in these United States. This the year ISRAEL will observe a JUBILEE in 2920 years. If we fail to get a man of God into office; THE TRIBULATION will be upon us IN A FEW SHORT YEARS; and many christians who are not watching and waiting for THE RAPTURE, are going to be left here on PLANET EARTH.

5. A Jewish Temple will be rebuilt. According to the bible, a Temple must be present in Jerusalem during the time of the Tribulation which we see in Daniel 9:27; Matthew 24:15; 2nd. Thessalonians 2:4; Revelation 11.
   The announcement that a new Jewish Temple was under construction in Jerusalem seemingly brought this prophecy near to fulfillment.
6. The man who will become the Antichrist will negotiate a treaty between Israel and Israel's enemies which we see in Daniel 9:27.The consideration that Israel will receive in the treaty will be secure borders and freedom from attack for 7 years. There is nothing implied in the prophecy, as far as I can determine, as to the nature of the consideration the opponents of the Jews will receive. In light of the current situation, the consideration is likely that there will be the creation of a Palestinian state.

7. The Antichrist breaks the treaty with Israel after 3 1/2 years and stops the worship of God in the Temple, and shows himself in the Temple to the whole world via satellite and television as the god of this world.

We know from subsequent prophetic events recorded in the Bible that a remnant of Israel will escape from the Antichrist which we see in Matthew 24:16–21; Revelation 12:14–16. God will protect the remnant in a secret place for 3 1/2 years; and then, Christ returns with the armies of heaven to destroy the Antichrist and his armies. All Israelites who accept Jesus Christ as Lord and Savior will be gathered back into the land of Israel as we see in Zechariah 12:10; Romans 11:26–27. Many have attempted to discredit the prophetic possibility that the building which was completed in December 1983, and which is identified as "The Great Synagogue", could be the Temple. It is argued that if this building is to be the Temple, then it must be built upon the Temple site which is located one mile to the east. Of course, we know that the Moslem Shrine, The Dome of the Rock, still stands on the Temple site till today. If the people of Israel were to destroy this Moslem Holy Place, this act would bring the combined armies of all the Arab states against them. But I suggested as long as 17 years ago that the Tribulation Temple would not be built on the Temple site. God asks of the people of Israel in regards to the new Tribulation Temple which we see in Isaiah 66:1.... "Where is the house that you build onto Me?... " There is also valid reason to believe that the Tribulation Temple will not be constructed on the Temple site, from a closer study of Revelation 11.

If, as I think probable, the Great Synagogue will be the Tribulation Temple, we should keep in mind that it WILL NOT BE THE MILLENNIAL Temple. Jesus Christ would never appear in a temple that had been defiled by the Antichrist. Jesus will build His own Temple as we see in Ezekiel 42–43–44 and Zechariah 6:12–13.

The destruction of the city and the sanctuary mentioned in Daniel 9:26 refers to the pillaging of Jerusalem and the burning of Herod's Temple by Titus in 70 A.D. The Antichrist will not destroy Jerusalem nor the Temple; for he sits in the Temple showing himself as God. The two witnesses of God will testify in Jerusalem during the last half of the Tribulation; and after they are killed and raised again we read in Revelation 11:13 that a great earthquake will shake the city; and Tribulation Temple will be destroyed in this earthquake.

That the Temple must be rebuilt is conclusive; and which I believe has been rebuilt and is The Great Jerusalem Synagogue. That it must be built upon the Temple site is a matter of disagreement. What many good Bible scholars overlook is the fact that it is not the Moslem building there that is important to the Arabs but rather the rock inside the building. The Building was originally constructed in 691 A.D. by an Arab leader, by the name of Omar the Magnificent, to keep so called Roman Christians from dumping garbage on "The Rock". This was where Abraham offered up Isaac onto the Lord. God told Abraham to travel 3 days journey to Mount Moriah; and there he was to sacrifice Isaac unto God. The Arabs till today argue with all Jews saying, that the Jewish people changed the scripture found in Genesis 22; stating that Abraham laid Ishmael upon "The Rock" as an offering onto the Lord and not Isaac. It was from "The Rock" that Mohammed, and his white steed the Arabs say, ascended into heaven. Even if an earthquake or some other catastrophe were to destroy the "Dome of The Rock", every devout Moslem in the world would rather die than see the Jews rebuild their Temple on this site. I see no possible religious or political development that will permit Israel to rebuild the Temple on the Temple site before Christ Returns. That is why I believe that The Great Jerusalem Synagogue which was built and completed in December 1983 is "THE TRIBULATION TEMPLE." On May 14th. 1948 after two thousands years of wandering and captivity, Israel became a recognized nation, actually "Born in one day," through the vote of the United Nations. After being away from their promised land for almost two thousand years, the people of Israel were given a national home land in Palestine by the Balfour Declaration in November 1917. In 1922 the League of Nations gave Great Britain the mandate over Palestine. On May 14th. 1948, Great Britain withdrew her mandate, and immediately Israel was declared a sovereign state, and her growth and her importance among the nations of the world has become astonishing. In Genesis 17:12, God commanded Abraham that all the children of Israel were to be circumcised on the eighth day of their life. On May 14th. 1948, Israel was born, but the tiny infant was surrounded by millions of Arabs who had sworn the destruction of the infant Israel. For eight days there was fierce battles, but on the eighth day the infant nation of Israel was circumcised and the fighting died down. In our Hebrew customs and traditions a boy does not begin his manhood until he starts his thirteenth year. Israel began her adulthood in 1960–61; which is thirteen years. In the book of Numbers chapter one verse three (Num. 1:3) We see God declaring to Moses and to Aaron that a man reaches the age that he may go to war, that age to be twenty (20). Because our Hebrew calendar being shorter than that of the western world we see this being fulfilled in the nation of Israel reaching her twentieth birthday in June 1967, and becoming "A man of war" according to scripture. In June 1967, we see that the city of Jerusalem, a city which was divided for many years, and also the West Bank of the Jordan river being restored to the land of Israel; as told by God Himself. In the areas of the West Bank we have places like Hebron, where Abraham, Isaac, and Jacob lived, and where they are buried. They are all buried in the cave of Machpelah which Abraham secured as a permanent burying place from the sons of Heth, according to Genesis 23:3–20. David also established his monarchy in Hebron seven years before he became king of all of Israel and moved his capital to Jerusalem. We have places in the West Bank like Bethlehem, which in the arabic language means "house of meat" and in the hebrew language means "house of bread." Ruth and David, and the Royal House of David were Bethlehemites. Jesus was born in Bethlehem. We have places in the West Bank like Ramathaim-Zophim in Samaria or as is known by the biblical name Ramah where the prophet and judge Samuel was born. We have places in the West Bank in Samaria like Jacob's well, right outside of Shechem or as the New Testament calls it "Shycar" or "Sycar". This is where Jesus spoke to the woman at Jacob's well and told her all about herself and she became a believer. In the book of Numbers chapter four, God tells Moses that those who were to enter the Holy of Holies had to be thirty years of age in their priesthood. We see that since the going down of Israel into Egypt and the great exodus and redemption of Israel by God; that no Pharaoh or leader of Egypt ever set foot in the land of Israel. Again, because of the shorter hebrew calendar the state of Israel reached her age of priesthood in the year 1977. When Anwar Sadat, president of Egypt, made peace with Israel he went to Jerusalem and worshiped. So, my beloved, in God's prophetic stage, the time is ripe for the anti-christ.

THE GREAT TRIBULATION is entirely different from the Greek Word "Tribulum". Let us see how the Word Tribulum applies to us as we read God's Word written to us today by The Apostle Paul in his letter to the Romans:

ROM 5:1 Therefore, since we have been justified through faith, we have peace with God through our Lord Jesus Christ, through whom we have gained access by faith into this grace in which we now stand. And we rejoice in the hope of the glory of God. Not only so, but we also rejoice in our sufferings, (Tribulum) because we know that suffering (Tribulum) produces perseverance; perseverance, character; and character, hope. And hope does not disappoint us, because God has poured out his love into our hearts by the Holy Spirit, whom he has given us. You see, at just the right time, when we were still powerless, Christ died for the ungodly. Very rarely will anyone die for a righteous man, though for a good man someone might possibly dare to die. But God demonstrates his own love for us in this: While we were still sinners, Christ died for us. Since we have now been justified by his blood, how much more shall we be saved from God's wrath through him! For if, when we were God's enemies, we were reconciled to him through the death of his Son, how much more, having been reconciled, shall we be saved through his life! Not only is this so, but we also rejoice in God through our Lord Jesus Christ, through whom we have now received reconciliation. Therefore, just as sin entered the world through one man, and death through sin, and in this way death came to all men, because all sinned—for before the law was given, sin was in the world. But sin is not taken into account when there is no law. Nevertheless, death reigned from the time of Adam to the time of Moses, even over those who did not sin by breaking a command, as did Adam, who was a pattern of the one to come. But the gift is not like the trespass. For if the many died by the trespass of the one man, how much more did God's grace and the gift that came by the grace of the one man, Jesus Christ, overflow to the many! Again, the gift of God is not like the result of the one man's sin: The judgment followed one sin and brought condemnation, but the gift followed many trespasses and brought justification. For if, by the trespass of the one man, death reigned through that one man, how much more will those who receive God's abundant provision of grace and of the gift of righteousness reign in life through the one man, Jesus Christ. Consequently, just as the result of one trespass was condemnation for all men, so also the result of one act of righteousness was justification that brings life for all men. For just as through the disobedience of the one man the many were made sinners, so also through the obedience of the one man the many will be made righteous. The law was added so that the trespass might increase. But where sin increased, grace increased all the more, so that, just as sin reigned in death, so also grace might reign through righteousness to bring eternal life through Jesus Christ our Lord."

FAITH IS THE CATALYST THAT PLACES YOU AND ME ON THE CROSS WITH JESUS

As Jesus became sin for you and me; **THE WRATH OF GOD** was poured out on Him in full force. This is the same **WRATH OF GOD** which will be poured out on all of mankind during the time of **THE GREAT TRIBULATION.**

FAITH, IS WHAT CAUSED YOU AND ME TO BE BAPTIZED INTO JESUS, WHERE HE IMPUTED ALL OF HIS RIGHTEOUSNESS UNTO US AS HE TOOK OUR SIN, AND FORGAVE US OF ALL.

GOD WILL ONLY ALLOW JESUS TO BE STRUCK ONE TIME AND ONE TIME ONLY

EXO 17:1 The whole Israelite community set out from the Desert of Sin, traveling from place to place as the Lord commanded. They camped at Rephidim, but there was no water for the people to drink. So they quarreled with Moses and said, "Give us water to drink." Moses replied, "Why do you quarrel with me? Why do you put the Lord to the test?" But the people were thirsty for water there, and they grumbled against Moses. They said, "Why did you bring us up out of Egypt to make us and our children and livestock die of thirst?" Then Moses cried out to the Lord, "What am I to do with these people? They are almost ready to stone me." The Lord answered Moses, "Walk on ahead of the people. Take with you some of the elders of Israel and take in your hand the staff with which you struck the Nile, and go. I will stand there before you by the rock at Horeb. STRIKE THE ROCK, and water will come out of it for the people to drink." So Moses did this in the sight of the elders of Israel. And he called the place Massah and Meribah because the Israelites quarreled and because they tested the Lord saying, "Is the Lord among us or not?"

MOSES WAS ALLOWED BY GOD TO STRIKE THE ROCK; THE ROCK BEING JESUS; THE FIRST TIME WHEN THEY HAD JUST LEFT EGYPT; TO BRING FORTH THE LIVING WATER.

NUM 20:1 In the first month the whole Israelite community arrived at the Desert of Zin, and they stayed at Kadesh. There Miriam died and was buried. Now there was no water for the community, and the people gathered in opposition to Moses and Aaron. They quarreled with Moses and said, "If only we had died when our brothers fell dead before the Lord! Why did you bring the Lord's community into this desert, that we and our livestock should die here? Why did you bring us up out of Egypt to this terrible place? It has no grain or figs, grapevines or pomegranates. And there is no water to drink!" Moses and Aaron went from the assembly to the entrance to the Tent of Meeting and fell facedown, and the glory of the Lord appeared to them. The Lord said to Moses, "Take the staff, and you and your brother Aaron gather the assembly together. SPEAK to THAT ROCK before their eyes and it will pour out its water. You will bring water out of the rock for the community so they and their livestock can drink." So Moses took the staff from the Lord's presence, just as he commanded him. He and Aaron gathered the assembly together in front of the rock and Moses said to them, "Listen, you rebels, must we bring you water out of this rock?" Then Moses raised his arm and struck the rock twice with his staff. Water gushed out, and the community and their livestock drank. But the Lord said to Moses and Aaron, "Because you did not trust in me enough to honor me as holy in the sight of the Israelites, you will not bring this community into the land I give them." These were the waters of Meribah, where the Israelites quarreled with the Lord and where he showed himself holy among them.

MOSES WAS NOT ALLOWED TO ENTER THE PROMISED LAND BECAUSE HE STRUCK JESUS TWICE; HE HAD TO WAIT 1400 YEARS TO ENTER IN; UNTIL JESUS CALLED HIM TO THE MOUNT OF TRANSFIGURATION.

By FAITH when we enter the waters of Baptism we become **THE BODY OF CHRIST** and GOD will NOT allow THE BODY OF HIS BELOVED SON TO BE STRUCK MORE THAN ONCE. **That is the reason why The Saints of Jesus Christ will be Caught Up, RAPTURED, and will not be here on PLANET EARTH, but WILL be with Jesus dur-**

ing the time of THE GREAT TRIBULATION, when God's Wrath is being poured out in full force on all those who have not accepted JESUS AS LORD AND SAVIOR. We will be with JESUS at His Marriage Supper! PRAISE GOD. If a friend or a loved one gave you this book to read; or if you yourself ARE NOT SURE, THAT YOU ARE SURE, THAT YOU HAVE BEEN "BORN AGAIN"; WHY NOT GIVE YOUR HEART TO JESUS RIGHT NOW AND MAKE HIM LORD OF YOUR LIFE, and you will never be an outcast or banished again; for wherever you are you are never alone, Jesus is always with you never leaving you nor forsaking you: Just repeat this simple prayer with me:

My Dear Gracious Heavenly Father, I Come To You In Jesus' Name, And I Ask You To Forgive Me Of All Of My Sin, And I Ask Jesus The Christ To Come Into My Life And Be Lord Of My Life. I Acknowledge And Profess What It States In Romans 10:9–10; "I Confess With My mouth Jesus As Lord, And Believe In My Heart That God Raised Him From The Dead And I Am Saved; For With The Heart Man Believes, Resulting In Righteousness, And With The Mouth He Confesses, Resulting In Salvation." I thank you JESUS for forgiving me of all my sin, and I covenant and promise that I will walk hand in hand with you all the rest of my life; for I remember all too well what it's like without you: Despair, Frustration, Oppression, Depression, Paranoia, Schizophrenia, Drugs of Downers to sleep, Drugs of Uppers to wake up. I THANK YOU JESUS!

Chapter 20

Seven Personages During the Last Days of the Tribulation

Revelation 12:1–2

The First Person—The Woman, Miriam (Mary) Israel.

A great and wondrous sign appeared in heaven: A woman clothed with the sun, with the moon under her feet and a crown of twelve stars on her head. She was pregnant and cried out in pain as she was about to give birth. The great "wonder" here is or "sign" is the "woman." She symbolizes Israel, as she is dressed in royal splendor, and the twelve stars upon her representing the twelve tribes of Israel, as Joseph's dream showed us in Genesis 37:9. The travail of the woman refers to Israel's agony during the great Tribulation, as the context of this scripture clearly shows us. The symbol of birth was a common old testament picture used to portray acute suffering, es-

141

pecially "the time of Jacob's trouble." We see this in Isaiah 26:17–18 also in Jeremiah 30:5–7. During this time of unheard of agony and travail, the nation of Israel will give birth to the godly Jewish remnant, which will be closely associated with the Male Child, Jesus Christ Himself as we see in 12:5 of this Revelation.

Revelation 12:3–4

Then another sign appeared in heaven: an enormous red dragon with seven heads and ten horns and seven crowns on his heads. His tail swept a third of the stars out of the sky and flung them to the earth. The dragon stood in front of the woman who was about to give birth, so that he might devour her child the moment it was born. She gave birth to a son, a male child, who will rule all the nations with an iron scepter. Micah 5: 2. "But you, Bethlehem, though you are small among the clans of Judah, out of you will come for Me one who will be ruler over Israel, whose origins are from old, from ancient times." And her child was snatched up to God and to His throne. The woman fled into the desert to a place prepared for her by God, where she might be taken care of for 1,260 days.

The Second Person—The Dragon, Satan

Revelation 12:3–4

The dragon is identified as that "old serpent, called the Devil, the Accuser, and Satan." He is "the great red dragon," which symbolizes him as the proud, cruel energizer of "the beast." Red portrays his murderous character, which is now featured. The seven diadems on his head, and ten horns identify him with the final form of Gentile world power centered in the beast as we see in Daniel 7:15–25.

The Third Person—The Male Child, Jesus

Revelation 12:5–6

The Male Child: There are four things that are announced to us: One, the birth of Jesus, Two, His destiny, which is to break His enemies in pieces, and then to rule in righteousness; Three, His ascension, Four, His position on God's throne. Jesus is destined to rule yet. Satan knows this, and chases the woman who is Godly Israel.

The Woman's Flight: The woman's flight into the desert, is

describing to us Israel's flight into the wilderness during the time of the Tribulation, Israel will be sustained by God for three and a half years during Satan's terrible persecution of the Jewish people, which Satan effects through the beast. 2nd. Thessalonians 2: 3–4 "Don't let anyone deceive you in any way, for that day will not come until the rebellion occurs and the man of lawlessness is revealed, the man doomed to destruction. He opposes and exalts himself over every thing that is called God or is worshiped, and even sets himself up in God's temple, proclaiming himself to be God.

Revelation 12: 7–12

"And there was war in heaven. Michael and his angels fought against the dragon, and the dragon and his angels fought back. But he was not strong enough, and they lost their place in heaven. The great dragon was hurled down-that serpent called the devil or Satan, who leads the whole world astray. He was hurled to the earth, and his angels with him." John says, "Then I heard a loud voice in heaven say: Now have come the salvation and the power and the kingdom of our God, and the authority of His Christ. For the accuser of our brothers, who accuses them day and night before our God, has been hurled down. They overcame him by the blood of the Lamb and by the word of their testimony; they did not love their lives so much as to shrink from death. Therefore rejoice, you heavens and you who dwell in them! But woe to the earth and the sea, because the devil has gone down to you! He is filled with fury, because he knows that his time is short."

The Fourth Person—Michael, The Archangel

Revelation 12:7–12

The Archangel Michael is the guardian angel of all of Israel; and the special protector of the Jewish people. He is involved in the war when Satan's expulsion from the heavenlies is at hand. Since his original rebellion, Satan and his host's have been loose in the heavenlies. In the middle of The Great Tribulation he and his angles will be expelled and cast down to earth. All of heaven rejoices and there is a joyous shout which is a prelude to the establishment of Christ's kingdom, which begins with the return of Jesus. Victory is on the basis of the accomplished sacrifice of Jesus, by a faithful testimony, and by martyrdom. Satan's expulsion means terrible woe to the earth. Satan's wrath and anger is spurred on by his knowledge of the shortness of his time. Satan knowing that his defeat had been brought about by the exaltation of the Man Child, Jesus, the dragon vents his fury on the sun-clothed woman who is Miriam (Mary), who is Israel, who gave birth to the Man Child. The eagle wings given to the woman to escape to the wilderness recall how the Lord delivered Israel from Egypt and bore her "on eagles' wings." This is the period of the "abomination of desolation" and The Great Tribulation spoken to us by our Lord Jesus Christ in Matthew 24:15–22. Satan, that old serpent spewed out of his mouth "water like a river," symbolizing Gentile nations energized by Satan himself with anti-Semitic hatred to destroy all Jews. "The earth opened her mouth and swallowed the flood." This points to friendly nations, who having listened and obeyed the preaching of the Gospel of the Kingdom, protect these persecuted Jews, as they did during World War II.

The Fifth Person—The Remnant Of Israel

Revelation 12:17

Satan now turns against the godly remnant of Jews who are still in the land. These are individual godly Jews who had not escaped to safety when The Tribulation broke out. These keep the commandments of God, the mark of godliness common to all true believers of all ages, and "have the testimony of Jesus and bear faithful witness to Him." Jesus tells us we must love one another as He loved us, **Not In Theory But In Practice And In Action.** Where would we be if Jesus stopped at the cross?

REV 13:1 And the dragon stood on the shore of the sea. And I saw a beast coming out of the sea. He had ten horns and seven heads, with ten crowns on his horns, and on each head a blasphemous name. The beast I saw resembled a leopard, but had feet like those of a bear and a mouth like that of a lion. The dragon gave the beast his power and his throne and great authority. One of the heads of the beast seemed to have had a fatal wound, but the fatal wound had been healed. The whole world was astonished and followed the beast. Men worshiped the dragon because he had given authority to the beast, and they also worshiped the beast and asked, "Who is like the beast? Who can make war against him?" The beast was given a mouth to utter proud words and blasphemies and to exercise his authority for forty-two months. He opened his mouth to blaspheme God, and to slander his name and his dwelling place and those who live in heaven. He was given power to make war against the saints and to conquer them. And he was given authority over every tribe, people, language and nation. All inhabitants of the earth will worship the beast—all whose names have not been written in the book of life belonging to the Lamb that was slain from the creation of the world. He who has an ear, let him hear. If anyone is to go into captivity, into captivity he will go. If anyone is to be killed with the sword, with the sword he will be killed. This calls for patient endurance and faithfulness on the part of the saints. Then I saw another beast, coming out of the earth. He had two horns like a lamb, but he spoke like a dragon. He exercised all the authority of the first beast on his behalf, and made the earth and its inhabitants worship the first beast, whose fatal wound had been healed. And he performed great and miraculous signs, even causing fire to come down from heaven to earth in full view of men. Because of the signs he was given power to do on behalf of the first beast, he deceived the inhabitants of the earth. He ordered them to set up an image in honor of the beast who was wounded by the sword and yet lived. He was given power to give breath to the image of the first beast, so that it could speak and cause all who refused to worship the image to be killed. He also forced everyone, small and great, rich and poor, free and slave, to receive a mark on his right hand or on his forehead, so that no one could buy or sell unless he had the mark, which is the name of the beast or the number of his name. This calls for wisdom. If anyone has insight, let him calculate the number of the beast, for it is man's number. His number is 666.

The Sixth Person—The Beast Out Of The Sea

Revelation 13: 1–10

This last great ruler of Gentile world power arises out of an unsettled political condition. He is the head of a confederated ten-kingdom empire covering the area of the ancient Roman empire, which we see is the fourth beast in Daniel's prophecy; Daniel 7:23–25. The ten horns are ten kingdoms and the diadems on the horns speak of despotic power. The dragon having seven heads and ten horns, and diadems upon his heads is the power behind the beast. The beast is in complete defiance of God which is indicated by the names of blasphemy upon his seven heads. His empire partakes of all the beastly qualities of the preceding world empires of the times of the Gentiles as we saw in Daniel 7: 4–6. His empire has the lionlike strength of the Babylonian empire, the bearlike voracity of the Persian empire, the leopardlike agility of conquest, like the Macedonian empire. His kingdom represents the restoration of the imperial power of the Roman Empire. The head which was wounded onto death symbolizes the seventh and last form of government of the Roman Empire, but the deadly wound yet to be healed indicates the imperial form of government will be restored under the beast. The beast is worshiped together with the dragon who energizes the beast. The beast becomes utterly defiant of God and destructive during the final three and a half years of The Great Tribulation. He blasphemes God and those who belong to God. To this end the beast makes war against the saints. This beast is permitted unrestrained power over all the earth's dwellers except over the elect of God, who are the saved remnant of Israel that Jesus saved. As we know God the Father, God the Son, and God the Holy Spirit, at this time the world will see the great counterfeit: Satan who is The Dragon, The Anti-Christ who is the Beast, and, The False Prophet. At one time you were "The Elect of God" but now, by your acceptance of Jesus Christ you have been installed in office as one of His saints; you are no longer the elect but a saint. The children of Israel are the promised elect Jesus said He would save if they would accept Him as Lord and Savior; for there are not many roads to heaven but One, and His Name is Jesus The Son of God, Himself God, who came into our world and took and put on a tent of human flesh. "John 1:1 In the beginning was the word, and the word was with God, and the word was God. He was with God in the beginning. Through Him all things were made; without Him nothing was made that has been made."

The Seventh Person—The Beast Out Of The Earth, The False Prophet

Revelation 13:11–18

This third member of the **UNHOLY** trinity arises out of the earth. He is the prophet of the first beast who is the Antichrist, even though he is disguised as a lamb. In this disguise he directs worship to the first beast by miraculous powers, and giving life to the image of the beast and killing those who do not worship the image. He compels men to be branded with "the number of man" and incompleteness. The number 666 is a triad, the meaning being that, which is a group of three, especially of three closely related or associated persons or things; or a set of three elements with similar properties; and who fall short of the real thing, for as far as God is concerned His perfect number is Three which indicates completeness! Father, Son, and Holy Spirit, Three in One. One God, One Lord, One Savior: Whereas the number 666 reveals to us; a counterfeit of three closely related or associated persons who are not one, but three separate beings who are totally wicked and incomplete.

REV 14:1 Then I looked, and there before me was the Lamb, standing on Mount Zion, and with him 144,000 who had his name and his Father's name written on their foreheads. And I heard a sound from heaven like the roar of rushing waters and like a loud peal of thunder. The sound I heard was like that of harpists playing their harps. And they sang a new song before the throne and before the four living creatures and the elders. No one could learn the song except the 144,000 who had been redeemed from the earth. These are those who did not defile themselves with women, for they kept themselves pure. They follow the Lamb wherever he goes. They were purchased from among men and offered as first fruits to God and the Lamb. No lie was found in their mouths; they are blameless. Then I saw another angel flying in midair, and he had the eternal gospel to proclaim to those who live on the earth—to every nation, tribe, language and people. He said in a loud voice, "Fear God and give him glory, because the hour of his judgment has come. Worship him who made the heavens, the earth, the sea and the springs of water." A second angel followed and said, "Fallen! Fallen is Babylon the Great, which made all the nations drink the maddening wine of her adulteries." A third angel followed them and said in a loud voice: "If anyone worships the beast and his image and receives his mark on the forehead or on the hand, he, too, will drink of the wine of God's fury, which has been poured full strength into the cup of his wrath. He will be tormented with burning sulfur in the presence of the holy angels and of the Lamb. And the smoke of their torment rises for ever and ever. There is no rest day or night for those who worship the beast and his image, or for anyone who receives the mark of his name." This calls for patient endurance on the part of the saints who obey God's commandments and remain faithful to Jesus. Then I heard a voice from heaven say, "Write: Blessed are the dead who die in the Lord from now on." "Yes," says the Spirit, "they will rest from their labor, for their deeds will follow them." I looked, and there before me was a white cloud, and seated on the cloud was one "like a son of man" with a crown of gold on his head and a sharp sickle in his hand. Then another angel came out of the temple and called in a loud voice to him who was sitting on the cloud, "Take your sickle and reap, because the time to reap has come, for the harvest of the earth is ripe." So he who was seated on the cloud swung his sickle over the earth, and the earth was harvested.

Another angel came out of the temple in heaven, and he too had a sharp sickle. Still another angel, who had charge of the fire, came from the altar and called in a loud voice to him who had the sharp sickle, "Take your sharp sickle and gather the clusters of grapes from the earth's vine, because its grapes are ripe." The angel swung his sickle on the earth, gathered its grapes and threw them into the great winepress of God's wrath. They were trampled in the winepress outside the city, and blood flowed out of the press, rising as high as the horses' bridles for a distance of 1,600 stadia.

The Lamb And His 144,000

Revelation 14:1–5

"Then I looked, and there before me was the Lamb, standing on Mount Zion, and with Him 144,000 who had his name and his Father's name written upon their foreheads." John had just seen a vision of a beast pretending to be the lamb. Here is a vision of the Lamb Himself. The 144,000, the Lamb's Faithful Followers, were marked with the Lamb's name, as the followers of the pretender lamb were marked with his name: the Lamb's True Church, in contrast to the false church of the pretender church: the Faithful Wife in the wilderness, while the unfaithful wife was reveling in her adulteries with the world. The 144,000 were free from falsehood, in contrast to the lying wonders and false teachings of the pretender lamb. They were virgins true to Christ, in contrast to the harlotry of the false church. Their practical godliness is shown in: their separation in virgin purity from the wickedness and idolatry around them, their obedience and discipleship, their redemption, their destiny, to be the first fruits to God and the Lamb of the earth's coming kingdom when all will bow to God and the Lamb; their truthfulness, clinging to God's word, their profession and their life, when the whole world believes the devil's lie.

The Fall Of Babylon Foreseen:
Revelation 14: 6–8

This gospel proclaims mercy in the midst of judgment, calling men in this terrible time to abandon the worship of the beast, and reverence God, giving the glory to Him, not the beast, for the hour of God's judgment has come. Babylon is a symbol of the Satanic world system, the center of all that is evil and false, of idolatry and oppression. It consists of the order of UNREGENERATE HUMANITY organized under evil principals with Satan as its head, with emphasis given to the ecclesiastical, political, and commercial aspects of this system. "Fallen, fallen is a Hebrew way of saying, "completely fallen." Many of the children that are disappearing, never to be seen or heard of again, are being used as live human sacrifices to Satan. You parents **must cover your children with your prayers, and take the authority that Jesus gave you, and bind and rebuke Satan from your children, your family and your home:** you are to do this the first thing every morning and the last thing every night. Jesus says, I give you power and authority to do greater things than that which I have done, in My Name rebuke the devil and he SHALL flee from you. Command Satan, his workers, his cohorts, his demons, his spirits, those sent out on assignments against you and your family, and the assignments themselves to be canceled in Jesus name and to go back to the pit of Hell where they came from. There IS power in the Name of Jesus. In John 16:33 Jesus says, "In this world you will have trouble. But take heart! I have overcome the world."

The Punishment Of The Wicked
Revelation 14: 9–20

The doom of the worshipers of the beast is announced by an angel "with a loud voice" so all may hear and be without excuse. It entails the full fury of God's wrath.

REV 15:1 I saw in heaven another great and marvelous sign: seven angels with the seven last plagues—last, because with them God's wrath is completed. And I saw what looked like a sea of glass mixed with fire and, standing beside the sea, those who had been victorious over the beast and his image and over the number of his name. They held harps given them by God and sang the song of Moses the servant of God and the song of the Lamb: "Great and marvelous are your deeds, Lord God Almighty. Just and true are your ways, King of the ages. Who will not fear you, O Lord, and bring glory to your name? For you alone are holy. All nations will come and worship before you, for your righteous acts have been revealed." After this I looked and in heaven the temple, that is, the tabernacle of the Testimony, was opened. Out of the temple came the seven angels with the seven plagues. They were dressed in clean, shining linen and wore golden sashes around their chests. Then one of the four living creatures gave to the seven angels seven golden bowls filled with the wrath of God, who lives for ever and ever. And the temple was filled with smoke from the glory of God and from his power, and no one could enter the temple until the seven plagues of the seven angels were completed.

REV 16:1 Then I heard a loud voice from the temple saying to the seven angels, "Go, pour out the seven bowls of God's wrath on the earth." The first angel went and poured out his bowl on the land, and ugly and painful sores broke out on the people who had the mark of the beast and worshiped his image. The second angel poured out his bowl on the sea, and it turned into blood like that of a dead man, and every living thing in the sea died. The third angel poured out his bowl on the rivers and springs of water, and they became blood. Then I heard the angel in charge of the waters say: "You are just in these judgments, you who are and who were, the Holy One, because you have so judged; for they have shed the blood of your saints and prophets, and you have given them blood to drink as they deserve." And I heard the altar respond: "Yes, Lord God Almighty, true and just are your judgments." The fourth angel poured out his bowl on the sun, and the sun was given power to scorch people with fire. They were seared by the intense heat and they cursed the name of God, who had control over these plagues, but they refused to repent and glorify him. The fifth angel poured out his bowl on the throne of the beast, and his kingdom was plunged into darkness. Men gnawed their tongues in agony and cursed the God of heaven because of their pains and their sores, but they refused to repent of what they had done. The sixth angel poured out his bowl on the great river Euphrates, and its water was dried up to prepare the way for the kings from the East. Then I saw three evil spirits that looked like frogs; they came out of the mouth of the dragon, out of the mouth of the beast and out of the mouth of the false prophet. They are spirits of demons performing miraculous signs, and they go out to the kings of the whole world, to gather them for the battle on the great day of God Almighty. "Behold, I come like a thief! Blessed is he who stays awake and keeps his clothes with him, so that he may not go naked and be shamefully exposed." Then they gathered the kings together to the place that in Hebrew is called Armageddon. The seventh angel poured out his bowl into the air, and out of the temple came a loud voice from the throne, saying, "It is done!" Then there came flashes of lightning, rumblings, peals of thunder and a severe earthquake. No earthquake like it has ever occurred since man has been on earth, so tremendous was the quake. The great city split into three parts, and the cities of the nations collapsed. God remembered Babylon the Great and gave her the cup filled with the wine of the fury of his wrath. Every island fled away and the mountains could not be found. From the sky huge hailstones of about a hundred pounds each fell upon men. And they cursed God on account of the plague of hail, because the plague was so terrible."

DEMONS AND HOW THEY INVADE YOUR HOME

FROGS	PSALMS 78:45	PSALMS 105:30	REVELATION 16:13
RAVENS	ISAIAH 34:11		
UNICORNS	DEUTERONOMY 33:17	NUMBERS 23:22	NUMBERS 24:8
	JOB 39:9–10	PSALMS 29:6	PSALMS 92:10
	DEUTERONOMY 33:17	PSALMS 22:21	ISAIAH 34:7
BUTTERFLY	2nd.CHRONICLES 11:15	ISAIAH 34:14	ISAIAH 13:21

IN THESE 3 VERSES OF SCRIPTURE IN THE KING JAMES BIBLE WE SEE THE SCRIPTURE POINTING TO A SATYR: WE NOW LOOK IN WEBSTER'S DICTIONARY FOR THE MEANING.
SATYR: A SYLVAN DEITY OR DEMIGOD OF THE GREEKS AND ROMANS, HALF MAN AND HALF GOAT; A LECHER. A "BUTTERFLY" OF THE FAMILY SATYRIDAE, MARKED WITH SMALL EYELIKE SPOTS ON THE WINGS. A MAN WITH SATYRIASIS.
SATYRIASIS AN UNCONTROLLABLE SEXUAL APPETITE IN MALES

VULTURES	ISAIAH 34:13–15	JEREMIAH 50:39	MICAH 1:8
OWLS	LEVITICUS 11:17	PSALMS 102:7	
DRAGONS	REVELATION 20:2	ISAIAH 51:9	REVELATION 12:3
	REVELATION 12:9	DEUTERONOMY 32:33	JOB 30:29
	PSALMS 44:19	PSALMS 74:13	PSALMS 91:13

151

DRAGONS	PSALMS 148:7	ISAIAH 13:22	ISAIAH 27:1
	ISAIAH 34:13	ISAIAH 35:7	ISAIAH 43:20
	JEREMIAH 9:11	JEREMIAH 10:22	JEREMIAH 49:33
	JEREMIAH 51:34	EZEKIEL 29:3	MICAH 1:8
	MALACHI 1:3	REVELATION 16:13	
SORCERY	DEUTERONOMY 18:10–12	ACTS 8:9–24	ACTS 13:6–8
	REVELATION 9:21	REVELATION 21:8	REVELATION 22:15
	REVELATION 18:23	ISAIAH 47:9–12	JEREMIAH 27:9
ASTROLOGY	ISAIAH 47:1	ISAIAH 47:12–15	DANIEL 2:27–28
	DANIEL 2:2	DANIEL 1:20	DANIEL 2:10–13
	DANIEL 4:7	DANIEL 5:7–8	DANIEL 5:11

MUSIC WEBSTER'S DICTIONARY'S DEFINITION OF MUSIC: THE ART OF ORGANIZING OR ARRANGING SOUNDS INTO MEANINGFUL PATTERNS OR FORMS, INVOLVING PITCH, MELODY, HARMONY AND RHYTHM.

ROCK AND ROLL The synonyms are these: **SWAY, AGITATE, DERANGE, DISORDER, SICKEN, UNHINGE, UPSET, GYRATE, SECT, MOB, GANG, FACTION, FLUSTER, RUFFLE, UNSETTLE, CRAP, CRUD, AND LAST BUT NOT LEAST:** *A COVEN AND A CULT*!!
IN CHRISTIAN WORSHIP EPHESIANS 5:19 COLOSSIANS 3:16

Being we have reached the place in The Revelation where Demons are coming out of the pit of Hell to attack the unsaved that are left here on earth during the time of The Great Tribulation; I am being led by the Lord to warn all believers about the fact that **DEMONS CAN AND DO INVADE** their homes! As Billie Jean, Deborah, and myself MINISTER throughout this ENTIRE country we see the garbage that many Christians have accumulated in their homes. The Garbage I have just enumerated. **THESE ARE OPEN *RECEIVERS* FOR SATAN TO ENTER YOUR HOME AND ATTACK YOU!**

The greatest argument we get from Christians is in regards to "THE BUTTERFLY". Some clown out of the pit of Hell has sold the Christian community that the butterfly is a beautiful picture of THE RESURRECTION OF JESUS; "A METAMORPHOSIS OF JESUS". I have Good News for you today! Your Jesus and MY JESUS did not go through any "METAMORPHOSIS". Here is Websters' definition!!

METAMORPHOSIS: "Denoting change, change of form, structure, or substance; TRANSFORMATION by MAGIC or WITCHCRAFT; any complete change in appearance, character, or circumstance.

PRAISE GOD THAT JESUS IS THE SAME, YESTERDAY, TODAY, AND FOREVER!!!!

Chapter 21

The Seven Bowls—The Final Plagues

Revelation Chapters 15 & 16

Bowls One To Six

Revelation 16:1–12

The bowl judgments are the consummation of the wrath of God poured out on the wickedness of men and characterized by severity, finality, and brevity. They continue to very end of the Tribulation period, for the angels do not return to heaven. Chronologically, the next event following the outpouring of the bowls is the coming of Jesus in victory as we will see in chapter 19. The command from heaven in verse 1, indicates that God's long-suffering is ended and His judgment can no longer be delayed. His glory demands that His Name and His Honor be vindicated.

The First Bowl Is Poured Out On Upon The Earth: on the organized government under the leadership of the beast. A grievous ulcer is inflicted on those bearing the mark of the beast. This constitutes God's judgment on those who have rejected His Grace and rebelled against His worship. The affliction is moral, and spiritual, as well as physical.

The Second Bowl Is Poured Out Upon The Sea: this now becomes blood, and is symbolic of the complete moral and spiritual death of the godless society.

The Third Bowl Is Poured Out On The Rivers And Springs Of Water: these now become blood, and in the midst of such judgment there is a proclamation of the righteousness of God who has judged. Justice has been done, for the dwellers of planet earth on whom such retribution falls have shed the innocent blood of the prophets and the saints, and God has given them blood to drink as they deserve. The altar of God now responds by saying, "Yes, Lord God Almighty, just and true are your judgments, because the prayers of the saints under the altar are now answered."

The Fourth Bowl Is Now Poured Out On The Sun: God's absolute authority over creation is here and now shown, and the sun is given power to scorch people with fire. The people are seared by the intense heat and they cursed the name of God, who had control over these plagues, and they still refused to repent and glorify Him. They harden their hearts and their true character is revealed.

The Fifth Bowl Is Now Poured Out On The Throne Of The Beast: Darkness now falls over the empire of the beast, and the center of his power is now affected. God now answers the taunt of the blasphemers we saw in 13: 4 "Who is like the beast? Who can make war against him?" Morally, politically and spiritually the kingdom of the beast is plunged into solitary darkness, and men gnaw their tongues in agony and curse the God of heaven because of their pains and their sores, but they still refuse to repent of what they had done.

The Sixth Bowl Is Now Poured Out On The River Euphrates: The drying up of the Euphrates River, which is 1,780 miles long, the largest stream in Western Asia, symbolizes the removal of every barrier for the advance of "the kings from the east" to Armageddon. This great river formed the eastern boundary of the Roman Empire and is stipulated as the eastern limit of enlarged Palestine as we see in Genesis 15:18. It was a natural barrier in Antiquity to invading armies from the east. No longer shall it be a barrier when the Lord Jesus gathers His hosts to Armageddon, and when He gathers Israel back into the Kingdom. The kings from the east are the rulers of powers east of the Euphrates.

The Three Frogs

Revelation 16:13-16

The Satanic Trinity now bring forth frogs, out of the mouth of the dragon, out of the mouth of the beast, and out of the mouth of the false prophet. Frogs symbolize the demons who will be the spiritual dynamic behind Armageddon. The dragon (Satan), the beast (the anti-christ), and the false prophet symbolize the Satanic Trinity of evil, the source of the demon spirits. These demons form the delusive means of persuading the nations to gather for the supreme folly of Armageddon: man's insane fight against God and Christ's sovereignty over the earth. Armageddon, known as "The Valley Of Jezreel, The Valley Of Megiddo," is the ancient battlefield and site of several decisive battles in Israel's History. Judges 5:19, The Battle of Deborah at Megiddo, 2nd. Kings 9:27, Ahaziah king of Judah died at the battle at Megiddo, 2nd Chronicles 35:22, Josiah king of Judah wounded at the battle at Megiddo died in Jerusalem. This valley of Megiddo symbolizes the place of the gathering of the nations, as the Valley Of Jehoshaphat, we see in Joel 3: 2,12; symbolizes the place of slaughter in the final end time battle. This battle decides the governmental question of the sovereignty of the earth. The warning is now given to the remnant of Israel that the darkness and deception of that hour would be so great that they are to be prepared for the coming of Christ. For Jesus says, "Behold, I come like a thief! Blessed is he who stays awake and keeps his clothes with him, so that he may not go naked and be shamefully exposed."

The Seventh Bowl

Revelation 16:17-21

The seventh angel pours out his bowl upon the air, the realm of Satan, who now having been driven out of the heavenlies onto the earth, and operates through the beast, the false prophet and their followers. The judgment of hailstones fall on the organized crime and evil on the earth. "It is done!" proclaims the completion of God's wrath upon those who have refused Jesus' cry from The Cross, "It Is Finished!" God's voice from His Temple, which is the place of His Presence, and The Throne, which is the seat of His Administration is now heard. His judicial action symbolized by voices, thunders, and lighting's, precede the great earthquake. This earthquake is a physical reality. Jerusalem "the great city" is divided into three parts. "The cities of the nations" also fall. "Great Babylon," the counterfeit political, and religious center of planet earth, now experiences God's full wrath. The earthquake is worldwide, and only one "Kingdom," meaning, "The Kingdom of Jesus on Earth," escapes, for it cannot be shaken. I now quote Daniel 2:40–44. "Finally Daniel, there will be a fourth kingdom, strong as iron—for iron breaks and smashes everything—and as iron breaks things to pieces, so it will crush and break all the others. Just as you saw that the feet and toes were partly of baked clay and partly of iron, so this will be a divided kingdom; yet it will have some of the strength of iron in it, even as you saw iron mixed with clay. As the toes were partly iron and partly clay, so this kingdom will be partly strong and partly brittle. And just as you saw the iron mixed with baked clay, so the people will be a mixture and will not remain united, any more than iron mixes with clay. In the time of those kings, the God of heaven will set up a kingdom that will never be destroyed, nor will it be left to another people. It will crush all those kingdoms and bring them to an end, but it will itself endure forever." From the sky huge hailstones of about a hundred pounds each fell upon men, which recalls the defeat of Israel's enemies at Beth-Horon which we see in Joshua 10:1–11. "Now Adoni-Zedek king of Jerusalem heard that Joshua had taken Ai and totally destroyed it, doing to Ai and its king as he had done to Jericho and its king, and that the people of Gibeon had made a treaty of peace with Israel and were living with them. He and his people were very much alarmed at this, because Gibeon was an important city, like one of the royal cities; it was larger than Ai, and all its men were good fighters. So Adoni-Zedek king of Jerusalem appealed to Hoham king of Hebron, Piram king of Jarmuth, Japhia king of Lachish and Debir king of Eglon. Come up and help me attack Gibeon, he said, because it has made peace with Joshua and the Israelites. Then the five kings of the Amorites—the kings of Jerusalem, Hebron, Jarmuth, Lachish and Eglon—joined forces. They moved up with all their troops and took positions against Gibeon and attacked it. The Gibeonites then sent word to Joshua in the camp at Gilgal: Do not abandon your servants. Come up to us quickly and save us! Help us, because all the Amorite kings from the hill country have joined forces against us. So Joshua marched from Gilgal with his entire army, including all the best fighting men. The Lord said to Joshua, Do not be afraid of them; I have given them into your hand. Not one of them will be able to withstand you. After an all-night march from Gilgal Joshua took them by surprise. The Lord threw them into confusion before Israel, who defeated them in a great victory at Gibeon. Israel pursed them along the road going up to Beth-Horon and cut them down all the way to Azekah and Makkedah. As they fled before Israel on the road down from Beth-Horon to Azekah, the Lord hurled large hailstones down on them from the sky, and more of them died from the hailstones than were killed by the swords of the Israelites. On the day the Lord gave the Amorites over to Israel, Joshua said to the Lord in the presence of Israel: O sun, stand still over Gibeon, O moon, over the valley of Aijalon. So the sun stood still, and the moon stopped, till the nation of Israel avenged itself on its enemies as it is written in the book of Jashar. *The sun stopped in the middle of the sky and delayed going down about a full day.* There has never been a day like it before or since, a day when the Lord listened to a man. Surely the Lord was fighting for Israel!"

REV 17:1 One of the seven angels who had the seven bowls came and said to me, "Come, I will show you the punishment of the great prostitute, who sits on many waters. With her the kings of the earth committed adultery and the inhabitants of the earth were intoxicated with the wine of her adulteries." Then the angel carried me away in the Spirit into a desert. There I saw a woman sitting on a scarlet beast that was covered with blasphemous names and had seven heads and ten horns. The woman was dressed in purple and scarlet, and was glittering with gold, precious stones and pearls. She held a golden cup in her hand, filled with abominable things and the filth of her adulteries. This title was written on her forehead: MYSTERY BABYLON THE GREAT THE MOTHER OF PROSTITUTES AND OF THE ABOMINATIONS OF THE EARTH. I saw that the woman was drunk with the blood of the saints, the blood of those who bore testimony to Jesus. When I saw her, I was greatly astonished. Then the angel said to me: "Why are you astonished? I will explain to you the mystery of the woman and of the beast she rides, which has the seven heads and ten horns. The beast, which you saw, once was, now is not, and will come up out of the Abyss and go to his destruction. The inhabitants of the earth whose names have not been written in the book of life from the creation of the world will be astonished when they see the beast, because he once was, now is not, and yet will come. "This calls for a mind with wisdom. The seven heads are seven hills on which the woman sits. They are also seven kings. Five have fallen, one is, the other has not yet come; but when he does come, he must remain for a little while. The beast who once was, and now is not, is an eighth king. He belongs to the seven and is going to his destruction. "The ten horns you saw are ten kings who have not yet received a kingdom, but who for one hour will receive authority as kings along with the beast. They have one purpose and will give their power and authority to the beast. They will make war against the Lamb, but the Lamb will overcome them because he is Lord of lords and King of kings—and with him will be his called, chosen and faithful followers." Then the angel said to me, "The waters you saw, where the prostitute sits, are peoples, multitudes, nations and languages. The beast and the ten horns you saw will hate the prostitute. They will bring her to ruin and leave her naked; they will eat her flesh and burn her with fire. For God has put it into their hearts to accomplish his purpose by agreeing to give the beast their power to rule, until God's words are fulfilled. The woman you saw is the great city that rules over the kings of the earth."

The Woman On The Beast
Revelation 17: 1–6

The Harlot represents ecclesiastical Babylon, which is personified religious revolt against God in its form, ripe for judgment. She stands for corrupt religion, a great harlot denoting a religious system that compromises truth for worldly power; and any kind of power. She exploits the peoples of the earth, and she is guilty of prostituting truth and purity, intoxicating men by her doctrines and practices which violate the Word of God. She is spiritually destitute, and the desert symbolizes the place of drought, where those who are thirsty can never be satisfied. She dominates and uses state government whenever possible. She comes into power in political Babylon, the beast's kingdom, the final form of Gentile world government. She heads up the corrupt religious system of the end time. Scarlet denotes her sin and adultery. She has influence, she is wealthy, and she has power. The golden cup in her hand being filled with abominable things and the filth of her fornication tells of her gross sin against God and His Word. She represents in the fullest extent, outlook, and application all apostate religious movements, from the time of Nimrod of ancient Babylon to the present time of apostate christianity in these end times. Her greatest and most horrible sin is the blood of the saints that she has murdered. Both Old Testament Saints and New Testament Saints suffered and died under this harlot. There were seven million christians and six and a half million Jews who suffered and died because of this harlot; THREE MILLION CATHOLICS AND FOUR MILLION PROTESTANTS; WHO DIED PROTECTING THEIR BROTHER AND SISTER JEWS; THROUGH Adolph Hitler of Germany, whose power came to him out of the pit of Hell by Satan himself. During the persecution of the end times, this evil system will participate with the beast in the mass murders of the true followers of Jesus Christ.

The Doom Of The Harlot

Revelation 17: 7–18

I believe there is only one city in the world that this is a description of: A city with its CIA, FBI, IRS, COVERT Operations, with its Computers which have a make on every person in the world, including you and me, and every new born baby, which now must have a social security number, a city which makes or breaks the economy of the world, which controls world wide inflation and deflation, world wide interest rates, a city whose influence and dominion extends to all capitals of the world, a city which sits upon the waters, and whose spiritual name is COMPROMISE!! When God says in verse sixteen that the ten horns, and the beast who is the anti-christ will hate the harlot which I believe to be Washington D.C.; the scripture says they will strip her, eat up her flesh, and utterly consume her with fire. I believe the first nuclear bombs will land on Washington D.C. with all of its attributes of Harlotry, immorality, murder; the aborting of 5,000 BABIES A DAY, 1,825,000 BABIES slaughtered YEARLY, homosexuals and lesbians being condoned and overlooked; when God in His revulsion of Homosexuality destroyed Sodom and Gomorrah and six of the plain cities. *The Unholy Spirit,* The Prince Demon which controlled Babylon, then controlled the kingdom of the Medes and Persians, then controlled the Greek Empire under

Alexander the Great, then controlled the Roman Empire, and which now controls Washington D.C. the city of the cherry blossoms on the Potomac.

REV 18:1 After this I saw another angel coming down from heaven. He had great authority, and the earth was illuminated by his splendor. With a mighty voice he shouted: "Fallen! Fallen is Babylon the Great! She has become a home for demons and a haunt for every evil spirit, a haunt for every unclean and detestable bird. For all the nations have drunk the maddening wine of her adulteries. The kings of the earth committed adultery with her, and the merchants of the earth grew rich from her excessive luxuries." Then I heard another voice from heaven say: "Come out of her, my people, so that you will not share in her sins, so that you will not receive any of her plagues; for her sins are piled up to heaven, and God has remembered her crimes. Give back to her as she has given; pay her back double for what she has done. Mix her a double portion from her own cup. Give her as much torture and grief as the glory and luxury she gave herself. In her heart she boasts, 'I sit as queen; I am not a widow, and I will never mourn.' Therefore in one day her plagues will overtake her: death, mourning and famine. She will be consumed by fire, for mighty is the Lord God who judges her. "When the kings of the earth who committed adultery with her and shared her luxury see the smoke of her burning, they will weep and mourn over her. Terrified at her torment, they will stand far off and cry: " 'Woe! Woe, O great city, O Babylon, city of power! In one hour your doom has come!' " The merchants of the earth will weep and mourn over her because no one buys their cargoes any more—cargoes of gold, silver, precious stones and pearls; fine linen, purple, silk and scarlet cloth; every sort of citron wood, and articles of every kind made of ivory, costly wood, bronze, iron and marble; cargoes of cinnamon and spice, of incense, myrrh and frankincense, of wine and olive oil, of fine flour and wheat; cattle and sheep; horses and carriages; and bodies and souls of men. "They will say, 'The fruit you longed for is gone from you. All your riches and splendor have vanished, never to be recovered.' The merchants who sold these things and gained their wealth from her will stand far off, terrified at her torment. They will weep and mourn and cry out: " 'Woe! Woe, O great city, dressed in fine linen, purple and scarlet, and glittering with gold, precious stones and pearls! In one hour such great wealth has been brought to ruin!' "Every sea captain, and all who travel by ship, the sailors, and all who earn their living from the sea, will stand far off. When they see the smoke of her burning, they will exclaim, 'Was there ever a city like this great city?' They will throw dust on their heads, and with weeping and mourning cry out: " 'Woe! Woe, O great city, where all who had ships on the sea became rich through her wealth! In one hour she has been brought to ruin! Rejoice over her, O heaven! Rejoice, saints and apostles and prophets! God has judged her for the way she treated you.' " Then a mighty angel picked up a boulder the size of a large millstone and threw it into the sea, and said: "With such violence the great city of Babylon will be thrown down, never to be found again. The music of harpists and musicians, flute players and trumpeters, will never be heard in you again. No workman of any trade will ever be found in you again. The sound of a millstone will never be heard in you again. The light of a lamp will never shine in you again. The voice of bridegroom and bride will never be heard in you again. Your merchants were the world's great men. By your magic spell all the nations were led astray. In her was found the blood of prophets and of the saints, and of all who have been killed on the earth." Believe me Saints when I tell you that God is calling you and me to a RENEWAL OF HOLINESS, the time of playing church is over WITH, "GAMESMANSHIP" if it ever was worth anything is now done away with. You can no longer compromise, the day is upon us when we are going to be asked who do we belong to? *AS FOR ME AND MY HOUSE THIS DAY WE WILL SERVE THE LORD JESUS!!!*

Chapter 22

The Judgment of the Commercial System and "Babylon"

Revelation 18:1–24

A great angel announces the ruin of commercial Babylon because of her sin of corruption and of her commercialism. God's people are commanded to separate from her, for her iniquity is full, and her pride calls for full and immediate punishment. All those who grew wealthy in their trafficking with her now bewail her. All heaven is summoned to rejoice over her destruction together with the saints, apostles, and the prophets. The reason for such joy is the fact that God has avenged us on her. This shows us that God, and only God, is the real destroyer of the Satanic world system, both religious and commercial. The millstone which we saw thrown into the sea is the symbol of Babylon's utter destruction, for she was and is guilty of the blood of the people of God. The Babylon of this chapter is the Satanic world system in all of its godless commercial and economic aspects. The macho dog eat dog mentality; man's inhumanity to man is the underlying attitude in today's world whether it be in the commercial or communist system of world power. This system is honeycombed throughout all phases of life of unregenerate mankind organized as a world system under Satan. We saw the religious aspects of Babylon in chapter 17; and in this chapter we are looking at the ramifications of cultural, scientific, educational, as well as governmental. The Satanic world system of Babylon with Satan as its directing head is mentioned more the 30 times in the New Testament. This system is pronounced by God as being totally evil, and is temporary and limited and is doomed to destruction at the second coming of Jesus The Christ, which will bring an end to greed, the thought of thinking we are better than our fellow man, pride, and war which has been a snare to God's people since the fall of man in The Garden of Eden.

REV 19:1 After this I heard what sounded like the roar of a great multitude in heaven shouting: "Hallelujah! Salvation and glory and power belong to our God, for true and just are his judgments. He has condemned the great prostitute who corrupted the earth by her adulteries. He has avenged on her the blood of his servants." And again they shouted: "Hallelujah! The smoke from her goes up for ever and ever." The twenty-four elders and the four living creatures fell down and worshiped God, who was seated on the throne. And they cried: "Amen, Hallelujah!" Then a voice came from the throne, saying: "Praise our God, all you his servants, you who fear him, both small and great!" Then I heard what sounded like a great multitude, like the roar of rushing waters and like loud peals of thunder, shouting: "Hallelujah! For our Lord God Almighty reigns. Let us rejoice and be glad and give him glory! For the wedding of the Lamb has come, and his bride has made herself ready. Fine linen, bright and clean, was given her to wear." (Fine linen stands for the righteous acts of the saints.) Then the angel said to me, "Write: 'Blessed are those who are invited to the wedding supper of the Lamb!' " And he added, "These are the true words of God." At this I fell at his feet to worship him. But he said to me, "Do not do it! I am a fellow servant with you and with your brothers who hold to the testimony of Jesus. Worship God! For the testimony of Jesus is the spirit of prophecy." I saw heaven standing open and there before me was a white horse, whose rider is called Faithful and True. With justice he judges and makes war. His eyes are like blazing fire, and on his head are many crowns. He has a name written on him that no one knows but he himself. He is dressed in a robe dipped in blood, and his name is the Word of God. The armies of heaven were following him, riding on white horses and dressed in fine linen, white and clean. Out of his mouth comes a sharp sword with which to strike down the nations. "He will rule them with an iron scepter." He treads the winepress of the fury of the wrath of God Almighty. On his robe and on his thigh he has this name written: KING OF KINGS AND LORD OF LORDS. And I saw an angel standing in the sun, who cried in a loud voice to all the birds flying in midair, "Come, gather together for the great supper of God, so that you may eat the flesh of kings, generals, and mighty men, of horses and their riders, and the flesh of all people, free and slave, small and great." Then I saw the beast and the kings of the earth and their armies gathered together to make war against the rider on the horse and his army. But the beast was captured, and with him the false prophet who had performed the miraculous signs on his behalf. With these signs he had deluded those who had received the mark of the beast and worshiped his image. The two of them were thrown alive into the fiery lake of burning sulfur. The rest of them were killed with the sword that came out of the mouth of the rider on the horse, and all the birds gorged themselves on their flesh."

As we stated earlier; THE SCRIPTURES in DANIEL pointed out to us that THE ANTI-CHRIST will come out of SYRIA. President Hafez Al-Assad of Syria has recently made the decision to commit over 50% of Syria's gross national income to defense. Syria has in her possession chemical weapons and is continuing to produce them. Nerve gas which leaves the victim dead in 10 minutes has been supplied by Russia to Libya, and Lybia has delivered a huge amount of this nerve gas to Syria. The SOVIETS have been teaching THE SYRIAN'S to fire missiles from NAVAL SHIPS; so that the possibility, of any attack upon "THE THREE KINGDOMS" we spoke about earlier could take place from LEBANON which Syria controls. New Naval Cruisers delivered by RUSSIA to SYRIA, plus the latest defense system in ANTI-AIRCRAFT Weaponry, chemical weapons, BACTERIOLOGICAL weapons, make this time, about the MOST CRITICAL TIME IN THE HISTORY OF THE WORLD! *REPENT, "THE KINGDOM OF GOD IS AT HAND."*

LOOK UP CHRISTIAN, YOUR REDEMPTION DRAWETH NIGH UNTO THEE!

1KI 18:1 After a long time, in the third year, the word of the Lord came to Elijah: "Go and present yourself to Ahab, and I will send rain on the land." So Elijah went to present himself to Ahab. Now the famine was severe in Samaria, and Ahab had summoned Obadiah, who was in charge of his palace. (Obadiah was a devout believer in the Lord. While Jezebel was killing off the Lord's prophets, Obadiah had taken a hundred prophets and hidden them in two caves, fifty in each, and had supplied them with food and water.) Ahab had said to Obadiah, "Go through the land to all the springs and valleys. Maybe we can find some grass to keep the horses and mules alive so we will not have to kill any of our animals." So they divided the land they were to cover, Ahab going in one direction and Obadiah in another. As Obadiah was walking along, Elijah met him. Obadiah recognized him, bowed down to the ground, and said, "Is it really you, my lord Elijah?" "Yes," he replied. "Go tell your master, 'Elijah is here.' " "What have I done wrong," asked Obadiah, "that you are handing your servant over to Ahab to be put to death? As surely as the Lord your God lives, there is not a nation or kingdom where my master has not sent someone to look for you. And whenever a nation or kingdom claimed you were not there, he made them swear they could not find you. But now you tell me to go to my master and say, 'Elijah is here.' I don't know where the SPIRIT OF THE LORD MAY CARRY YOU when I leave you. If I go and tell Ahab and he doesn't find you, he will kill me. Yet I your servant have worshiped the Lord since my youth. Haven't you heard, my lord, what I did while Jezebel was killing the prophets of the Lord? I hid a hundred of the Lord's prophets in two caves, fifty in each, and supplied them with food and water. And now you tell me to go to my master and say, 'Elijah is here.' He will kill me!" Elijah said, "As the Lord Almighty lives, whom I serve, I will surely present myself to Ahab today." So Obadiah went to meet Ahab and told him, and Ahab went to meet Elijah. When he saw Elijah, he said to him, "Is that you, you troubler of Israel?" "I have not made trouble for Israel," Elijah replied. "But you and your father's family have. You have abandoned the Lord's commands and have followed the Baals. Now summon the people from all over Israel to meet me on Mount Carmel. And bring the four hundred and fifty prophets of Baal and the four hundred prophets of Asherah, who eat at Jezebel's table." So Ahab sent word throughout all Israel and assembled the prophets on Mount Carmel. Elijah went before the people and said, "How long will you waver between two opinions? If the Lord is God, follow him; but if Baal is God, follow him." But the people said nothing. Then Elijah said to them, "I AM THE ONLY ONE of the Lord's prophets left, but Baal has four hundred and fifty prophets. Get two bulls for us. Let them choose one for themselves, and let them cut it into pieces and put it on the wood but not set fire to it. I will prepare the other bull and put it on the wood but not set fire to it. Then you call on the name of your god, and I will call on the name of the Lord. The god who answers by fire—he is God." Then all the people said, "What you say is good." Elijah said to the prophets of Baal, "Choose one of the bulls and prepare it first, since there are so many of you. Call on the name of your god, but do not light the fire." So they took the bull given them and prepared it. Then they called on the name of Baal from morning till noon. "O Baal, answer us!" they shouted. But there was no response; no one answered. And they danced around the altar they had made. At noon Elijah began to taunt them. "Shout louder!" he said. "Surely he is a god! Perhaps he is deep in thought, or busy, or traveling. Maybe he is sleeping and must be awakened." So they shouted louder and slashed themselves with swords and spears, as was their custom, until their blood flowed. Midday passed, and they continued their frantic prophesying until the time for the evening sacrifice. But there was no response, no one answered, no one paid attention. Then Elijah said to all the people, "Come here to me." They came to him, and he repaired the altar of the Lord, which was in ruins. Elijah took twelve stones, one for each of the tribes descended from Jacob, to whom the word of the Lord had come, saying, "Your name shall be Israel." With the stones he built an altar in the name of the Lord, and he dug a trench around it large enough to hold two seahs of seed. He arranged the wood, cut the bull into pieces and laid it on the wood. Then he said to them, "Fill four large jars with water and pour it on the offering and on the wood." "Do it again," he said, and they did it again. "Do it a third time," he ordered, and they did it the third time. The water ran down around the altar and even filled the trench. At the time of sacrifice, the prophet Elijah stepped forward and prayed: "O Lord, God of Abraham, Isaac and Israel, let it be known today that you are God in Israel and that I am your servant and have done all these things at your command. Answer me, O Lord, answer me, so these people will know that you, O Lord, are God, and that you are turning their hearts back again." Then the fire of the Lord fell and burned up the sacrifice, the wood, the stones and the soil, and also licked up the water in the trench. When all the people saw this, they fell prostrate and cried, "The Lord—he is God! The Lord—he is God!" Then Elijah commanded them, "Seize the prophets of Baal. Don't let anyone get away!" They seized them, and Elijah had them brought down to the Kishon Valley and slaughtered there. And Elijah said to Ahab, "Go, eat and drink, for there is the sound of a heavy rain." So Ahab went off to eat and drink, but Elijah climbed to the top of Carmel, bent down to the ground and put his face between his knees. "Go and look toward the sea," he told his servant. And he went up and looked. "There is nothing there," he said. Seven times Elijah said, "Go back." The seventh time the servant reported, "A cloud as small as a man's hand is rising from the sea." So Elijah said, "Go and tell Ahab, 'Hitch up your chariot and go down before the rain stops you.' " Meanwhile, the sky grew black with clouds, the wind rose, a heavy rain came on and Ahab rode off to Jezreel. THE POWER OF THE LORD came upon Elijah and, tucking his cloak into his belt, he ran ahead of Ahab all the way to Jezreel. Now Ahab told Jezebel everything Elijah had done and how he had killed all the prophets with the sword. So Jezebel sent a messenger to Elijah to say, "May the gods deal with me, be it ever so severely, if by this time tomorrow I do not make your life like that of one of them." Elijah was afraid and ran for his life. When he came to Beersheba in Judah, he left his servant there, while he himself went a day's journey into the desert. He came to a broom tree, sat down under it and prayed that he might die. "I have had enough, Lord," he said. "Take my life; I am no better than my ancestors." Then he lay down under the tree and fell asleep. All at once an angel touched him and said, "Get up and eat." He looked around, and there by his head was a cake of bread baked over hot coals, and a jar of water. He ate and drank and then lay down again. The angel of the Lord came back a second time and touched him and said, "Get up and eat, for the journey is too much for you." So he got up and ate and drank. Strengthened by that food, he traveled forty days and forty nights until he reached Horeb, the mountain of God. There he went into a cave and spent the night. And the word of the Lord came to him: "What are you doing here, Elijah?" He replied, "I have been very zealous for the Lord God Almighty. The Israelites have rejected your covenant, broken down your altars, and put your prophets to death with the sword. I AM THE ONLY ONE LEFT, and now they are trying to kill me too." The Lord said, "Go out and stand on the mountain in the presence of the Lord, for the Lord is about to pass by." Then a great and powerful wind tore the mountains apart and shattered the rocks before the Lord, but the Lord was not in the wind. After the wind there was an earthquake, but the Lord was not in the earthquake. After the earthquake came a fire, but the Lord was not in the fire. And after the fire came a gentle whisper. When Elijah heard it, he pulled his cloak over his face and went out and stood at the mouth of the cave. Then a voice said to him, "What are you doing here, Elijah?" He replied, "I have been very zealous for the Lord God Almighty. The Israelites have rejected your covenant, broken down your altars, and put your prophets to death with the sword. I AM THE ONLY ONE LEFT, and now they are trying to kill me too." The Lord said to him, "Go back the way you came, and go to the Desert of Damascus. When you get there, anoint Hazael king over Aram. Also, anoint Jehu son of Nimshi king over Israel, and anoint Elisha son of Shaphat from Abel Meholah to succeed you as prophet. Jehu will put to death any who escape the sword of Hazael, and Elisha will put to death any who escape the sword of Jehu. Yet I reserve seven thousand in Israel—all whose knees have not bowed down to Baal and all whose mouths have not kissed him." So Elijah went from there and found Elisha son of Shaphat. He was plowing with twelve yoke of oxen, and he himself was driving the twelfth pair. Elijah went up to him and threw his cloak around him. Elisha then left his oxen and ran after Elijah. "Let me kiss my father and mother good-by," he said, "and then I will come with you." "Go back," Elijah replied. "What have I done to you?" So Elisha left him and went back. He took his yoke of oxen and slaughtered them. He burned the plowing equipment to cook the meat and gave it to the people, and they ate. Then he set out to follow Elijah and became his STUDENT."

HOW MANY GLORIOUS MINISTRIES HAVE BEEN HURT AND CURTAILED BECAUSE OF ONE WOMAN MOVING IN THE BLACK WIDOW SYNDROME OF JEZEBEL?? Where are the **SEVEN THOUSAND KNEES** that are known to GOD only? Where are these **SEVEN THOUSAND KNEES** that should have helped these ministries? **ELIJAH** COMMANDED BY GOD had to turn his ministry over to ELISHA after he ran! STAND UP SAINT.

Chapter 23

The Second Coming of Jesus and Two Hallelujah Choruses

Revelation 19:1–10

The first chorus, expresses heaven's joyous celebration over the destruction of Babylon and of the harlot church. "Hallelujah! salvation and glory and power belong to our God, for true and just are His judgments. He has condemned the great prostitute who corrupted the earth by her adulteries. He has avenged on her the blood of His servants." The second chorus, is a swell of voices like the roar of the ocean and the roll of thunder, announcing the Marriage of the Lamb to His True Bride. "Hallelujah! For our Lord God Almighty reigns. Let us rejoice and be glad and give Him glory! For the wedding of the Lamb has come, and His bride has made herself ready. Fine linen, bright and clean, was given her to wear. (fine linen stands for the righteous acts of the saints).

THE MARRIAGE SUPPER OF THE LAMB

Revelation 19:9-10

"Then the angel said to me, write: Blessed are those who are invited to the wedding supper of the Lamb! And he added, these are the true words of God. At this I fell at his feet to worship him. But he said to me, do not do it! I am a fellow servant with you and your brothers who hold to the testimony of Jesus. Worship God! for the testimony of Jesus is the spirit of prophecy." The grand event of the wedding is preluded by the announcement that God Almighty assumes Kingly Power in Jesus christ. There are guests that are invited to this wedding supper, and it is important for us to understand who they are, that's why John receives the command "write." The blessed happiness of the invited guests is stressed in the scripture, showing us that they are to be distinguished from The Bride for they are Old Testament Saints. This is called a marriage supper, as it is the blessed reward to those who belong to God in contrast to the supper of judgment which we will see later in the scripture.

THE SECOND COMING OF JESUS, KING OF KINGS AND LORD OF LORDS

At this point let us look at the only physical description of The Second Coming of Jesus, which is FOUND ONLY in The Old Testament in The Book of The Prophet Zechariah.

ZEC 12:1 This is the word of the Lord concerning Israel. The Lord, who stretches out the heavens, who lays the foundation of the earth, and who forms the spirit of man within him, declares: "I am going to make Jerusalem a cup that sends all the surrounding peoples reeling. Judah will be besieged as well as Jerusalem. On that day, when all the nations of the earth are gathered against her, I will make Jerusalem an immovable rock for all the nations. All who try to move it will injure themselves. On that day I will strike every horse with panic and its rider with madness," declares the Lord. "I will keep a watchful eye over the house of Judah, but I will blind all the horses of the nations. Then the leaders of Judah will say in their hearts, 'The people of Jerusalem are strong, because the Lord Almighty is their God.' "On that day I will make the leaders of Judah like a firepot in a woodpile, like a flaming torch among sheaves. They will consume right and left all the surrounding peoples, but Jerusalem will remain intact in her place. "The Lord will save the dwellings of Judah first, so that the honor of the house of David and of Jerusalem's inhabitants may not be greater than that of Judah. On that day the Lord will shield those who live in Jerusalem, so that the feeblest among them will be like David, and the house of David will be like God, like the Angel of the Lord going before them. On that day I will set out to destroy all the nations that attack Jerusalem. "And I will pour out on the house of David and the inhabitants of Jerusalem a spirit of grace and supplication. They will look on me, the one they have pierced, and they will mourn for him as one mourns for an only child, and grieve bitterly for him as one grieves for a first-born son. On that day the weeping in Jerusalem will be great, like the weeping of Hadad Rimmon in the plain of Megiddo. The land will mourn, each clan by itself, with their wives by themselves: the clan of the house of David and their wives, the clan of the house of Nathan and their wives, the clan of the house of Levi and their wives, the clan of Shimei and their wives, and all the rest of the clans and their wives.

ZEC 13:1 "On that day a fountain will be opened to the house of David and the inhabitants of Jerusalem, to cleanse them from sin and impurity. "On that day, I will banish the names of the idols from the land, and they will be remembered no more," declares the Lord Almighty. "I will remove both the prophets and the spirit of impurity from the land. And if anyone still prophesies, his father and mother, to whom he was born, will say to him, 'You must die, because you have told lies in the Lord's name.' When he prophesies, his own parents will stab him. "On that day every prophet will be ashamed of his prophetic vision. He will not put on a prophet's garment of hair in order to deceive. He will say, 'I am not a prophet. I am a farmer; the land has been my livelihood since my youth.' If someone asks him, 'What are these wounds on your body?' he will answer, 'The wounds I was given at the house of my friends.' " Awake, O sword, against my shepherd, against the man who is close to me!" declares the Lord Almighty. "Strike the shepherd, and the sheep will be scattered, and I will turn my hand against the little ones. In the whole land," declares the Lord, "two-thirds will be struck down and perish; yet one-third will be left in it. This third I will bring into the fire; I will refine them like silver and test them like gold. They will call on my name and I will answer them; I will say, 'They are my people,' and they will say, 'The Lord is our God.' "

ZEC 14:1 A day of the Lord is coming when your plunder will be divided among you. I will gather all the nations to Jerusalem to fight against it; the city will be captured, the houses ransacked, and the women raped. Half of the city will go into exile, but the rest of the people will not be taken from the city. Then the Lord will go out and fight against those nations, as he fights in the day of battle. On that day his feet will stand on the Mount of Olives, east of Jerusalem, and the Mount of Olives will be split in two from east to west, forming a great valley, with half of the mountain moving north and half moving south. You will flee by my mountain valley, for it will extend to Azel. You will flee as you fled from the earthquake in the days of Uzziah king of Judah. Then the Lord my God will come, and all the holy ones with him. On that day there will be no light, no cold or frost. It will be a unique day, without daytime or nighttime—a day known to the Lord. When evening comes, there will be light. On that day living water will flow out from Jerusalem, half to the eastern sea and half to the western sea, in summer and in winter. The Lord will be king over the whole earth. On that day there will be one Lord, and his name the only name. The whole land, from Geba to Rimmon, south of Jerusalem, will become like the Arabah. But Jerusalem will be raised up and remain in its place, from the Benjamin Gate to the site of the First Gate, to the Corner Gate, and from the Tower of Hananel to the royal winepresses. It will be inhabited; never again will it be destroyed. Jerusalem will be secure. This is the plague with which the Lord will strike all the nations that fought against Jerusalem: Their flesh will rot while they are still standing on their feet, their eyes will rot in their sockets, and their tongues will rot in their mouths. On that day men will be stricken by the Lord with great panic. Each man will seize the hand of another, and they will attack each other. Judah too will fight at Jerusalem. The wealth of all the surrounding nations will be collected—great quantities of gold and silver and clothing. A similar plague will strike the horses and mules, the camels and donkeys, and all the animals in those camps. Then the survivors from all the nations that have attacked Jerusalem will go up year after year to worship the King, the Lord Almighty, and to celebrate the Feast of Tabernacles. If any of the peoples of the earth do not go up to Jerusalem to worship the King, the Lord Almighty, they will have no rain. If the Egyptian people do not go up and take part, they will have no rain. The Lord will bring on them the plague he inflicts on the nations that do not go up to celebrate the Feast of Tabernacles. This will be the punishment of Egypt and the punishment of all the nations that do not go up to celebrate the Feast of Tabernacles. On that day holy to the Lord will be inscribed on the bells of the horses, and the cooking pots in the Lord's house will be like the sacred bowls in front of the altar. Every pot in Jerusalem and Judah will be holy to the Lord Almighty, and all who come to sacrifice will take some of the pots and cook in them. And on that day there will no longer be a Canaanite in the house of the Lord Almighty.

JOHN'S VISION OF JESUS' COMING

John sees the heavens open, and his vision is the departure of Jesus from heaven with His saints and angels to claim His Kingship over the earth. We denote His victory by His sitting on a white horse, which is symbolic of a conquest of victory. His triumph is based on Him being faithful and true to the will of God in every respect. He comes to judge and to make war, and He comes in absolute righteousness. He brings with Him the All Knowing judgment symbolized by His eyes, which are like blazing fire and He comes in absolute authority, which is symbolized by the many crowns He has on His Head. The saints wear a victor's crown and not a monarch's crown, symbolizing that the saints belong to The Monarch who is King Jesus. He comes in vengeance upon His enemies denoted by His garment dipped in the blood of His enemies. His name is the Word of God, which now proclaims Him as God and Creator as well as Redeemer. He has the double right to rule the earth as The Creator and Redeemer. The armies of heaven which are the saints and the angels are associated with Him in His victory. He comes to earth on a white horse with His redeemed who are also on white horses and who share in His victorious conquest. Upon the return of Jesus to planet earth He conquers supernaturally, the sharp sword we see in this chapter is the Omnipotent word of God that spoke the universe into existence. With His Word He slays His enemies. He rules with sternness but at the same time He rules peacefully, as a shepherd, but those who are rebellious will find His shepherd staff a rod of iron. He deals with unsparing vengeance on evil. The entire universe and universal dominion is His. His name denotes His full Kingship and Lordship over all the earth, and all of mankind which is His right as The Creator and Redeemer.

ARMAGEDDON, AND THE FINAL DOOM OF THE BEAST AND THE FALSE PROPHET

Revelation 19:17-21

The supper of God is in great contrast to The Marriage Supper of The Lamb. One shows us the blissful fellowship of the righteous saints in heaven; and the other shows us the destruction of the enemies of Jesus Christ on earth. The catastrophic event of Armageddon is brought about by the word from the mouth of the returning Christ, which we saw in the scripture to be the sharp sword with which to strike down the nations. The four enemies of the Lamb, were the dragon, the beast, the false prophet and Babylon. In chapter 18 Babylon the working ally of the beast and false prophet fell. Then the beast and the false prophet, the government and the apostate church, dissolved their alliance, but they continued for a while each one in his own field. Now in this chapter their destruction is foretold. And we will see in chapter 20 the Dragon, Satan, the Evil Spirit that prompted it all go to their final doom.

REV 20:1 And I saw an angel coming down out of heaven, having the key to the Abyss and holding in his hand a great chain. He seized the dragon, that ancient serpent, who is the devil, or Satan, and bound him for a thousand years. He threw him into the Abyss, and locked and sealed it over him, to keep him from deceiving the nations anymore until the thousand years were ended. After that, he must be set free for a short time. I saw thrones on which were seated those who had been given authority to judge. And I saw the souls of those who had been beheaded because of their testimony for Jesus and because of the word of God. They had not worshiped the beast or his image and had not received his mark on their foreheads or their hands. They came to life and reigned with Christ a thousand years. (The rest of the dead did not come to life until the thousand years were ended.) This is the first resurrection. Blessed and holy are those who have part in the first resurrection. The second death has no power over them, but they will be priests of God and of Christ and will reign with him for a thousand years.

When the thousand years are over, Satan will be released from his prison and will go out to deceive the nations in the four corners of the earth—Gog and Magog—to gather them for battle. In number they are like the sand on the seashore. They marched across the breadth of the earth and surrounded the camp of God's people, the city he loves. But fire came down from heaven and devoured them. And the devil, who deceived them, was thrown into the lake of burning sulfur, where the beast and the false prophet had been thrown. They will be tormented day and night for ever and ever. Then I saw a great white throne and him who was seated on it. Earth and sky fled from his presence, and there was no place for them. And I saw the dead, great and small, standing before the throne, and books were opened. Another book was opened, which is the book of life. The dead were judged according to what they had done as recorded in the books. The sea gave up the dead that were in it, and death and Hades gave up the dead that were in them, and each person was judged according to what he had done. Then death and Hades were thrown into the lake of fire. The lake of fire is the second death. If anyone's name was not found written in the book of life, he was thrown into the lake of fire."

THE WAR OF GOG AND MAGOG

This war will not take place until The 1,000 years of The Millennium are completed and fulfilled! I repeat **THIS WAR WILL NOT TAKE PLACE UNTIL THE 1,000 YEARS OF THE MILLENNIUM ARE COMPLETED AND FUL-FILLED!** Let us see what God says through the Prophet Ezekiel in chapter 38.

EZE 38:1 The word of the Lord came to me: "Son of man, set your face against Gog, of the land of Magog, the chief prince of Meshech and Tubal; prophesy against him and say: 'This is what the Sovereign Lord says: I am against you, O Gog, chief prince of Meshech and Tubal. I will turn you around, put hooks in your jaws and bring you out with your whole army—your horses, your horsemen fully armed, and a great horde with large and small shields, all of them brandishing their swords. Cush and Put will be with them, all with shields and helmets, also Gomer with all its troops, and Beth Togarmah from the far north with all its troops—the many nations with you. " 'Get ready; be prepared, you and all the hordes gathered about you, and take command of them. After many days you will be called to arms. In future years you will invade a land that has recovered from war, whose people were gathered from many nations to the mountains of Israel, which had long been desolate. They had been brought out from the nations, and now all of them live in safety. You and all your troops and the many nations with you will go up, advancing like a storm; you will be like a cloud covering the land. " 'This is what the Sovereign Lord says: On that day thoughts will come into your mind and you will devise an evil scheme. You will say, "I will invade a land of unwalled villages; I will attack a peaceful and unsuspecting people—all of them living without walls and without gates and bars. I will plunder and loot and turn my hand against the resettled ruins and the people gathered from the nations, rich in livestock and goods, living at the center of the land." Sheba and Dedan and the merchants of Tarshish and all her villages will say to you, "Have you come to plunder? Have you gathered your hordes to loot, to carry off silver and gold, to take away livestock and goods and to seize much plunder?" ' "Therefore, son of man, prophesy and say to Gog: 'This is what the Sovereign Lord says: In that day, when my people Israel are living in safety, will you not take notice of it? You will come from your place in the far north, you and many nations with you, all of them riding on horses, a great horde, a mighty army. You will advance against my people Israel like a cloud that covers the land. In days to come, O Gog, I will bring you against my land, so that the nations may know me when I show myself holy through you before their eyes. " 'This is what the Sovereign Lord says: Are you not the one I spoke of in former days by my servants the prophets of Israel? At that time they prophesied for years that I would bring you against them. This is what will happen in that day: When Gog attacks the land of Israel, my hot anger will be aroused, declares the Sovereign Lord. In my zeal and fiery wrath I declare that at that time there shall be a great earthquake in the land of Israel. The fish of the sea, the birds of the air, the beasts of the field, every creature that moves along the ground, and all the people on the face of the earth will tremble at my presence. The mountains will be overturned, the cliffs will crumble and every wall will fall to the ground. I will summon a sword against Gog on all my mountains, declares the Sovereign Lord. Every man's sword will be against his brother. I will execute judgment upon him with plague and bloodshed; I will pour down torrents of rain, hailstones and burning sulfur on him and on his troops and on the many nations with him. And so I will show my greatness and my holiness, and I will make myself known in the sight of many nations. Then they will know that I am the Lord."

By the same token; as God gave us Methuselah who was the longest living person on Planet Earth; and who's life span overlapped that of Adam by 243 years and that of Shem by 98 years, thus showing us; that He God formed a connecting link between The Garden of Eden and The Post Flood World; showing us that His Word is True and Infallible and without error and that The Garden of Eden did exist. He left the account which was given first hand by Adam to Methuselah who's witness and testimony was to tell His Grandson Noah, who would tell The Post Flood World about The Garden of Eden. He now explains to us who Gog and Magog are and the other nations:

MESHECH—MOSCOW
TUBAL-SCYTHIANS—ARMENIA
PERSIA—IRAN
CUSH—ETHIOPIA
PUT—LIBYA
GOMER-CIMMERANIANS—GERMANY
BETH TOGARMAH—GREATER ARMENIA

*****GOG—CHINA*****
*****MAGOG—RUSSIA*****

When The Prophet and Law Giver Moses descended from Mount Sinai, he gave us a peculiar name; which was Gog and he told us these were The People of Sinim whom we know to be –CHINA.– Quite obviously a reconciliation between the Communism of Red China and the Communism of Russia after The Millennium in The War of Gog and Magog against all that is Holy, and God and His People!!!

Chapter 24

The Millennium and the Final Judgment

Revelation 20:1–3

Satan Bound : John sees an angel coming down out of heaven, and this vision symbolizes an event which is the outcome of the events we saw in chapter 19: Satan, the main culprit, and the instigator of all the evil on earth, and all opposition to God, must be dealt with before the Kingdom of Jesus Christ can be established on earth. The angel represents the agent of God's authority over the nether world. The key and the chain in Hebrew thought shows us the divine authority given to him by God. The angel is seen by John coming down from heaven to take Satan, because Satan had been expelled from heaven to the earth.

There are five things in the Hebrew that reveal Satan's character to us:

1: The Dragon   = Denoting his cruelty
2: The Serpent   = Denoting his deceptions

3: Old	= Denoting his operating in the Garden of Eden
4: The Devil	= Denoting his slander
5: The Satan	= Denoting his opposition to God's Will

The length of Satan's imprisonment is the length of The Millennium, One Thousand years. The place of imprisonment is The Abyss which in the Hebrew is called "Tehom". The prison place of the demons. We saw "Tehom" in the very first two verses of Genesis; which in the original Hebrew reads this way: "In the beginning God created the heavens and the earth. Now the earth was unformed, void, and chaotic and darkness was upon the face of The Tehom." Satan is then loosed for a final revolt after the thousand year period; then he is cast into Eternal Hell, which in the Hebrew is called Gehenna to share the fate of The Beast, The False Prophet, and all unsaved people. I now quote Jesus in Matthew 25:31, "When the Son of Man comes in His glory and all the angels with Him, He will sit on His throne in heavenly glory. All the nations will be gathered before Him, and He will separate the people one from another as a shepherd separates the sheep from the goats. He will put the sheep on the right and the goats on His left. Then the King will say to those on His right, come, you who are blessed by my Father; take your inheritance, the kingdom prepared for you since the creation of the world. For I was hungry and you gave Me something to eat, I was thirsty and you gave me something to drink, I was a stranger and you invited Me in, I needed clothes and you clothed Me, I was sick and you looked after Me, I was in prison and you came to visit Me. Then the righteous will answer Him, Lord, when did we see You hungry and feed You, or thirsty, and give you something to drink? When did we see You a stranger and invite You in, or needing clothes and clothe you? When did we see You sick or in prison and go to visit You? The King will reply, I tell you the truth, **what ever you did for one of the least of these brothers of mine, you did for Me.** Then He will say to those on His left, depart from Me, you who are cursed, into the eternal fire prepared for the devil and his angels. For I was hungry and you gave Me nothing to eat, I was thirsty and you gave Me nothing to drink, I was a stranger and you did not invite Me in, I needed clothes and you did not clothe Me, I was sick and in prison and you did not look after Me. They also will answer, Lord, when did we see You hungry or thirsty or a stranger or needing clothes or sick or in prison, and did not help you? He will reply, I tell you the truth, whatever you *Did Not* do for one of the least of these, you *Did Not Do For Me.* Then they will go away to eternal punishment, but the righteous to eternal life."

Do you know that every Secular Army and Heathen Army protects its wounded! There is only one Army in the world that kills its wounded and enjoys doing it: **THE CHRISTIAN ARMY IS THE ONLY ARMY IN THE WORLD THAT KILLS ITS WOUNDED!**

The Saints Rule With Christ

Revelation 20:4–6

There Are Three Distinct Groups of Saints.

1st. Group = This group consists of all of the redeemed from Abel to the Rapture of The Church.

2nd. Group = This group consists of the souls of the martyrs of the early part of The Tribulation Period. They had died for their witness of Jesus and for The Word of God.

3rd. Group = This group consists of the souls who had not worshiped the beast and they belong to the martyrs of the last part of The Tribulation Period. And they the martyred of The Tribulation Period lived and were resurrected. Their resurrection therefore takes place after the marriage of The Lamb and at the beginning of the kingdom. Therefore they are distinct from The Bride, who is The Church, and distinct from the guests who have been invited to The Wedding Supper of The Lamb, who are The Old Testament Saints, but all three groups make up those in The First Resurrection. These are they who are blessed and holy, and they are to be distinguished from the rest of the dead, who are the unsaved, and who will not be resurrected until after The Millennium, which is The Second Resurrection to Perdition, (Lake of Fire). Those of The First Resurrection, who are the ones that are saved in Jesus Christ, The Second Death, which is The Lake of Fire, this has no power over them, but they shall be priests of God and of Christ and will reign and rule with Him for a thousand years.

THE LAST REBELLION OF SATAN

Revelation 20:7–10

Satan was first cast out of heaven, now he is consigned to

his fate, The Lake of Fire. Verse 7, resumes the history of Satan which was begun in verse 3, of this chapter, which was interrupted by the account of the saints' reign with Christ during the Millennium. After Satan's 1000 year imprisonment, Satan is liberated from the abyss to test man's loyalty to God under the most ideal conditions of the last of God's ages, before the eternal state. The result is Satan's successful deception of the nations in man's final human confederacy against God, in the final war after The Millennium, which is the War of Gog and Magog. After The Millennium Satan's rebellion will be similar to before the Millennium. This rebellion will be world wide and will consist of the final coalition against God, His people and the Holy City, Jerusalem. The rebels will be people among the nations who played the game of being loyal to Jesus during the 1000 year reign. Israel will be loyal to her Messiah as we see in Jeremiah 31:31–34; and Romans 11:26. The final end of the revolt of the rebels against Jesus will be their complete supernatural destruction and the end of divine toleration of evil upon earth. Satan's predestined judgment which was shown to us by God in Genesis 3:15 is now executed. We first saw Satan cast out of the heavenlies; then we saw Satan imprisoned in the abyss for a 1000 years, now we see him consigned to his eternal fate, The Lake of Fire. The Lake of Fire will contain the Beast and the False Prophet, who are already there and the unsaved.

THE GREAT WHITE THRONE JUDGMENT
Revelation 20:11–15

This final scene of judgment closes the millennium and marks the beginning of eternity. Babylon, The Beast, The False Prophet, Satan, and all of his evil influences, are now out of the way and the time has come for the assignment of each Human Individual to his final habitation. A great white throne now describes to us the greatest judgment ever held, white denoting God's divine purity and righteousness. Those who had already been judged as worthy of The First Resurrection will now have their judgment confirmed in the presence of the assembled universe. The judgment will be complete.

Every person from every age and from every nation will be there. Every deed and every motive will have been recorded. It will be the day when God shall judge the secrets of men spoken of by Paul in Romans 2:16. There will be only two classes of people: The Saved and The Lost. The books will have all the records of all men's lives. The Book of Life will have the entire list of the saved written in it with the blood of Jesus and in His own handwriting. The Book of Life is now opened which is the register of all the saved. It does not contain the name of one unsaved person. The subjects of this Great White Throne Judgment are those who are physically and spiritually dead. All the unsaved are included both the small and the great, no matter what their position on earth might have been. They stand alone, in the shame, and in the agony of their sins, before the Throne of God. They have neither the altar nor the blood of Jesus for forgiveness.

Every sinner is face to face with God alone. They are faced with their works, and they are lost because they did not accept God's plan of salvation for them. "For God so loved them that He gave His only begotten Son, so that if they did believe in Him they would never perish but have everlasting life." As lost souls they are judged on what they did in this life. It is strictly the sinners judgment. The wicked dead are raised, as death holding the body, which was buried in the earth, and Hell and Hades, which was holding the soul, now surrender their prisoners. Death and Hell are finally done away with at the completion of the first resurrection. The doom of the unsaved is the lake of fire—the second death, the place of isolation of evil and all sinners from God in eternity. To better understand this, we take the words The Holy Spirit gave to Saint Paul in Second Corinthians 5:8, " To be absent from the body is to be with the Lord Jesus Christ." Also First Thessalonians 4:16, "For the Lord Himself will descend from heaven with a loud cry of summons, with the shout of an archangel, and with the blast of the trumpet of God. And those who have departed this life in Christ will rise first." When the Rapture takes place those who died in Christ, their bodies which were buried in the earth, and held by death, are now resurrected by Jesus, and the soul which was with Him is now reunited with the physical body that has been released from death, according to His command to become Glorified bodies to be with Him forever. By the same token at The Great White Throne Judgment, we see death commanded by God to give up its' dead, and also Hades, is commanded to give up its' souls. So as it was with the saved, it is also with the unsaved. The saved were with Christ, the unsaved were in Hell. There is now no longer any need for death or Hell and they are thrown into the lake of fire by God.

REV 21:1 Then I saw a new heaven and a new earth, for the first heaven and the first earth had passed away, and there was no longer any sea. I saw the Holy City, the new Jerusalem, coming down out of heaven from God, prepared as a bride beautifully dressed for her husband. And I heard a loud voice from the throne saying, "Now the dwelling of God is with men, and he will live with them. They will be his people, and God himself will be with them and be their God. He will wipe every tear from their eyes. There will be no more death or mourning or crying or pain, for the old order of things has passed away." He who was seated on the throne said, "I am making everything new!" Then he said, "Write this down, for these words are trustworthy and true." He said to me: "It is done. I am the Alpha and the Omega, the Beginning and the End. To him who is thirsty I will give to drink without cost from the spring of the water of life. He who overcomes will inherit all this, and I will be his God and he will be my son. But the cowardly, the unbelieving, the vile, the murderers, the sexually immoral, those who practice magic arts, the idolaters and all liars— their place will be in the fiery lake of burning sulfur. This is the second death." One of the seven angels who had the seven bowls full of the seven last plagues came and said to me, "Come, I will show you the bride, the wife of the Lamb." And he carried me away in the Spirit to a mountain great and high, and showed me the Holy City, Jerusalem, coming down out of heaven from God. It shone with the glory of God, and its brilliance was like that of a very precious jewel, like a jasper, clear as crystal. It had a great, high wall with twelve gates, and with twelve angels at the gates. On the gates were written the names of the twelve tribes of Israel. There were three gates on the east, three on the north, three on the south and three on the west. The wall of the city had twelve foundations, and on them were the names of the twelve apostles of the Lamb. The angel who talked with me had a measuring rod of gold to measure the city, its gates and its walls. The city was laid out like a square, as long as it was wide. He measured the city with the rod and found it to be 12,000 stadia in length, and as wide and high as it is long. He measured its wall and it was 144 cubits thick, by man's measurement, which the angel was using. The wall was made of jasper, and the city of pure gold, as pure as glass. The foundations of the city walls were decorated with every kind of precious stone. The first foundation was jasper, the second sapphire, the third chalcedòny, the fourth emerald, the fifth sardonyx, the sixth carnelian, the seventh chrysolite, the eighth beryl, the ninth topaz, the tenth chrysoprase, the eleventh jacinth, and the twelfth amethyst. The twelve gates were twelve pearls, each gate made of a single pearl. The great street of the city was of pure gold, like transparent glass. I did not see a temple in the city, because the Lord God Almighty and the Lamb are its temple. The city does not need the sun or the moon to shine on it, for the glory of God gives it light, and the Lamb is its lamp. The nations will walk by its light, and the kings of the earth will bring their splendor into it. On no day will its gates ever be shut, for there will be no night there. The glory and honor of the nations will be brought into it. Nothing impure will ever enter it, nor will anyone who does what is shameful or deceitful, but only those whose names are written in the Lamb's book of life."

ETERNITY is now shown to us as "A New Heaven and a New Earth. The old heaven and earth are completely renovated by fire, BUT NOT ANNIHILATED. This renovation includes the elimination of all the oceans, which are necessary NOW AND IN THE KINGDOM, but are not necessary in Eternity. THE NEW JERUSALEM, represents THE GLORIFED CHURCH after The Millennial Reign. The CHURCH comes out of HEAVEN where she has been with JESUS. She is called HOLY because she is GLORIFIED AND WITHOUT SIN, and she is joined to JESUS in administrative and ruling capacity. GOD'S dwelling is now with men, because ADAM'S SIN HAS BEEN REMOVED, SATAN has been JUDGED, the WICKED punished, and The Universe sinless, except "FOR THE LAKE OF FIRE." In The Millennium GOD spread HIS TABERNACLE over His People; HE NOW TABERNACLES with them.

THE SEPARATED LIFE

As Christians many of us find ourselves captives in this life of worldliness and pleasure that surrounds us, and many of us instead of being **TRANSFORMED** are being **CONFORMED** to this world. We have entered in with **THE SPIRIT OF THIS PRESENT EVIL AGE,** and we are living a life of **COMPROMISE,** the outcome of which is a life of POWERLESSNESS and SPIRITUAL BARRENNESS. We will FAIL to see what GOD is waiting to reveal to us out of HIS HOLY WORD and by THE POWER OF HIS HOLY SPIRIT! Some of us have learned to become IDIOTS by watching the

IDIOT BOX most of our free time. Many will get audited by the I.R.S. BECAUSE THEY FAIL TO "GIVE TO CAESAR WHAT IS DUE CAESAR. Many receive PLAYBOY MAGAZINE in a brown wrapper and then they wonder why "A SPIRIT OF REBELLION AND LUST ENTER INTO THEIR CHILDREN! GOD IS NOT MOCKED!

Chapter 25

The New Heaven and the New Earth

In the Garden of Eden man was driven from the actual, immediate presence of God. Here in the new earth he is restored to the immediate presence of God.

In the new earth we shall actually see God, and be with Him in loving fellowship through out all of eternity. No more death, no tears, no heartaches, nor sorrow. A new universe comes into existence.

THE NEW JERUSALEM

Revelation 21:9–27

One of the seven angels, the same angel who had invited John to see the judgment of religious and political Babylon, here invites John to see the Lamb's wife, the Bride. This is now a reference to the city of the Lamb, which in Hebrew thought we see the city being wed to the ruler. John is now carried away in the Spirit to a good vantage point from which he sees the descent of The Holy City, Jerusalem. This new city takes the place of and supersedes the old historical Jerusalem which passed away with the first earth. The city is the most beautiful symbol of the eternal home and destiny of the redeemed of God of all ages. The inhabitants of this city will be God the Father, in full revelation of divine light and glory, glorified old testament saints, new testament church saints, who is the Bride, the Lamb's wife, myriads of **unfallen angels**, and Our Lord and Savior, and redeemer Jesus Himself. Both Israel and the church appear prominently in the city. The measurement of the city reveal a solid cube of golden construction of 1,500 miles long, 1,500 miles wide, and 1,500 miles high. This would mean 2,250,000 square miles on each tier of the cube extending 1,500 miles upward. Each gate was a pearl. The twelve foundations were each built on a precious stone. They are similar to the names of the twelve stones on the Breastplate of the High Priest with the names of the twelve tribes of Israel as recorded in Exodus 28:15–30 which was intended as a picture prophecy of The New City of Jerusalem. Our Encyclopedia Judaica, recording our Hebrew History reveals to us the colors of these precious stones which we see on the breastplate of the High Priest and in The New City of Jerusalem.

Reuben's stone was Carnelian and it had a red color.

Simeon's stone was Chrysolite and it had a yellowish green color.

Levi's stone was Emerald and it had a green color.

Judah's stone was Sardonyx and it had a brownish red color.

Zebulun's stone was Sapphire and it had a rich blue color.

Issachar's stone was Jacinth and it had the color of a blue white diamond.

Dan's stone was Topaz and it had an amber color.

Gad's stone was Chalcedony and it had a grayish color.

Asher's stone was Amethyst and it had a light purple color.

Naphtali's stone was Beryl and it had a sea green color.

Joseph's stone was Jasper and it had the color of a black onyx.

Benjamin's stone was Chrysopraze and it had a apple green color.

Life Within The New City

There will be no temple in this new city, for there is no need for a place of worship. God The Father and God The Son dwell there with the redeemed and there is direct access to God. An indirect access through a temple with its altar is entirely unnecessary. There will be no need for the sun, the moon, and the stars, for The Radiant Glory of God will illuminate the entire city. The gates of the new city have no need of ever being closed, for all of her enemies have been destroyed, and nothing unclean will ever be found in The New City of Jerusalem.

REV 22:1 Then the angel showed me the river of the water of life, as clear as crystal, flowing from the throne of God and of the Lamb down the middle of the great street of the city. On each side of the river stood the tree of life, bearing twelve crops of fruit, yielding its fruit every month. And the leaves of the tree are for the healing of the nations. No longer will there be any curse. The throne of God and of the Lamb will be in the city, and his servants will serve him. They will see his face, and his name will be on their foreheads. There will be no more night. They will not need the light of a lamp or the light of the sun, for the Lord God will give them light. And they will reign for ever and ever. The angel said to me, "These words are trustworthy and true. The Lord, the God of the spirits of the prophets, sent his angel to show his servants the things that must soon take place."

"Behold, I am coming soon! Blessed is he who keeps the words of the prophecy in this book." I, John, am the one who heard and saw these things. And when I had heard and seen them, I fell down to worship at the feet of the angel who had been showing them to me. But he said to me, "Do not do it! I am a fellow servant with you and with your brothers the prophets and of all who keep the words of this book. Worship God!" Then he told me, "Do not seal up the words of the prophecy of this book, because the time is near. Let him who does wrong continue to do wrong; let him who is vile continue to be vile; let him who does right continue to do right; and let him who is holy continue to be holy." "Behold, I am coming soon! My reward is with me, and I will give to everyone according to what he has done. I am the Alpha and the Omega, the First and the Last, the Beginning and the End. "Blessed are those who wash their robes, that they may have the right to the tree of life and may go through the gates into the city. Outside are the dogs, those who practice magic arts, the sexually immoral, the murderers, the idolaters and everyone who loves and practices falsehood. "I, Jesus, have sent my angel to give you this testimony for the churches. I am the Root and the Offspring of David, and the bright Morning Star." The Spirit and the bride say, "Come!" And let him who hears say, "Come!" Whoever is thirsty, let him come; and whoever wishes, let him take the free gift of the water of life.

I warn everyone who hears the words of the prophecy of this book: If anyone adds anything to them, God will add to him the plagues described in this book. And if anyone takes words away from this book of prophecy, God will take away from him his share in the tree of life and in the holy city, which are described in this book. He who testifies to these things says, "Yes, I am coming soon." Amen. Come, Lord Jesus.

"The grace of the Lord Jesus be with God's people.
Amen."

THE TREE OF LIFE

Revelation 22:1-21

We first saw The Tree of Life in Genesis 2:9-10 in the Garden of Eden which was denied to all mankind on account of his sin; But now for the redeemed of the Lord Jesus Christ, the Tree of Life standing by the water of life is now available to all of the redeemed through God the Father, and through God the Son. The final invitation at the close of this Revelation is given by Jesus Himself and I quote, "I Am the Root and Offspring of David, the bright and Morning Star," means that Jesus is The Only One that all prophecy pointed to in the entire bible and in Whom all prophecy is fulfilled. Jesus alone is Savior. Without Him there is no hope. Without Him there is a dark abyss! To all who will listen and humble themselves as they read the words of this prophecy, may now receive the greatest gift that God has ever offered; for God so loved **YOU** that He gave **YOU** Jesus, and Jesus says to **YOU**,

**"COME, AND TAKE OF THE WATER OF LIFE
FREELY!"
"HIS HOLY SPIRIT SAYS, COME!"
"HIS CHURCH SAYS, COME!"**

Any and everyone may receive everlasting life with Jesus, by making Him your Savior and Lord of your life in accordance with Romans 10:9–10. "That if you confess with your mouth, Jesus is Lord, and believe in your heart that God raised Him from the dead, you will be saved. For it is with your heart that you believe and are justified, and it is with your mouth that you confess and are saved.

"THERE IS A GLORIOUS WORLD AHEAD!"
"COME, BEFORE IT IS TOO LATE!"
EVEN SO, COME QUICKLY, LORD JESUS.

ANY COUNSELING REQUESTS
COMMENTS,
INQUIRIES FOR SPEAKING ENGAGEMENTS,
OR ORDERS FOR TAPES SHOULD BE DIRECTED
TO,
DR. MICHAEL ESSES
P.O. BOX 849
PEORIA, ARIZONA 85345

Other books by Dr. Michael Esses:

Michael, Michael, Why Do You Hate Me?
The Phenomenon of Obedience
Jesus In Genesis
Jesus In Exodus
Next Visitor To Planet Earth
The Battle Is Not Yours, Its the Lord's
The Father Never Forsake Jesus and He Will Never
Forsake you!
All The Promises Of God Are Yours, For Just Saying
Yes And Amen Lord–

TAPES BY DR. MICHAEL ESSES
OF THE
BOOKS OF THE BIBLE

A verse-by-verse study taught "live" to different classes all over the world. Dr. Esses uses as his source material the Bible: The Old and New Testaments in the original Hebrew, The Torah, The Mishnah, Jewish History, The Talmud, The Zohar, The Encyclopedia Judaica, and many other sources.

THE OLD TESTAMENT:

_____#100   GENESIS
16 cassettes, $4.00 each or $64.00 for album

_____#101   EXODUS
18 cassettes, $4.00 each or $72.00 for album

_____#102   JUDGES and 1st. and 2nd. SAMUEL
12 cassettes, $4.00 each or $48.00 for album

_____#103   ESTHER and RUTH
4 cassettes, $4.00 each or $16.00 for album

_____#104   1st. and 2nd. KINGS
12 cassettes, $4.00 each or $48.00 for album

_____#105   EZRA and NEHEMIAH
6 cassettes, $4.00 each or $24.00 for album

_____#106   PSALMS
24 cassettes, $4.00 each or $96.00 for album

_____#107   PROVERBS
18 cassettes, $4.00 each or $72.00 for album

_____#108   ISAIAH
24 cassettes, $4.00 each or $96.00 for album

_____#109   ECCLESIASTES
3 cassettes, $4.00 each or $12.00 for album

_____#110   JEREMIAH
30 cassettes, $4.00 each or $120.00 for album

____#111   EZEKIEL
12 cassettes, $4.00 each or $48.00 for album

____#112   DANIEL
6 cassettes, $4.00 each or $24.00 for album

____#113   HABAKKUK, JONAH, ZEPHANIAH, HAG-
GAI and MALACHI
6 cassettes, $4.00 each or $24.00 for album

____#114   ZECHARIAH
6 cassettes, $4.00 each or $24.00 for album

____#115   HOSEA and MICAH
6 cassettes, $4.00 each or $24.00 for album

____#116   JOEL, AMOS, OBADIAH, NAHUM, DE-
BORAH and BALAAM
6 cassettes, $4.00 each or $24.00 for album

MAIL YOUR SELECTIONS TO
P.O. BOX 849
PEORIA, ARIZONA 85345

BOOKS BY DR. MICHAEL ESSES
ON PAGE 198

THE NEW TESTAMENT

____#117   THE GOSPEL ACCORDING TO MATTHEW
16 cassettes, $4.00 each or $64.00 for album

____#118   THE GOSPEL ACCORDING TO MARK
8 cassettes, $4.00 each or $32.00 for album

____#119   THE GOSPEL ACCORDING TO LUKE
12 cassettes, $4.00 each or $48.00 for album

____#120   THE GOSPEL ACCORDING TO JOHN
12 cassettes, $4.00 each or $48.00 for album

____#121   ACTS OF THE APOSTLES
6 cassettes, $4.00 each or $24.00 for album

____#122   ROMANS
8 cassettes, $4.00 each or $32.00 for album

____#123   1st. CORINTHIANS
6 cassettes, $4.00 each or $24.00 for album

____#124   2nd. CORINTHIANS
4 cassettes, $4.00 each or $16.00 for album

____#125   GALATIANS, EPHESIANS, JUDE
and PHILEMON
6 cassettes, $4.00 each or $24.00 for album

____#126   1st. and 2nd. THESSALONIANS
2 cassettes, $4.00 each or $8.00 for album

____#127   1st. and 2nd. TIMOTHY and JAMES
6 cassettes, $4.00 each or $24.00 for album

____#128   THE EPISTLE to TITUS
1 cassette, 4.00

____#129   HEBREWS
6 cassettes, $4.00 each or $24.00 for album

____#130   1st.PETER
6 cassettes, $4.00 each or $24.00 for album

THE NEW TESTAMENT CONTINUED

____#131   REVELATIONS
8 cassettes, $4.00 each or $32.00 for album

OUTSTANDING SERIES TAUGHT BY DR. ESSES

____#132   THE PHENOMENON OF OBEDIENCE
12 cassettes, $4.00 each or $48.00 for album

____#133   WHO IS JESUS ?
4 cassettes, $4.00 each or $16.00 for album
IS HE GOD ?
IS HE THE SON OF GOD ?
IS JESUS EQUAL WITH GOD ?
IS HE THE SAVIOR ?

____#134   THE HOLY SPIRIT TODAY
6 cassettes, $4.00 each or $24.00 for album
HIS OFFICE
HIS PERSONALITY
HIS DIVINITY
HOW HE IS GIVEN AND RECEIVED
HIS EFFECT IN YOUR LIFE
HOW HE IS RESISTED

____#135   THE HOLY SPIRIT IN THE OLD TESTAMENT
4 cassettes, $4.00 each or $16.00 for album

____ #136   SIGNS OF THE END TIMES
4 cassettes, $4.00 each or $16.00 for album
THE SIGNS OF THE END TIMES
THE TRIBULATION TEMPLE
HOW TO FIGHT SATAN IN THESE END TIMES
AFTER ALL IS SAID AND DONE, HOW TO STAND IN THESE END TIMES

____#137   CHRIST IN THE PASSOVER CEREMONY
Listen to the Passover and go into The Last Supper
2 cassettes, $4.00 each or $ 8.00 for album

OUTSTANDING SERIES TAUGHT BY DR. ESSES CONTINUED

____#138　　SONGS OF PRAISE and THANKSGIVING 2
　　　　　　cassettes, $4.00 each or $ 8.00 for album

____#139　　ORIGINAL HEBREW SONGS FROM IS-
　　　　　　RAEL
　　　　　　Sung in Hebrew and recorded in Israel
　　　　　　2 cassettes, $4.00 each or $ 8.00 for album

____#140　　THE **MARRIAGE SEMINAR** AT COUPLES
　　　　　　ADVANCE WITH **DR. MICHAEL AND
　　　　　　MRS. BILLIE JEAN ESSES**
　　　　　　2 cassettes, $4.00 each or $ 8.00 for album

THE FOLLOWING SINGLE CASSETTES ARE ALL $4.00 EACH
please order by name and number

____#141　　LEARN HOW TO UNDERSTAND THE
　　　　　　10 COMMANDMENTS

____#142　　LEARN HOW TO RECEIVE
　　　　　　YOUR HEALING

____#143　　LEARN HOW TO RECEIVE YOUR JOY
　　　　　　FROM THE LORD

____#144　　HOW TO UNDERSTAND THE SERMON ON
　　　　　　THE MOUNT

____#145　　HOW TO APPLY THE 23rd. PSALM AS A
　　　　　　PRESCRIPTION FOR YOUR LIFE

____#146　　PERSONAL TESTIMONY OF
　　　　　　DR. MICHAEL ESSES

____#147　　HOW TO PRAY WITH POWER

____#148　　WAS JESUS FORSAKEN BY GOD
　　　　　　ON THE CROSS ?

_____#149   ***"HEALED"*** FINANCIALLY, PHYSICALLY, SPIRITUALLY, EMOTIONALLY

_____#150   HOW TO LOVE YOURSELF BEFORE YOU CAN LOVE YOUR NEIGHBOR

_____#151   COUNTDOWN TO THE RAPTURE

_____#152   HOW TO LEARN TO LOVE THOSE WHO USE US

_____#153   HOW TO SURVIVE IN YOUR MARRIAGE IN THESE END TIMES

_____#154   HOW TO SURRENDER THE ROOT OF BITTERNESS NOW

_____#155   A MEDICAL REPORT ON THE CRUCIFIXION OF JESUS

_____#156   WHAT ABOUT THE FRUIT OF THE HOLY SPIRIT ?

_____#157   THE SPIRIT OF THE ANTI-CHRIST IN THE WORLD TODAY

_____#158   WILL JESUS HEAL AND SAVE YOUR LOVED ONES BY YOUR PRAYERS ?

_____#159   HOW TO RELEASE, AND FORGIVE, AND FORGET

_____#160   HOW JESUS PRAYS FOR US TODAY

_____#161   DOES GOD EVER TEMPT MAN?

_____#162   COMPLACENT CHRISTIANITY

_____#163   LEARN HOW TO LIVE AN OVERCOMERS LIFE

____#164   FAITH IN THESE END TIMES

____#165   HOW TO PRAY THE FATHER IN JESUS NAME PRESENTING ALL THAT HE IS

____#166   THE FOUR THINGS THAT LOCK UP THE PERSONALITY

____#167   SPIRITUAL BLINDNESS

____#168   LEARN HOW TO RECEIVE THE HOLY SPIRIT AND YOUR PRAYER LANGUAGE

____ #169   WILL JESUS HEAL A NON-BELIEVER TO SAVE HIM ?

____#170   WHAT IS LOVE ?

____#171   THE HISTORIC LIFE OF JESUS

____#172   THE BATTLE IS NOT YOURS ITS THE LORD'S

____#173   HOW DEMONS INVADE YOUR HOME

____#174   HOLINESS! BAH! HUMBUG

____#175   WHEN JESUS CAME TO YOUR TOWN

BOOKS BY DR. MICHAEL ESSES

MICHAEL, MICHAEL, WHY DO YOU HATE ME?	$5.00
THE PHENOMENON OF OBEDIENCE	$5.00
JESUS IN GENESIS	$5.00
JESUS IN EXODUS	$5.00
NEXT VISITOR TO PLANET EARTH	$5.00
THE BATTLE IS NOT YOURS, ITS THE LORD'S	$2.00
THE FATHER NEVER FORSAKE JESUS AND HE WILL NEVER FORSAKE YOU	$2.00

ALL OF GOD'S PROMISES ARE YOURS FOR
   JUST SAYING *"YES AND AMEN LORD"* $3.00
DEATH OF A WORLD $7.00

THE TEACHING MINISTRY OF BILLIE JEAN ESSES

____#176   WHY, WOMAN ?
            8 cassettes, $4.00 each or $32.00 for album
            WHY, WOMAN ?
            THE MINISTRY OF THE WOMAN
            BEST FRIENDS EQUALS COMMUNICA-
            TION (WHETHER MARRIED OR SINGLE)
            HOW TO DEAL WITH INSECURITY AND
            THE WOUNDED SPIRIT
            THE ROLE OF THE WIFE
            THE WOMAN'S OUTWARD COVERING
            NOT A HOUSE BUT A HOME
            THE ROLE OF THE MOTHER

____#177   THE POUTING CHRISTIAN
            1 cassette, $4.00

and now **"MAY THE LORD BLESS THEE, AND KEEP THEE; MAY THE LORD MAKE HIS FACE TO SHINE UPON THEE, AND BE GRACIOUS UNTO THEE; MAY THE LORD LIFT UP HIS COUNTENANCE UPON THEE, AND GIVE THEE PEACE." AMEN**

**MAIL YOUR SELECTIONS TO
DR. MICHAEL ESSES
P.O. BOX 849
PEORIA, ARIZONA 85345**

"SO YOU WANT TO BE LIKE JESUS"

If you really believe that God has called you to be really like Jesus in all of your spirit, He will draw you into such a life of crucifixion and humility, and put on you such demands of obedience, that He will never allow you to follow other Christians, and in many ways He will seem to let other good people do things which He will never let you do. Other christians and ministers who seem to be very religious and useful may push themselves, pull wires and work schemes to carry out their plans, but you cannot do it; and if you do attempt it, you will meet with such failure and rebuke from the Lord as to make you sorely penitent. Others can brag on themselves, on their work, on their success, on their writings, but the Holy Spirit will never allow you to do any such thing, and if you do begin it, He will lead you into some deep mortification that will make you despise yourself and all of your good works. Others will be allowed to succeed in making great sums of money, or having a legacy left to them or in having luxuries; but God may supply you daily, because He wants you to have something far better than gold and that is a helpless dependence on Him, that He may have the privilege of providing your needs day by day out of the unseen treasury in heaven. The Lord may let others be honored, and put forward, and He may keep you hidden away in obscurity, because He wants to produce some choice, fragrant fruit for His coming glory, which can only be produced in the shade. God may let others be great, but He may keep you small. He may let others do a work for Him, and get the credit for it, but He might make you work and toil on without knowing how much you are doing; and then to make your work still more precious; He will let others get the credit for the work which you have done, and this will make your reward ten times greater when Jesus comes. The Holy Spirit will put a strict watch on you, with a jealous love, and He will rebuke you for little words and feelings or for wasting your time, which other christians never seem to get distressed over. So make up your mind that God is an infinite Sovereign, and He does have a right to do as He pleases with His own, and He will never explain to you a thousand things which may puzzle your reason in His dealings with you. God will take you at your word; and if you absolutely sell yourself to be His slave, He will wrap you up in a jealous love, and let other people say and do many things that you cannot do or say. Therefore, settle it forever, that you are to deal directly with the Holy Spirit, and that He is to have the privilege of tying your tongue, or chaining your hands, or closing your eyes, in ways that others are never dealt with. Now when you are so possessed with the living God that you are, in your secret heart, pleased and delighted over this peculiar, personal, private, jealous guardianship and management of the Holy Spirit over your life, you will have found the vestibule of heaven!!!

Shalom

BIBLIOGRAPHY

THE ENCYCLOPEDIA JUDAICA
KETER PUBLISHING HOUSE LTD; JERUSALEM,ISRAEL

THE CODE OF JEWISH LAW
HEBREW PUBLISHING COMPANY; NEW YORK, NEW YORK

THE ZOHAR-THE SONCINO PRESS;
LONDON, JERUSALEM, NEW YORK

THE YALE JUDAICA SERIES
YALE UNIVERSITY PRESS; NEW HAVEN AND LONDON

THE MIDRASH RABBAH
THE SONCINO PRESS; LONDON

THE GUIDE FOR THE PERPLEXED-by RABBI MOSES MAIMONIDES;
P.SHALOM; BROOKLYN

THE BABYLONIAN TALMUD
THE SONCINO PRESS; LONDON

THE LEGENDS OF THE JEWS
JEWISH PUBLICATION SOCIETY OF AMERICA; PHILADELPHIA

THE INTERLINEAR GREEK-ENGLISH NEW TESTAMENT
ZONDERVAN; GRAND RAPIDS,MICHIGAN

THE WORKS OF FLAVIUS JOSEPHUS-BAKER BOOK HOUSE;
GRAND RAPIDS, MICHIGAN

THE INTERPRETER'S BIBLE-ABINGDON;
NASHVILLE,TENNESSEE

THE INTERPRETER'S DICTIONARY OF THE BIBLE-ABINGDON;
NASHVILLE,TENNESSEE

THE NEW INTERNATIONAL VERSION
NEW YORK INTERNATIONAL SOCIETY; ZONDERVAN

THE HOLY BIBLE-THOMAS NELSON INC.
NASHVILLE, CAMDEN, NEW YORK

HARPER STUDY BIBLE-ZONDERVAN PUBLISHING HOUSE;
GRAND RAPIDS, MICHIGAN

THE CLEAR WORD BIBLE-ROYAL PUBLISHERS INC.
NASHVILLE, TENNESSEE

THOMPSON'S CHAIN REFERENCE BIBLE-B. B. KIRKBRIDE BIBLE CO.
INDIANAPOLIS, IND.

NEW ANALYTICAL BIBLE-JOHN A. DICKSON PUBLISHING CO.
CHICAGO,ILLINOIS

DANIEL AND THE REVELATION-REVIEW HERALD PUBLISHING CO.
1897 WASHINGTON,D.C.

NEW AMERICAN STANDARD BIBLE-THE LOCKMAN FOUNDATION;
LA HABRA, CALIFORNIA

THE BOOK OF JASHAR-REFERRED TO IN JOSHUA AND 2nd.SAMUEL;
M. M. NOAH 1840 N.Y.

THE NEW ENGLISH BIBLE-OXFORD UNIVERSITY PRESS,
CAMBRIDGE UNIVERSITY PRESS

THE JERUSALEM BIBLE-DOUBLEDAY AND CO, INC.
GARDEN CITY, NEW YORK

THE TORAH: THE FIVE BOOKS OF MOSES: A NEW TRANSLATION OF
THE HOLY SCRIPTURES ACCORDING TO THE MASORETIC TEXT.
PHILADELPHIA: THE JEWISH PUBLICATION SOCIETY OF AMERICA

CHRISTIANITY THROUGH THE CENTURIES
ZONDERVAN PUBLISHING; GRAND RAPIDS, MI.

Shalom